# Complexities and Dangers of Remembering and Forgetting in Rwanda

Sidestone Press

# COMPLEXITIES AND DANGERS OF REMEMBERING AND FORGETTING IN RWANDA

OLIVIER NYIRUBUGARA

MEMORY TRAPS
VOLUME I

© 2013 O. Nyirubugara

Published by Sidestone Press, Leiden
    www.sidestone.com

ISBN 978-90-8890-110-2

Photographs cover: Anna Omelchenko | Dreamstime.com
Cover design: K. Wentink, Sidestone Press
Lay-out: F. Stevens & P.C. van Woerdekom, Sidestone Press

# Contents

| | |
|---|---|
| Acknowledgments | 9 |
| Introduction | 11 |
|    1 Tales and Myths as Memory | 13 |
|    2 The Meanings of Memory | 15 |
|       Artifacts | 15 |
|       Process | 16 |
|    3 Characterising Memory | 17 |
|       Presentism | 18 |
|       Futurism | 19 |
|       Multiplicity | 21 |
|    4 Memory and History | 22 |
|       Exclusiveness | 22 |
|       Marriage | 23 |
|       Suspiciousness | 25 |
|    5 This Book and Its Author | 26 |
| **Part One - Memory Policing** | **31** |
|    1 Dual Interpretations | 33 |
|       1.1 Earlier Times | 33 |
|       1.2 The 'True Story' | 38 |
|       1.3 Controlling Memory through Education | 41 |
|       1.4 Inheriting a Heavy Past | 43 |
|    2 Parallel Remembrances | 47 |
|       2.1 Remember the 'Right' Past | 47 |
|       2.2 Imposed Amnesia | 48 |
|       2.3 Self-Imposed Amnesia | 53 |
|       2.4 Overcoming Amnesia through Language | 54 |
|    3 Ethnic Guilt | 59 |
|       3.1 The *Gacaca* Pedagogy | 59 |
|       3.2 Collective Guilt | 64 |
|       3.3 Some Are Guiltier Than Others | 66 |
|       3.4 Scapegoating | 69 |
|       Summary | 71 |
| **Part Two - Memory Transmission** | **75** |
|    4 Oral Traditions and the Representation of the Past | 77 |
|       4.1 Myths Are not Just Myths | 78 |
|       4.2 Clue-Providers | 80 |

|  |  |
|---|---:|
| 4.3 Mapping Ancient Rwanda | 83 |
| 4.4 Myths as Source of Divergence | 86 |
| **5 The Reminders** | **89** |
| 5.1 The Drum Impasse | 89 |
| 5.2 The Drum as a Symbol of the Golden Age | 92 |
| 5.3 Memory Reminders in Independent Rwanda | 93 |
| **6 Name as a Memory Keeper** | **97** |
| 6.1 Name is Man | 98 |
| 6.2 Memory in a Nutshell | 100 |
| 6.3 The Selective Character of the Name | 102 |
| 6.4 Personal Name and Collective Memory | 104 |
| **7 Name as Mission Statement** | **107** |
| 7.1 Sealing and Unsealing Fate | 107 |
| 7.2 I Am My Past | 110 |
| 7.3 The Name 'Rwanda' | 113 |
| **8 Names as a Form of Dialogue** | **117** |
| 8.1 Coding the Message | 117 |
| 8.2 Decoding and Responding to the Message | 121 |
| 8.3 Language Subtleties | 123 |
| Summary | 125 |
| **Part Three - Memory at Work** | **127** |
| **9 Memories, the Self, and the Collectivity** | **129** |
| 9.1 Autobiography as Memory | 130 |
| 9.2 Society and Pursuit of Happiness | 132 |
| 9.3 'We' and 'They' | 135 |
| 9.4 Horizontality and Verticality | 138 |
| **10 Backgrounding the Self** | **141** |
| 10.1 All In Common Except… | 142 |
| 10.2 The Relevant Past | 144 |
| 10.3 One Event, Two Perspectives | 145 |
| Summary | 149 |
| **11 Concluding Remarks** | **151** |
| 11.1 Remembering | 151 |
| 11.2 Forgetting | 153 |
| 11.3 Conciliation | 156 |
| 11.4 The Way Forward | 159 |
| References | 165 |

*To my father whose passion for Rwanda's history, culture, and oral traditions continues to inspire me;*

*to Stella.*

## *Acknowledgments*

I started working on this book in 2007, which is more than five years before its initial publication, and many people have helped me shape my ideas or otherwise enrich the work. Although this work is entirely mine, it would be unfair not to mention and thank those people. I would like to thank prof. dr. Eric Ketelaar, prof. dr. Frank van Vree, prof. dr. Annemiek Richters, and dr. Jean-Valéry Turatsinze for their critical reading of the manuscript [or part of it]. Their tough questions and insightful observations have allowed me to sharpen my arguments. I am indebted to Clare Martin-Bell who has gone through this manuscript to make sure that it reads smoothly. I am grateful to my publishers Corné van Woerdekom and Karsten Wentink for their inspiring thoughts about the manuscript and the tremendous work they have completed to turn it into the book you have in your hands. Finally, let me express my gratitude to my family, my wife, my daughters, my mother, brothers, sisters, aunts, uncles, and my friends, for having provided me the opportunity to test my analyses, my arguments, and my ideas, without necessarily knowing that I was working on this book. The discussions took place in informal settings but were highly useful since they helped me detect some holes in my arguments.

# Introduction

On 31st May 1994, as the genocide was in its second month in Rwanda, Gaspard Gahigi, the Editor-in-Chief of *Radio Television Libre des Milles Collines* (RTLM) made a one-century dive into the past to explain the news from that day. He was trying to provide an historical context to the alleged recruitment of the Tutsi in the Great Lakes Region by the Rwandese Patriotic Front (RPF), a Tutsi-dominated rebel movement that was at war against the Hutu-dominated army. Gahigi made a comparison between that campaign and a similar one carried out by King Kigeri IV Rwabugiri [1853–1895],[1] who was facing the White Man's invasion:

> I would like to *remind* you that the Tutsi's arrogance started a long time ago. I don't know if you *remember* the greatest Tutsi warrior, Rwabugiri. The Inkotanyi [RPF fighters] want to replicate his bravery. Rwabugiri fought in Uganda, [and] here in the country… and at Ijwi Island [in the middle of Lake Kivu]. I also hope that you *remember* the story of Kabego. One day, Rwabugiri was informed that white men had attacked, and that they were carrying thunder-bows [*Imiheto irimo inkuba*]. He resolved to fight them, and you *know* how that all ended. *It was exactly like the [current] suicide of the Inkotanyi*. I hope that you have *heard* about the Shangi attack… This attack *brings to mind* the stories of [General Fred] Rwigema [the first RPF Commander-in-Chief killed on the battle field on the second day of the war on 2nd October 1990] and [Paul] Kagame; … Rwabugiri gathered 10 battalions, placed them under the command of his own sons, with Muhigirwa, Sharangabo, Inyonza, and another one who grew up at the court, namely Bisangwa son of Rugombituri… All Rwabugiri's sons were killed together with all the combatants. All those Tutsi were exterminated… Let me *remind* you dear [colleague] Kantano, that the Inkotanyi against whom we are fighting, have been through all those countries that Rwabugiri had conquered: Ijwi, the Bwisha – you *know* that Rwabugiri had occupied a considerable part of Zaire [now Democratic Republic of Congo] – and a large territory of the Bufumbira. They [Inkotanyi] have gone there to tell the Rwandans living in those areas: "you should know that we are all Rwandans and that we are preparing a war to liberate Rwanda. You are all Rwandans and you should help us liberate Rwandans [Emphasis added].[2]

---

[1] Rwanda was a hereditary monarchy until 1961 when the Republic of Rwanda was proclaimed. Until that time, the King of Rwanda –*umwami* – came exclusively from the Tutsi clan of Abanyinginya. Each King had a dynastic name that conferred to him a special mission. The dynastic names of Kigeri, which Rwabugiri bore, and of Mibambwe, gave the Kings the mission to wage wars [*abami b' intambara*], while those of Mutara and Cyilima gave the mission to take care of, and improve the welfare of cattle [*abami b' inka*]. On its part, the name of Yuhi, conferred the mission to perpetuate the dynasty [*abami b'umuriro*] (See Nkurunziza, 2004).

[2] Gaspard Gahigi. RTLM recording. P103-17 KT00-03373, 31 May 1994. Translation from Kinyarwanda is mine.

Gahigi's account of the White Men's attack, the attempts at resistance, and subsequent heavy battles that were lost by Rwabugiri's troops might be correct, but the easy analogy made between that event and the war and the genocide underway at that very moment is an interesting point to reflect upon. The point Gahigi wanted to make, at least as far as I understand it, was that the Tutsi have always been arrogant, and that examples abounded. One of them was Rwabugiri's arrogance to counter the far stronger and better-armed white invaders. The other was RPF's 1st October 1990 attack, which, like the White Men's attack in the late-19th century, cost the lives of the most senior commanders. At that time, the Tutsi were committing suicide by facing the thunder-bow-carrying White Men. Gahigi implicitly induced the listener to conclude that the Inkotanyi [RPF fighters] in particular, and the Tutsi in general, were committing suicide by waging war against the Hutu regime. History repeats itself! This was the conclusion Gahigi expected the listeners to draw.

The excerpt presented above is far from being the most hatred-loaded broadcast. There is no direct, explicit message calling the Hutu to take up machetes and kill their 'arrogant' Tutsi neighbours. Nonetheless, the conviction power of memory is likely to play a more significant role in fueling violence than the direct, non-memory-backed, 'kill them' messages proffered by Gahigi's most known colleague Habimana Kantano. The danger resides in the fact that the public is provided with a precedent and urged to act accordingly. Gahigi was making sweeping statements and conclusions – e.g., that 'the Tutsi's arrogance started a long time ago – but did not necessarily invent an event that did not take place. In his view, he was just *reminding* the listeners what they were supposed to already *know* and to have *heard* of. This is a clear instance of ethnic identity and related memory at work, of the way in which past events can be brought back to fit in, and serve, present-day ideological purposes for the worse and for the better.³ Gahigi and RTLM were doing what I would call memory journalism – which took up new but equally dangerous forms in post-genocide Rwanda – whereby [ethnically-coloured] memory is an unquestionable source of historical background for current affairs and news items.

As this book will show, ethnic identities and related memories are pervasive in Rwanda and no genuine effort has been made to ensure that they do not continue to fuel hatred. From the cultural studies perspective, to have an identity is to have a certain past, a certain golden age, with which one or a community identifies oneself (Ingimundarson, 2007: 96). Historian Georg Iggers (1999: 49) defined identity as 'a whole set of attitudes and values which are accepted as right without requiring [national] justification'. Since cultural memory serves as a reservoir of values and attitudes considered by individuals and communities as exemplary and

---

3   Another case worth mentioning here is the way the exile in Karagwe and return to Rwanda of King Ruganzu Ndoli [circa 1580] was at the centre of the Tutsi students' ideology in Belgium in the 1960s. Servilien Manzi Sebasoni, a Tutsi exile at that time and future RPF and Rwandan government senior official, said in a recent interview that 'I and other students formed small groups and wondered how we would return to our country, Rwanda. Our reasoning was guided by the thought that *in the past Ruganzu, whom they had forced into exile, finally returned home; we convinced ourselves that cost what it costs, we will return home*' (Ngarambe, 2012. Emphasis added).

worth imitating, it follows that memory is an integral, key part of present identities (Zerubavel 2003: 38). This book, therefore, is a contribution to the understanding of some of the ways in which cultural memories interact with ethnic identities, and how both work and manifest themselves in Rwanda, resulting in, or fueling, open or latent conflicts. It should be noted that sometimes ethnic identities and related memories are rooted in events that actually took place in the past – like the attack and resistance mentioned above – while at other times they are grounded in legends, myths, and tales, which are often interpreted as reflecting social realities of the past in coded ways.

## 1 Tales and Myths as Memory

On 14th January 1994, three months before the Genocide against the Tutsi kicked off in Rwanda, and more than three years after the war between the Hutu dominated-government and the Tutsi-dominated RPF now in power, a presenter of RTLM, Noël Hitimana verbally attacked a Belgian priest, who had criticised the radio station during one Sunday's preaching. According to Hitimana, the priest had said during the homily that all RTLM staff members were dogs, spending their time barking and pissing on their neighbours' fence as they passed. Hitimana commented:

> Daring to say, in a church, to Christians, that Noheli [Hitimana] and colleagues are like dogs pissing on neighbours' fences. In a church! My God [*Mwokabyara mwe*! literally: May you have children!], that's an unacceptable provocation [*agasumburutso*]. Those who heard it remember how they gazed at him. He will realise that they will no longer attend his masses.[4]

This priest lived in Kicukiro, a neighbourhood of the capital Kigali. That neighbourhood is the scene of Michael Caton-Jones' 2005 film *Shooting Dogs*, but it is not certain, nor am I suggesting here, that Father Christopher [in the film] represents the priest that Hitimana was verbally attacking. In the film, Father Christopher stayed with the Tutsi displaced at the Kicukiro vocational school and was shot dead by militiamen at a nearby roadblock as he was attempting to rescue Tutsi children out of the city.

Obviously, Hitimana was upset by the priest's statement which he refused to consider as a mere comment, without any hidden message. However, as I will later discuss in this book, the comment became an unforgiveable insult in Hitimana's mind most probably because of its memory connotation: in various myths and legends of Rwanda, the dog and all its shortcomings and vices represent the Hutu, which, to a greater extent, could explain the use of the word *agasumburutso* or 'unacceptable provocation' by Hitimana. Ethical issues and fire-lighting broadcasts by the RTLM have been abundantly discussed, but the feeling one has is that those undeniable issues have blinded us from further analysing RTLM's connections to Rwanda's hate memories. Amongst other ways, Rwandans repeat and transmit

---

4   Noel Hitimana. RTLM recording P36-34 KT00-0511, 14 January 1994. Translation from Kinyarwanda is mine.

'hatred' to one another by just introducing a certain kind of tales – *imigani* – like this:

> Let me tell you a story,
> Let me awaken you with a story
> So that even he who will come from the
> land of stories can find an adult and
> vigorous story tied to the hut's pillar.
> *There was, let there be no more!*
> *The dogs and rats are now dead,*
> *Only the drum and the cow prevailed*
> …
> Once upon a time… (Smith, 1975: 11. Emphases added).

This apparently innocent once-upon-a-time opening is a sort of allegiance to a sacred but blood-tainted past marked by ethnic conflict. Verses 6, 7, and 8 [see italicised verses] remind us that the Hutu were once in control of the country, and that it should not have happened, and that it will not occur any more as they [dogs and rats] have been decimated to leave room for the royal drum [adorned with their genitals as we will see later] and the cow, the sign of the Tutsi's power and prestige (Maquet, 1955). One could wonder how the dog connects to the Hutu and the cow to the Tutsi. Memory provides the answer through Rwanda's oral traditions. Another popular myth suggests that Sabizeze, the ancestor of the Banyiginya dynasty [Tutsi], was born from the heart of a bull kept in a milk jar for nine months (Erny: 2005: 60; Coupez & Kamanzi, 1962: 60–68). As for the dog, another legend explains that it once had horns, but these were removed by God after the dog failed to keep a secret (Erny, 2005: 61). This curse, and how the dog became different from the cow by losing its horns due to some deficiency, comes back more clearly in another tale, according to which *Kibaza,* The Questioner, cursed the Hutu and the Twa, for failing to conduct a mission, while he blessed the Tutsi for intelligently fulfilling the mission he was not entrusted with in the first place.

It would be a mistake to automatically dismiss the impact of these tales because they are the most important and the first channels through which social and cultural knowledge is transmitted to the younger generation either at home or, to a lesser extent, at school. Some real-life examples show how the knowledge acquired through those channels made it to everyday life. For instance, after his return from exile in 1965, Valens Kajeguhakwa (2001: 95), a Tutsi, was told by one old Hutu that 'the dogs had devastated the country' and 'killed people and cattle'. The old man was referring to the 1959 Revolution during which the 'dogs' had destroyed Tutsi properties, killed them [people] and their cattle. The idea I want to make clear here is that 'dogs' in popular culture and cultural memories of those days, referred to the Hutu, and that the Hutu themselves seemed to have interiorised that situation. From here then, one understands why Hitimana assumed that the Kicukiro Christians, whom he presumed were mostly Hutu, would stay away from that church because of the unacceptable, memory-inspired provocation.

In this book, I aim to discuss ways in which Rwandans remember, that is, how they manage their memories and how external factors, such as politics, oral traditions, and other forces influence the process of remembering and forgetting. The suggestion I make throughout the book is that Rwandans remember and forget in complex ways that fuel and perpetuate ethnic conflicts, whether open or latent. Look at the once-upon-a-time formula. Check the names of individuals and political organisations. Consider any war poem – *icyivugo* – including comic ones meant for primary-school going children. Take the name 'Rwanda' itself, which on its own, summarises how memories can be silently but seriously harmful. What about swear phrases? However, memory itself is complex and multifaceted. One needs to first understand what it is, what it implies, and how it functions. In the following sections, therefore, I want to explore the contours of the concept of cultural memory and to discuss its main features.

## 2 The Meanings of Memory

Before social and cultural studies scholars started viewing society as a remembering entity, memory was an almost exclusive realm for psychologists, psychoanalysts, philosophers, and educationalists. These disciplines considered memory chiefly from the individual point of view, as the faculty to record, conserve, and then to evoke past experiences (Michaux, 1974: 18). In the mid-1920s Maurice Halbwachs extended the notion of memory beyond its individual scope. He was then arguing that 'autobiographical memory tends to fade with time unless it is periodically reinforced through contact with persons with whom one shared the experiences in the past' (Coser, 1992: 24). In both individual and collective senses, memory is first of all that content, those traces and vestiges of the past. When Halbwachs wrote, 'We preserve memories of each epoch in our lives, and these are continually reproduced', what he meant by memory was the 'vertebra of fossil animals which would in themselves permit reconstruction of the entities of which they were once part' (Halbwachs, [1925] 1992: 47). This section deals with these two major aspects: memory-artifact or memory-content, and memory-process, which can also be called memory-reconstruction.

### *Artifacts*

After completing his four-volume *Odes* in 13 B.C., Roman poet Horace exclaimed: *exegi monumentum aere perennius* [I have raised a monument more permanent than bronze]. With his numerous lyric poems that took him over a decade to lay down, he had built a solid and lasting monument that future generations would find intact. Horace perceived his texts as a monument, most likely because of their symbolic and physical hugeness. It is in this sense that historian Suzanne Citron (1987: 7) referred to Pierre Nora's four-volume *Lieux de mémoire* (1984 & 1986) and Fernand Braudel's three-volume *L'identité de la France* (1986) as 'textual monuments.' Roman history scholar Valerie Hope (2003: 113) called Cornelius Tacitus' *De vita Agricolae* (ca. 98 A.D.) 'a lasting memorial'. Hope borrowed this phrase from Cicero's *Ad familiares,* where the author stated that an aptly written text would achieve more than 'all the portraits and statues under the sun'. Two millennia after Horace, Tacitus, and Cicero, memory scholars reversed the metaphor: monuments and other objects or situations that have survived, and remind of, the past are memory texts that can be read and interpreted. This metaphor implies that there is a medium that carries symbolic texts. It also suggests that there are readers, individuals or groups, who are remembering subjects.

Archival studies and memory scholar Eric Ketelaar (2005: 1–2) explained those memory texts as being 'interfaces between an individual and the past'. They include landscapes, buildings, monuments, bodily gestures in commemorations, amongst others. Psychology scholar Jens Brockmeier (2002: 25–26), too, perceived memory as 'an array of texts', both in the literal and figurative senses, as involving not only identification and membership cards, birth certificates and documents from schools, universities and the like, but also 'tapes, videos and boxes with photographs'. In his study about 'the sociology of texts', Don Francis McKenzie (1999: 2) explored the latter perception of text, basing his argument on the term's Latin etymology – *textere*: to weave. He stressed not a specific material, but 'its woven state, the web or texture of the materials'.[5]

McKenzie's bibliographic definition can be extended to memory texts, which then would be viewed as woven materials that, in the end, ensure the presence of the past in the present (Nora, 1984b: XXXVII), in the same way texts – in the literal sense – ensure the presence in the mind of concepts and images behind each word, sentence or paragraph. Those woven materials include letters, words, sound waves, stones, bytes, soil, wood, paint, and any other materials that can [be used to] represent a past experience in a visible or audible way. In this case then, as Marcel Roncayolo (1986: 487) wrote, even landscapes are memory texts, as they serve as 'a mental map' and 'become source of knowledge, a living or material archive'. However, like the verses in Horace's poems or the ashes in the French Pantheon, the 'thoughts, sentiments, and actions' (Zelizer, 1995: 234) of the great figures they once were and remind of, need to be assigned a meaning to by the readers regarding both sorts of texts.

## Process

The above has suggested that memory texts, as the beginning point, are themselves memory. However, for those texts to yield some sense, they need to be read and interpreted. This 'meaning-making activity', either by society, its portion, or any of its members, is memory (Zelizer, 1995: 228), too. In this respect, the April 1791 legislation by the French National Assembly that turned the Saint Geneviève Church in Paris into the Pantheon is memory in at least two senses: firstly as archival text, and secondly, as a step in the meaning-making process of the French past (Monval, 1937: 6). The subsequent laws that authorised the burial of the relics of Voltaire, Jean-Jacques Rousseau, Victor Hugo, and many

---

5   Pierre Lévy (1998: 48 & 50) gave a similar definition based on the 'textile gestures' behind the concept of text. Like McKenzie, he suggested that text be defined 'in its most general sense' as 'an elaborated discourse or deliberated utterance'.

others, are equally memory texts and meaning-makers. Similarly, the numerous attempts, some successful, others not, to remove the statue and the relics of Saint Genevieve from the Pantheon were other meaning-making efforts that reflected how the process is vulnerable to external political, ideological, religious, and social parameters.

Another aspect – imagination – should be taken into account, as it greatly influences the memory process. Imagination and memory are two processes that have interconnected roles and aims, as 'those things that are essentially the objects of memory are also such of which there is imagination'.[6] Both aim to make the past and the present intelligible and meaningful, with the former 'assigning' meanings and the latter 'reading' the assigned meanings (Misztal, 2003: 119). The meaning resulting from the memory-text-reading process suffers the bias imposed by the reader's thoughts, world view, plans, and dreams, to the extent that 'of the text itself, nothing remains', as it has only helped 'adjust our models of the world… establish a resonance among the images and words already in our possession' (Lévy, 1998: 49).

Myths are one form of how imaginative representation intermingles with the memory process. In many societies – and Rwanda is a good illustration – they provide the basis for social and political organisation by legitimating certain ideas, 'drawing justification from invented heritage' (Kaschuba, 2000: 225). Far from being just remembering, forgetting, or just imagining, the memory process is all at once, to the extent that it simply becomes impossible to draw a clear line between mythic and real past and between imagination and actual situations (Huyssen, 2000: 26; Ricoeur, 2004: 5; Michaux, 1974: 18–19). Due to external political, ideological, religious or sociological factors, the memory process is fragmented into smaller frames, whereby a certain consensus exists among groups or individuals with converging interests and backgrounds. It is in this framework that ethnic identities and related memories in Rwanda should be understood and analysed. One thing is certain: however fragmentary and multi-directional the process might be, it takes place in one larger framework – society.

## 3 Characterising Memory

I would like to discuss some of the main features of memory using one concrete case that, in my view, helps understand the ways in which memory navigates between public and private spaces; between the past and the future passing through the present; and how politics interferes with remembrance. That case is Spain, where in early November 2007 the government passed a law to destroy all monuments and other objects that reminded of General Francisco Franco and his 1939–1975 fascistic administration. The bill also aimed to forbid all commemorations and gatherings in Franco's honour. The motivation of the government was to restore the memory of Franco's Republican victims. Until the passing of that bill, Franco's fanatics had been publicly perpetuating Franco's memory by singing his regime's

---

6   Aristotle, *De Memoria et Reminiscentia,* in Bloch, David, *Aristotle on Memory and Recollection* (Leiden: Brill, 2007), p. 29

fascist anthem, exhibiting its Imperial Eagle flag and organising pilgrimages to his imposing mausoleum overlooking Madrid. Authorities at all levels were requested to immediately start removing the statues of the *generalísimo* from public places and to make sure that no public homage was paid to him.[7] By doing so, the Spanish socialist government started a process of reinterpreting, some would even say of cutting off, about half a century of the country's past, taking into account present-day social and political concerns, among others, and hoping for a better, less tension-marked future for Spain.[8]

The political move described above strikingly resembles a common practice in ancient Rome known as *damnatio memoriae*, that consists of literally damning one's memory by toppling his statues and removing his name from public places to make the person 'infamous' and 'completely forgotten' (Hope, 2003: 115). The way the past is interpreted and its heroes, or those considered so, commemorated largely depends on present circumstances, and has far-reaching, future-oriented motivations. In this section, I review theories presenting cultural memory as being not a once-and-for-all fixed narrative, but as heavily dependent on external factors and agents in the present and in the future. These external, present, and future factors make memory fragmentary and multiple.

## *Presentism*

The Spanish anti-Franco memory law falls under what Halbwachs described as the rearrangement of recollections that society, in each period, operates 'in such a way as to adjust them to the variable conditions of its equilibrium' (Halbwachs, [1925] 1992: 182–183). Halbwachs highlighted five essential factors that, together and at the same time, enter into play to shape cultural memory: (1) rearrangement, by (2) society, operated in a given (3) [present] period of time, taking into account certain (4) variable conditions, to achieve (5) a certain equilibrium [in the future]. Memory scholars have almost unanimously adopted and built upon this description of memory, recognising its inherent presentist characteristic. Communications scholar Jill Edy (2006: 3) defined presentism as being 'the idea that the form of the past is largely determined by present needs, interests, and concerns'. Media and visual culture scholar José Van Dijck (2006: 362) went a step further to suggest that the content of memory is determined more by the present than by the past.

Presented as being inherently presentist, cultural memory would be summarised as the interpretation of the past as viewed and celebrated through present-day lenses (Lowenthal, 1985: XVI). It is meant to serve some educational, social, political, and ideological purposes in the near or distant future. The anti-Franco memory law has two obvious aims: the officially proclaimed social aim to rehabilitate the Republican victims' memory; and the unacknowledged – and

---

7   France2 news edition, 19 November 2007
8   The BBC reported that Jose Maria Aznar's conservative party in power in 2002 voted against proposals to remove street names, statues and other symbols of the Franco era. http://news.bbc.co.uk/2/hi/europe/4357373.stm (Accessed 2 December 2007).

thus debatable – political, ideological aim to weaken emerging nationalistic and conservative currents. Historian Jacques le Goff (1988: 195) explained presentism as playing a distorting role on the interpretation of the past, but stressed that it cannot be avoided. This unavoidability makes it what historians Jan Bank and Piet de Rooy called 'the dictatorship of the now and here'.[9] Discussing the present–past relationships, early-20th-century historians Johan Huizinga[10] and Carl Becker maintained that actually the present does not exist. What is called present is 'at best no more than an infinitesimal point in time, gone before we can note it as present', and which we create 'by robbing the past' (Becker, [1931] 1960: 6–7). P.J. Lee (1984: 5) shared this view that no neat line can be traced between the past and the present as 'understanding the one cannot be isolated from understanding the other'.

This argument suggests that by perpetually robbing the past to call it the present, those who rob telescope successive past events into a single instant, a philosophical phenomenon Becker referred to as 'specious present'. In cultural memory terms, this phenomenon is [very close to] presentism. Politics is one angle from which the past can be telescoped, given that it is the most powerful force that shapes cultural memory. Nora referred to political influence as a game involving forces that transform reality and memory into a *'lieu du pouvoir politique'* (Nora, 1984a: VIII & XII). Converging on the point that cultural memory is a political tool, memory scholars interpret the resulting transformations or distortions as reflecting the ever-changing relationships of power within society (Misztal 2003: 131; Confino, 1997: 1393; Strath, 2000: 22; Connerton, 2004: 1).

From the above, the initial past event or experience emerges as the starting point. Its rendition, either through mediation, testimonial, monuments, place re/naming and other memory keeping mechanisms, takes place in a certain present that has some contemporary social or political issues and concerns. The latter factors not only prevent those memory carriers from preserving [all] the past (Assmann & Czaplicka 1995: 130; Edy, 2006: 4), but also and above all, determine which version of the past is triumphant.[11]

## *Futurism*

It is widely argued and theorised that cultural memory is a bridge that links the past to the future passing through the present. Memory, by nature, is the perpetual effort, individual or collective, to preserve and then convey a certain version of the past to posterity. The preservers and conveyors of those memories, I should add the legislators and political authorities, who determine society's orientations,

---

9   Jan Bank and Piet de Rooy '*Wat iedereen moet weten van de vaderlandse geschiedenis: Een canon van het Nederlands verleden*', *NRC Handelsblad,* 30 October 2004, p. 3.
10  In his *Hoe bepaalt de geschiedenis het heden* ? [How does history influence the present?] (Amsterdam, [1940] 1988), p. 10, Dutch cultural historian Johan Huizinga argued about the non-existence of the present: '*Het heden. – Maar het heden, dat wil zeggen het nu, bestaat niet, want bestaan veronderstelt bestaan blijven en het nu blijft niet, dat is slechts een punt tusschen het eeuwig rustend verleden en de ongekende toekomst*'.
11  This answers Alon Cofino's (1997: 1390) interrogations as to 'Why is it that some pasts triumph while others fail? Why do people prefer one image of the past over another?'

are situated in the ever-changing present, but their eyes are directed to the future. In this sense, the present and the future influence each other because the pursued future dictates actions to be taken in the present, while present actions determine what the future will be like, by creating expectations.

Memory theorist Paul Connerton (2004: 6) suggested that humans fundamentally base their experiences on 'a prior context in order to ensure that they are intelligible at all'. This means that the past serves as the basis or reference for the present and the future. In their ethnographic study of memories and public politics in the post-Franco Catral area in Spain, Susana Narotzky and Gavin Smith (2002: 193) came across 'the very subtle ways in which memories of the past had changed, as the realities of the present and the expectations for the future gave them a new sense'. Beside the proclaimed aims, the anti-Franco memory law's ultimate aim is to have a country in the future, where the Francoist regime will be forgotten, or at least remembered in a certain way and under the terms defined – in the present – by the legislators or the government authorities.

Extending his thoughts on 'specious present', that is understood as the inclusion of the past in the present, Becker ([1931] 1960: 7) noted that futurism, just like presentism, is inherent to cultural memory as it 'refuses to be excluded' from it. He further stressed that 'the more of the past we drag into the specious present, the more a hypothetical, patterned future is likely to crowd into it also'. Becker refrained from discussing the primacy issue between the past and the future, that is, whether the past generates hopes and desires for the future, or reversely, whether the past is reconstructed to fit future hopes and desires. However, he suspected that 'memory of past and anticipation of future events work together, go hand in hand as it were in a friendly way, without disputing over priority and leadership' (*Ibid.*: 8). Writing in the same year [1931] and about the same subject [past-present-future], philosopher Paul Valéry (1931: 18–19) accorded primacy to the past, maintaining that it acts powerfully on the future, as sentiments and ambitions feed themselves more with remembrances of the past than with present perceptions. He further argued that the future can be imagined only in the light of past situations, catastrophes, acts, attitudes, decisions, etc. The past-future bridging role of cultural memories consists of 'stilled moments in the present' and of 'relevant stories' not only about the past but also about the future (Van Dijck, 2007: 8 & 21). In this respect then, as cultural historian and literary critic Andreas Huyssen (2003: 6) nicely put it, 'we actually do remember the future and try to envision alternatives to the current status quo'.

The Spanish government reversed the positions and statuses of the two conflicting interpretations of the Franco era, sending the Franco-the-hero version to the archival memory, and implicitly pushing the Franco-the-tyrant version into the active memory. Memory theorist Aleida Assmann (2006: 16–17) defined active memory as one that 'society consciously selects and maintains as salient and vital for a common orientation and a shared remembering', and archival memory as one that lingers in a state of latency and which does not circulate as common knowledge. The action of forbidding remembering took place at a certain [present] moment, now in the past, but paved the way to a certain future, where Franco's regime will be perceived differently or forgotten. The anticipated future consequences and impact are the key causes and aims of the action, as memories can help political authorities manage future events and situations (Edy, 2006: 2).

*Multiplicity*

Considered in the light of the presentist, futurist, and bridging theories discussed above, cultural memory constitutes a chain of different versions of the past deemed relevant for different, successive presents and for different, successive futures that society projects (Van Dijck 2007: 21). Defining the relevant versions and projecting them into the future imply both remembering and forgetting, the two sides of the same cultural-memory coin (Ricoeur, 2004: 87). Brockmeier (2002: 21) proposed that the two should not be viewed separately, but rather as 'two sides of one process, a process in which we give shape to our experience, thought and imagination in terms of past, present and future.'

It is often argued that the remembering-forgetting tandem is a natural process demanding little effort on the remembering/forgetting subject's part. Being 'both a biological and a cultural, social, historical being', man necessarily forgets and remembers (Schachtel, 1959: 317). Philosopher Friedrich Nietzsche ([1874] 1980: 10) contended that the above-mentioned tandem is not only natural but also essential and salutary both for individuals and communities, just like the light-darkness tandem is required for life by all organisms. Although he advised individuals and groups to be 'able to forget at the right time as well as to remember at the right time', he stressed that 'without forgetting it is quite impossible to live at all'. Nietzsche was suggesting that memory is much more useful and beneficial when forgetting overpowers remembering. Ernest Renan extended the reflection to the nation to suggest that 'In order to ensure national cohesion there is a need to forget events that represent a threat to unity' (quoted in Misztal 2003: 17).

In the same vein, philosopher Jacques Derrida wondered why it is necessary to have memory: 'You are never going to prove that memory is better than nonmemory. What is more, memory includes forgetting. If there is selectivity, it is because there is forgetting' (Derrida & Stiegler, [1993] 2002: 64). Drawing on the fact that there are remembered [relevant] versions and forgotten [irrelevant] ones, Van Dijck (2006: 370) remarked that there can be nothing like a 'unified collective memory', but rather 'numerous networks, platforms, and sites for constructing versions of a communal past'. Constructing these versions go through negotiation and consensus among remembering subjects.

Illustrating the potential harmful effects of multiple, conflicting memories of the past, Narotzky and Smith (2002: 213) noted that the Spanish post-Franco transitional leaders intentionally silenced those memories, aware that '"democracy" could only be attained by keeping the practices of the old regime off the agenda of public discussion'. Those practices have come back not only on the political agenda but also on the judicial one. Amnesia had been imposed by a legal text, namely the 1975 amnesty law, and was removed by another legal text, 32 years later, thereby allowing justice to look into repressed memory in search of criminal acts.

Since one of the arguments in this book is that the dominant memory in Rwanda is the one proclaimed as the official history of the nation, I would like to briefly and theoretically discuss the relationship between memory and history. In doing so, my intention is to pave the way for the discussions of real-life memory-history interactions in Rwanda.

## 4 Memory and History

In 1978, French writer André Castelot authored a monograph in which he put historical and cultural memory works side by side. It might be argued that the book's title – *DE L'HISTOIRE et des histoires…* – intends to anticipate any subsequent criticism from some exclusivist readers. The use of upper and lower case in this title is most likely meant to distinguish between *HISTOIRE* – the critical exercise that has to meet a set of intellectual and scholarly requirements – and *histoires* – cultural memories. Having clarified his choice and approach quite from the title page, Castelot mixed critical historical analyses and biographies and other memory works. For instance, he critically explored the first crusade, discussed the life and career of Napoleon Bonaparte's personal physician Corvisart, the early life of Honoré de Balzac, before making a documented analytical study of the Pearl Harbour air strike. Both historiography and memory scholars have abundantly theorised the relationships between History and cultural memory. While all agree on the fact that the past serves as the spinal column for both, their positions diverge considerably on other points. This section surveys these theories, starting with those about mutual exclusion, then those about the history-memory marriage, and closing with those about suspiciousness on the part of history.

### *Exclusiveness*

Theories of exclusiveness present History as aiming to be critical and as putting 'a premium on archival research and primary sources, the authenticity of documents and the reliability of witnesses, the need to obtain substantiating and countervailing evidence' (Himmelfarb, 1999: 74). From this perspective, [modernist] history and cultural memory appear to be irreconcilable as both their aims and methods diverge considerably. Their object is the same – the past – but their finality is different. Historian David Lowenthal (1985: 212) noted that although they both convey the knowledge of the past, history and memory diverge principally in their acquisition, validation, and transmission methods. From this point of view, history plays an informative role by reconstructing the 'historical contexts and trends of people's social, cultural, political, intellectual, and institutional lives' (Kors, 1999: 14-15), while cultural memory plays an organisational and socialising one.

Nora (1984b: XVIII & XIX) held this perception of exclusive history responsible for the destruction of the true, primitive memories, as it has profiled itself as just 'trace and selection'. Nora argued that as soon as it is a question of trace, distance, and mediation, one is no longer talking about true memory, but about history. It is suggested here that there is a conflictual relationship between memory – as representation of living groups' life resulting from remembering and amnesia and in permanent evolution – and history as the intellectual and critical representation of the past (*Ibid.*). Nora presented memory as being on the defensive and suspicious of history 'whose true mission is to *destroy and repress it*' (*Ibid.*: XX. Emphasis added). These exclusiveness theories build on the volatility of cultural memories, their exposure to presentist and futurist factors (see previous section), the combination of myths and reality, and thus consider all these features as opposed to the aim of historical work – one based on evidenced-description and explanation of past experiences. Pictured like this, history emerges as a unitary, critical, intellectual endeavour and as 'the primary mode of knowledge about the past', while cultural memories emerge as fragmentary and as many as the groups that create and maintain them (Misztal 2003: 101).

## *Marriage*

Historian Marc Bloch (1949: XIV), one of the leading figures of the *Annales* School, portrayed history as another means to an end, another tool at society's disposal, like memory. Putting Man, and by extension society, at the centre of the historian's preoccupation, he suggested that history 'is an effort towards a better being'. From the *Annales* school's perspective, 'where he [the historian] smells human flesh, there should be his prey' (*Ibid.*: 4). Like Bloch, his friend and co-founder of the *Annales* School Lucien Fèbvre (1948: VI–VII) perceived and described history in a way that almost entirely incorporates, and even turns cultural memory into history:

> History has not to be learnt. History has to be understood. As the science of Man, History studies in time and space the changes that differentiated – and keeps differentiating the various groups of Humanity. As Man is a living whole, it does not exclude from its research any functions, any manifestations of that living whole. In time and space, it studies their successive and simultaneous transformations, be they in politics, religion, the military or economic activity, the humblest technics or the most refined arts – the most modest folklore or the haughtiest philosophy.

Fèbvre defined the relationships between history and cultural memory as being one of a study – history – and its object – cultural memory. However, the study itself shares the same features with its object. Not only is 'history [is] the daughter of its time', but also historians' work is influenced by the needs of their country, their age, their century, which push them 'to reveal, from the immense film of the past, one part rather than another'. Like history itself, Fèbvre argued, historians, too, are the products of their time and space, from which they cannot free themselves. Merging the study and its object, Fèbvre (1948: VII–VII) came to the conclusion that history, in reality, 'is a reconstruction of the societies and people of the past by and for the people operating in a network of today's human realities'. Commenting on this *Annales* approach to history, Nora (1986b: XII) hailed its originality that brought about the amplest and most profound renewal of the national [French] memory, especially by placing Man at its centre, and by opening it up to a wider scope.

Le Goff and Nora, both adepts of the *Annales* School, referred to both memory and history as *histoires* – which Nora (1984b: XVIII) attributed to 'language infirmity'. They not only advocated the marriage between history and memory, but also explained how that marriage would take place. Although the collective memory *histoire* is essentially mythic, distorted, anachronistic, it represents the reality of the relationship between the past and the present (Le Goff, 1988: 194). As for the other *histoire*, Le Goff, like Becker ([1931] 1960: 16–17), referred to it as the one completed by professional historians and taught in schools, and which has to be the one to correct memory. According to Nora (1986a: 350), when the professional historian's *histoire* critically deepens the cultural memory *histoire*, it rids it of legends and rectifies facts; both become what he termed 'history-memory', whose structure does not violently shake the 'spontaneous articulations of memory'.

Arguing from the oral history perspective, Paul Thompson suggested that history and memory should be merged. Opening his 1978 oral history monograph, *The Voice of the Past: Oral History*, he wrote:

> ALL history depends ultimately upon its social purpose… Sometimes the social purpose of history is obscure… At the other extreme the social purpose of history can be quite blatant: used to provide justification for war and conquest, territorial seizure, revolution and counter-revolution, the rule of one class or race over another. Where no history is readily at hand, it will be created (Thompson, [1978] 1990: 1).

Thompson maintained that the historian should hear the stories from the under-classes, the unprivileged, and the defeated, so as to challenge the established account. That way, he concluded, 'the scope of historical writing itself is enlarged and enriched'. In short, 'history becomes… more democratic' (*Ibid.*: 6–8).

The history-memory marriage theories detect more similarities between the two components. Not only do they concern themselves with the past, but they also glamorise it (Lowenthal, 1985: 28). With half a century separating their works, memory scholar Zelizer and historian Bloch, complemented each other in almost similar terms. In Zelizer's (1995: 216) view, memory is 'a kind of history-in-motion', while in Bloch's (1949: XIV) view, history is 'something in motion'. Using different terms, but expressing the same point, Strath (2000: 26) suggested that 'history is in flux; it is, like the present, in a permanent state of transformation'. Flux or motion in time implies at least two points on the timeline, one in the past and another in the present, assuming that many other points spot that line, representing the different presents that now belong to the past. As such, 'history is duration, both the past and the present', and, since 'it is the past perceived in the present' (*Ibid.*), it has to meet the latter's interests.

*Suspiciousness*

Although defending diverging points of view, Paul Connerton (2004), Leo Ribuffo (1999), and James Wilkinson (1996) used the courtroom metaphor to elucidate their points about the relationships between history and cultural memory. Connerton (2004: 13–14) held that historians proceed like lawyers, investigating and cross-questioning evidence, and 'extracting from that evidence information which it does not explicitly contain'. Keeping in mind that cultural memory is 'one of the most evanescent forms of evidence' (Wilkinson, 1996: 86), the historian cross-questions cultural memory to extract information out of it. By doing so, the historian, who follows his 'criteria of historical truth' and conducts a 'critical examination', might reject the evidence, even the one provided by eye-witnesses to come out with his own interpretation (Connerton 2004: 13–14). Both Wilkinson and Ribuffo agreed that history is a sort of courtroom, but did not totally share Connerton's point on the criteria of historical truth. Wilkinson (1996: 80–81) stressed that the definition of evidence has expanded – it was previously limited to written documents, archives, and other primary sources whose authenticity has been proven (Himmelfarb, 1999: 74) – to include crop yields, peasant tales, popular culture such as movies, perfumes, and rock lyrics, and the like (Wilkinson, 1996: 80–81). For Ribuffo, criteria are not established in advance and depends on the ever-changing goals the historian, just like the lawyer, wants to achieve:

> A constitutional lawyer can argue passionately before Judge Smith on Tuesday that most authors and ratifiers of the First Amendment intended to protect obscenity and then argue passionately before Judge Jones on Wednesday that they did not. Indeed she might continue this process through a long, lucrative series of Tuesdays and Wednesdays without wondering which interpretation was true, let alone whether the question of truth made much historical sense (Ribuffo, 1999:145–146).

In any of these three courtroom metaphors, history appears to be an intellectual and critical effort that begins with an *a priori* principle that cultural memory is deficient and is not necessarily a carrier of historical facts. Writing from a different perspective, historical cognition scholar Sam Wineburg (2001: 77), too, used the courtroom metaphor to illucidate the efforts historians made when they engaged with historical documents that he presented to them for the purpose of his empirical research:

> Historians worked through these documents as if they were *prosecuting attorneys*; they did not merely listen to testimony but actively drew it out by putting documents side by side, locating discrepancies, and questioning sources and delving into their conscious and unconscious motives [Emphasis added].

Explaining what he termed recovered or critical history, Lewis (1975: 54–55) emphasised that it began with 'a dissatisfaction with memory and a desire to remedy its deficiency'. The deficiency of cultural memory being its inherent and intrinsic feature, analysing and questioning it to recover history by remedying it, is killing the past and its memory. Similarly, according to Nora (1984b: XXI), questioning a tradition is not plainly recognising oneself in it. Le Goff (1988: 170–171) did not consider this questioning of the past and its memory as their demise but rather as the creation of a new history, a scientific history based on memory, which he also calls 'the revolution of memory'. Unlike the exclusiveness approach to the memory-history relationship, the suspiciousness approach leaves room for memory but sets strict criteria against which memory materials should be weighed before they are taken into account.

## 5 This Book and Its Author

From this theoretical review of the concept of cultural memory, a number of key aspects emerge that will come back throughout this book. One of them is that memory can be conceived both as objects, events, experiences and as a meaning-making process. As such, it is exposed to external forces that keep it in a dynamic state. New social or political concerns lead to new meanings; new projections for the future equally result in new, revised or 'corrected' versions of the past. All these together make memory necessarily fragmentary, multiple and complex, turning it into a potential source of conflicts in societies like Rwanda. Ethnicity appears to be one of the most decisive factors causing memory fragmentation and multiplicity, to the extent of giving the impression that the Hutu and the Tutsi have two different pasts in the same country.

It is those ethnic identities and related memories that this book sets out to discuss, exploring some of the ways in which they manifest their multiple and fragmentary character in Rwanda. It offers an analysis and reflection on the complexity and dangers resulting from the ways in which their multiplicity and fragmentary character are managed both at personal and at collective levels. The main argument is that the various manifestations of collective and personal memories follow ethnic lines and dangerously lead to a state of permanent conflict – sometimes open and brutal, and at other times, latent and deeply heart-buried.

This book is primarily meant for scholars, researchers, experts, and students in disciplines such as cultural studies, [oral] history, memory studies, genocide studies, conflict management, as well as those among the wider public who want to understand how memory works and affects individuals and communities. It provides a new insight into the previously neglected memory dimension to the overall understanding of how a seemingly quiet society can suddenly and, to some extent, unpredictably, turn into a scene of the most horrible inter-ethnic crimes. Political leaders – not only in Rwanda but also in other countries with similar memory issues – and policy makers – both national and international – will also find this book relevant, as it critically addresses the relationships between politics and memory. My hope is that this will reach and capture the attention of the young generation in Rwanda and in other countries around the world where memory seems to be a burden and a cause for cultural hypocrisy. My major intention is to trigger discussion by shaking some of the assumptions so far taken for granted.

To try and discuss some complex memory issues I fetch from various theories and disciplines: psychology, philosophy, [oral] history, critical theory, cultural studies, memory studies, literature, linguistics, anthropology, etc. However, this book falls primarily in the memory studies category, as it aims at investigating how Rwandans live by their memories, how they are haunted by them, and how they use and abuse them (Assmann, [2006] 2008: 210). The readers will also realise that I make reference to, and use illustrations from, other countries and epochs. My aim in doing that is to invite the readers to compare the workings of memory in those countries and epochs with those in Rwanda now and then.

At this point, I would like to add a personal note meant to help the readers locate me, as a person, vis-à-vis this work and the subject it deals with. I am fully aware, as social science methodologists urge researchers to be, that I am researching something I am connected to. Aull Charlotte Davies (1998] 2008: 3–4; see also Creswell, 2007: 37) maintained that 'All researchers are to some degree connected to, or part of, the object of their research', a phenomenon known as 'reflexivity'. She held:

> If reflexivity is an issue for the[se] most objective sciences, then clearly it is of central importance for social research [in my case: cultural research], where the connection between the researcher and research setting – the social world – is clearly much closer and where the nature of research objects – as conscious and self-aware beings – make influences by the researcher and the research process on its outcome both more likely and less predictable (*Ibid.*).

The question, then, is: Who am I? I am Rwandan, Hutu, born in Northern Rwanda in what was formerly known as Byumba Prefecture. It is in this region that the RPF war started in October 1990. I was born in the mid-1970s, i.e., in the early years of Hutu President Juvénal Habyarimana's regime. Like millions of other Hutu, I [and my family] fled from war and genocide in April 1994, and since that time I have been living outside Rwanda. Another question is: Is my background likely to play a role in the arguments and discussions contained in this book? My position has some considerable advantages but also presents obvious challenges. The advantages are that I have some insider knowledge, including the language, the culture, and personal experiences, etc. The challenges are equally significant, as my very background might [unconsciously] influence and interfere with my choice of perspectives, especially when I discuss some controversial issues. What I am trying to explain here is that I wrote this book whilst being myself, and that should be assumed. However, being 'myself' is not limited to my earlier experiences alone. It also includes my academic experience that took me to the Amsterdam University's Institute for Culture and History, the Amsterdam School for Cultural Analysis, and the Erasmus School of History, Culture and Communication, among other institutions.

This brings me to the thorny subject of bias and objectivity, which philosophers, historians, social scientists, and scholars in many other disciplines have debated without ever coming to some consensus. In the social sciences, for instance, objectivity 'is attainable not through the exclusion of [personal] evaluations but through the *critical awareness and control of them*' (Mannheim, [1936] 1966: 5. Emphasis added). In this respect, 'Every view should be equated with the social position of the observer. If possible, it should be investigated in every case why the relations appear as they do from every given standpoint' (*Ibid.*: 153). In journalism, too, it has been argued that eliminating biases is both impossible and counterproductive. Instead, journalists are expected to be managers of their biases and those of their organizations (Kovach & Rosenstiel, [2001] 2007: 102). In the same vein, historians are aware that 'historical knowledge likewise is shaped by subjectivity' (Lowenthal, 1985: XXII; see also De Certeau, 1974: 5; Le Goff, 1988: 10; Trachtenberg, 1999: 9), and those personal value judgments affect their interpretation to some extent (Ribuffo, 1999: 143). On their side, philosophers [of history] maintain that the very fact of having a subject as an author turns any interpretation into a subjective exercise:

> ... the relationship between subjectivity and objectivity or, if one prefers, the place of the subject in his [historian's] own work, can no longer be thought of as in the halcyon days of positivist science... *Every utterance implies its own subject*, whether this subject is expressed in an apparently direct fashion, by the use of 'I', or indirectly, by being referred to as 'he', or avoided altogether by means of impersonal constructions... What is excluded [however] is always only the 'person', psychological, emotional or biographical, certainly not the subject... *objectivity is imaginary* as everything else (Barthes, 1970: 413–414. Emphasis added).

This book, then, does not have any *objectivistic* pretention whatsoever. It rather presents a reflection and arguments about, and analysis of, the role that cultural memories play[ed] in the age-long lack of harmony and full trust between the Hutu and the Tutsi. To some extent, my endeavour has the same aim as Jan Amos Comenius' *Magna Didactica* (1657), Jean-Jacques Rousseau's *Emile* (1768), Leo Tolstoy's *On Education* (1862), Helen Parkhurst's *Education on the Dalton Plan* (1922), amongst other works of the past. All these authors insightfully analysed and criticised the culture [namely the educational system] that had made them who they were. In my case, I am scrutinising a memory-marked situation in which I myself grew up. As sociologists Pierre Bourdieu and Jean-Claude Passeron (1977: 37) pointed out, 'The man who deliberates on his culture is already cultivated and the questions of the man who thinks questioning the principles of his upbringing still have their roots in his upbringing'. This book is an invitation to others to do a better job than I, to take enough distance where they suspect I embroiled myself too deeply, to provide thorough details where they feel I failed to do so and to discuss the issues they think I neglected. By doing this, they will have advanced this discussion, which is one important way of ridding Rwanda of its memory traps.

The book comprises three parts, but before outlining them, I have to admit that it was not easy to find a logical structure given the inter-connectedness of the different subjects I discuss. While a theoretical introduction appeared to be the most logical way to begin with, ordering subsequent parts was a challenging task. For instance, it took a long time of reflection to decide to put the study and analysis of autobiographical accounts at the end, even though those accounts are repeatedly referred to before reaching that end. My reasoning was that the selected autobiographies illustrate some of the ways in which the memory process discussed in the book culminates in something concrete, in a palpable commodity ready for consumption. Deconstructing them at the beginning of the book would confuse the reader, who would then wonder why I chose specifically autobiographies rather than novels, poetry, or folklore, for instance. Putting them at the end creates some logic: having gone through a certain past, heard certain accounts and certain interpretations of myths and tales, suffered certain injustices or enjoyed certain privileges, the authors come to a certain understanding of their own lives. In other words, autobiographies are used to illustrate in a concrete way most of the arguments discussed in the book.

Following that logic, Part One discusses mainly two memory phenomena that I call dual memory and parallel remembrance. Dual memory applies to the long-gone past and to the systematic divergence of views amongst the Hutu and the Tutsi. I focus on the *Ubuhake*, the social system that turned the entire society into a pyramid, with the Tutsi King on its top, and his vassals under him. According to the Hutu, at the lowest level, only the Hutu vassals or serfs would be subjected to hard labour for their Tutsi masters for protection and to eventually receive a cow. Moreover, the Hutu would say, no Hutu master had Tutsi vassals, simply because Hutu masters did not exist. For the Tutsi, the *Ubuhake* system presented an ideal social system that fostered harmony among all Rwandans. Each of them knew his place and role and all worked perfectly. I argue that this dualism has become one of the deadliest trap, as each ethnically based regime puts forward its own [equally ethnically-biased] version of the past forward. I use parallel remembrance to refer to the form of dual memory at the level of the individual. I use the example of the massacres committed by the Tutsi-dominated RPF rebel troops against Hutu populations, to maintain that the Tutsi-dominated regime force Hutu survivors to forget, not to remember their dead. The consequence is that each individual goes around with two memory accounts: the genuine version of what happened and the feel-good version the regime has preached since 1994. Knowing which past to lock or remember privately and which one to proclaim or remember publicly has become a matter of survival in modern-day Rwanda. In other words, the government-imposed amnesia has turned into self-imposed amnesia, which is maintained through, among other means, the judicial system.

Part Two explores a few channels through which ethnic identities and related memories are transmitted from one generation to another. These include oral traditions – the sole memory texts that coded past experiences into myths, tales and legends – but also significant memory reminders that, on their own, symbolised centuries of tension-marked ethnic relationships. Names are also discussed as serving not only as the family memory keepers but also as powerful mission statements, and fate-sealers. The main argument in this part is that myths, tales, proverbs, adages, names and the beliefs they convey and perpetuate are far from being mere superstition. I maintain that they reflect in some sophisticated ways how society perceives itself and wants to be remembered by its future members. In the particular case of names, I stress that they have some magical power as they somehow haunt the bearer, whether individuals, organizations, or the country itself, and tell them the path to follow. In this part, I suggest that Rwandans take time to think about the name 'Rwanda' itself and what it represents. In my view, and the memories behind that name should prove me right, the name Rwanda does not convey any peaceful, conciliation-fostering message. Since Rwandan traditions encourage the extension of male names into war poems [*ibyivugo*], I discuss the latter, mainly pointing out the danger they pose by turning the concepts of death, killing, and violence into social values.

In Part Three, ethnic identities and related memories are closely scrutinised through their constant intrusion into autobiographical writings. My analysis focuses on two autobiographic accounts and attempts to understand the ways in which the authors' Selves are shaped by, and backgrounded with, memories related to ethnic identities. While both authors consider the 1959 Hutu uprising as the starting point of their accounts, they diverge completely in its interpretation. The same memory lines discussed in Part One reappear with the Hutu author finding some grounded justifications for the uprising, and the Tutsi author defending the opposite. Yet the two authors belong to the same generation, attended the same school, and had a similar professional background. This pushes to believe that ethnic identities and related memories determine the path that the authors must follow in their effort to link the past to the present.

Let me end this introduction with a note about the next steps. This book is far from exhaustive and no one single book can ever manage to encapsulate all the complexities of remembering and forgetting in one given country or culture. This book is Volume One of the *Memory Traps* series that will allow me to share my thoughts, reflections, and analyses about other aspects of ethnic identities and related memories in Rwanda. Since my ultimate intention is to trigger a constructive discussion about ways in which Rwanda can tear apart the memory traps in which it has been stuck for centuries, I would highly appreciate any criticism and observations about this and upcoming volumes, so that each new volume or each new edition of the previous volumes can be improved. A website, www.memorytraps.com, has been designed to allow readers to provide their feedbacks, reviews, and observations, and to interact with the author more directly.

# Part One

## Memory Policing

*Chapter 1*

# Dual Interpretations

Not so much has been written about the role of cultural memory and remembrance in Rwanda's tragedies. The 1994 genocide was like the culmination of, or a step in, a process that was misunderstood. To use President Kagame's words, the genocide was the product of years of cultivated hatred, 'an explosion resulting from a process that lasted years' (Misser, 1995: 91). In fact, only little research has been timidly conducted about how and what Rwandans remember, and, above all, why they do remember what they remember at any given moment in history, and then forget it at a different time within that same history. To put it into more concrete terms, one needs to understand why the post-genocide regime prefers to remember 1959 as the starting point of the process that led to the genocide, while the previous Hutu dominated regimes considered that year as the beginning of the Hutu emancipation.

Timothy Longman and Theoneste Rutagengwa (2004: 164–165) noted that the memory of the past that is currently being promoted 'is widely accepted by former Tutsi refugees who have returned to Rwanda since the genocide and now dominate the country's social, political and intellectual life'. According to this official narrative, Rwandans were living harmoniously before the coming of the coloniser and the missionaries. The latter created ethnicity and the post-colonial governments of President Grégoire Kayibanda [1961–1973] and President Juvénal Habyarimana [1973–1994] took over and 'continued to use ethnicity as a wedge, falsely teaching that Tutsi were foreign invaders who had always subjugated and exploited the Hutu majority'. Choosing which version to adhere to is a political act, and 'reasoning on history, is, unmistakably, reasoning on power [struggle]' (Debord, 1967: 112). In this chapter, I discuss the dual memories of pre-colonial and colonial Rwanda, before looking into ways in which dominant memories turn into history, and the role education plays in that process. I close the chapter with an observation that most of these ethnic issues are to be partly blamed on the memories the successive leaders inherited, rather than on the sole colonisers, who became an easy scapegoat.

## 1.1 Earlier Times

Let me consider an earlier pre-colonial period, let's say, the 19$^{th}$ century, and analyse how the different ethnic groups experienced it, and then later interpreted it. The monarch still had the death right, a great part of Rwandans were serfs under the *Ubuhake* system, while a smaller portion had privileges within that same system. Depending on one's ethnic group, the Hutu servitude is praised by some, namely the Tutsi, as having contributed to social harmony and peace that lasted until the 'white man' decided to 'divide in order to rule' by inciting the Hutu to emancipate.[12] Others, the Hutu, call it nameless bondage. Perceived from a post-revolutionary nostalgic context, which seems to be the case of Anastase Shyaka, harmony refers to a situation in a given society 'where everyone is in their place, their class, taken up with the duty allocated to them, and equipped with the sensory and intellectual equipment appropriate to that place and duty'. In other words, pre-colonial Rwanda was a harmonious society because each Hutu, each Tutsi, and each Twa confined themselves into the places, privileges or disadvantages allotted to their groups, and manifested little willingness to reverse the situation. According to Shyaka and some other authors, 'the white man' who first collaborated to settle down, called for emancipation, which is nothing else but the reversal of the seemingly harmonious situation. According to philosopher Jacques Rancière (2009: 42) who recently dealt with both harmony and emancipation, though in another context, stated that emancipation refers to the 'emergence from a state of minority'. Minority in this context should be understood as implying any form of social, political, economic [or otherwise] imbalance.

A comparison between two Rwanda[n] scholars' understanding of the *Ubuhake* system should suffice to shed some more light on my point. Their understanding leaves no doubt as to the authors' ethnic backgrounds and memories.[13] These scholars are Anastase Shyaka, Director of the Centre for Conflict Management and lecturer at the National University of Rwanda [at least at the time he authored the document to which I am referring], and Charles Nkurunziza, former lecturer of Law (including Customary Law) at the same university, who also served in the government in the 1980s. Both authored two separate essays with the same title, *Le conflit rwandais*. For Shyaka:

> The *Ubuhake* refers to the system in ancient Rwanda, where cattle breeders granted cattle as usufruct to those who had none in return for services. It should be noted here that a similar system known as '*Ubukonde*' was in force among the cultivators in the Northwest of Rwanda. It consisted in renting arable plots of land in exchange for crops: the one who owned the most land offered a plot to a client to receive part of his harvests in return. The '*Ubuhake*' and '*Ubukonde*' have ceased to exist for tens of years. However, a mountain of differences distinguishes them in the Rwandan socio-political imagination. The *Ubuhake* system is still perceived as a source that still causes conflicts today, while the *Ubukonde* has no conflict generating feature whatsoever. This difference is the result of the radically opposite views of

---

12   Anastase Shyaka, *Le conflit rwandais: origines, développement et stratégies de sortie* (year ?), p.15.
13   Quoting a colleague of his from Nigeria who was attending a conference on Rwanda and Burundi in 1995, Mahmood Mamdani (2001: 42) wrote: He [the colleague] could close his eyes and tell the identity of a speaker by the twist of his or her argument: if a person claims that there was no difference between Hutu and Tutsi, or that the difference was one of class, the speaker was most likely a Tutsi. A Hutu intellectual was more likely to argue otherwise, that the difference was one of distinct groups, ethnic or even racial.

the two systems since the first encounters with Europe. The former system was radicalised, demonised, fetishised and given ideological significance. The latter received a different consideration and that is why it did not leave any conflict generating germs.[14]

Contrary to Shyaka, Nkurunziza described the *Ubuhake* as:

> A system governing socio-political relations among individuals or even among institutions. It was inspired by the *Ubugererwa* contract practiced in the Hutu kingdoms, the only difference being its object and its objective. The object of the *Ubuhake* system was the cow instead of the land, and it involved two individuals belonging to two different social categories. The most powerful offered protection to the weaker and his family under any circumstances and so long as their *Ubuhake* relationships were not definitively interrupted. The other party committed itself to perfectly executing all the orders given by his protector. Through this relationship, the serf ceased to belong to himself and to his family and was to be fully at his protector's disposal. It is worth mentioning here that the cow that was received under those circumstances remained part of the protector's property, the *Mugaragu* [serf] being only usufructuary. This means that under whatever pretext, the *Shebuja* [protector] could take back all the cows that the *Mugaragu* had received. Even for anyone owning cows obtained outside the *Ubuhake* system (cows known as *imbata*) could lose them to a more powerful person, without any means of getting them back. When all was well, the relationship between the two parties was transmitted from father to son for generations. Through *Ubuhake*, the Tutsi aimed to turn the Hutu into a subjugated man essentially dedicated to his [Tutsi's] service.[15]

The two quotes could be interpreted as follows: the son of the former *Umugaragu* and the one of the former *Shebuja* will hardly find a common ground as to the nature of the social relationships regarding those days. The reason is that the former suffered from it while the other benefited from it in one way or another, or at least, was not negatively affected by it. More interestingly, this diverging understanding was at the heart of the political crises of the late-1950s to the early-1960s and certainly during the early- and mid- 1990s. During the Hutu emancipation movement in the 1950s, the rejection of the *Ubuhake*-based system by the Hutu serfs and their sons who had managed to attend Roman Catholic seminaries (Gakusi & Mouzer, 2003: 51–52; Twagilimana, 2003: 69) served as the basis of the movement.[16] The Tutsi establishment who had benefited from the system defended it as being the result of centuries of their forefathers' relentless

---

14 Anastase Shyaka, *Le conflit rwandais*, p. 11.
15 Charles Nkurunziza, *Le conflit rwandais* (Brussels: 2006).
16 The 1957 *Manifeste des Bahutu* [Hutu Manifesto] served as the basis for the emancipationist movement. This document reads: The current situation presents a big misbalance created by the old socio-political structure in Rwanda, namely the Ubuhake… Without ignoring the Hutu's deficiencies, we think that each race and each class has its own and we would like to correct that instead of systematically pushing the Hutu back into the eternally inferior situation… (Nkundabagenzi, 1961: 21–29).

efforts.[17] Valens Kajeguhakwa, a Tutsi businessman, turned politician, who also sponsored the RPF war, and whose family owned cattle and large plots of land in the Northwest of Rwanda, looked back at the *Ubuhake* system with perceptible nostalgia. He maintained that the system was based on voluntarism on the part of the client seeking wealth, cattle and protection. During the colonisation, he claimed, even more land-ploughing Hutu voluntarily embraced the system, because they were the most exposed to the colonisers' abuse. The system is presented here as the sole protection on which the Hutu could count against the abuses of the coloniser (Kajeguhakwa, 2001: 96–97).

Western scholars, too, have grappled with the concept of *Ubuhake*. Law professor Filip Reytnjens (1985: 198) defined the *Ubuhake* as being a relationship system based on clientelism, which allowed the Tutsi to have the monopoly of economic resources and politics, and to appropriate themselves with all the considerable parts of the goods without participating in the production process. Similar to the way in which the modern economic system is based on money, the economic system in ancient Rwanda was based on cattle (Maquet, 1961: 82). The protecting Tutsi lord gave them to his serf in return for services, and this situation was binding for the next generation on both sides:

> The *buhake* relationship was perpetuated even after the death of both parties. The *shebuja*'s heirs inherited their father's relations of *buhake* vis-à-vis his clients, and the client's heirs kept the cows (and/or their progeny) granted to their father. But the *shebuja* had the right to refuse to recognise as successor of his client, a person without the proper qualities to be a good *garagu* (Maquet, 1961: 131; also see *Ibid*: 93–94)

In a 1955 documentary that portrayed Rwanda's cattle-based feudality, social anthropologist Jacques Maquet contended that, like the Hutu, the Tutsi needed more powerful Tutsi that would go on to become their clients, but who could never offer non-remunerated labour or offer part of their food provisions to their masters. Kajeguhakwa (2001: 97) contested this and suggested that both the Hutu and Tutsi were subjected to the same obligations vis-à-vis their masters. However, he failed to give an example of Tutsi serfs with Hutu masters.[18] It is relatively easy to have a broad picture of the *Ubuhake* system because many witnesses, beneficiaries and victims of the system are still alive. Born in the 1940s, Canisius Karake, a former Hutu diplomat, remembers that 'my grandfather was a serf of a

---

17  The conservative Tutsi élite reacted to the *Manifeste des Bahutu* with two letters, among others. The *Premier écrit de Nyanza* established the superiority of the Tutsi race and rejected demands for equality of the Hutu arguing: 'Since our kings conquered the Hutu's countries killing their kings and enslaved the Hutu, how can the latter now claim to be our brothers' (Nkundabagenzi, 1961: 35–36). The second letter – the *Deuxième écrit de Nyanza* – rejected another grievance of the Hutu who were demanding the sharing of pastures and cattle with their masters (Nkundabagenzi, 1961: 36–37).

18  It is important to note that a system similar to the *ubuhake* existed in Ankole, a kingdom in southern Uganda, where the *Omugabe* – the King – was necessarily from the cattle-rearing *Bahima* ethnic group. Like in Rwanda, he appointed chiefs among his relatives (Morris, 1964: 2) and maintained a system of dependence in which the *Bairu* – another ethnic group – 'had to render services to their Bahima masters, and, in particular, to provide them with beer. In return, the Muhima looked after the interests of the Bairu dependants and was responsible for their defense' (*Ibid*.: 1).

Tutsi master. When he became old, it was my father who replaced him'. He knows that if change had not occurred in the 1950s, he would have taken over from his father (Wambu, 2001).

The duality of Rwanda's past appears also whilst considering whether Rwanda became progressively what it is now, or whether it has always been what it is. Ferdinand Nahimana, a Hutu historian,[19] maintained that Rwanda, like its name indicates, has expanded along centuries, with the initial nuclear *Rwanda rwa Binaga* annexing neighbouring kingdoms. He considered the Bushiru, Bugoyi, and other northern and northwestern regions as independent Hutu kingdoms, which King Yuhi V Musinga had attempted to control in the early 1900s by appointing Tutsi chiefs to rule them in vain (Nahimana, 1993: 289). It is with the military support of the coloniser that he conquered the former kingdoms. Those kingdoms had dynastic drums, codes of succession and enthronisation whose names survived in oral traditions, and even royal staff (see Nahimana, 1993: 177; 180–187; 188–189). What is more, 'if these *abami* [kings] of the Northwest stayed on their thrones until the early twentieth century, it is because they resisted the progress of the Nyiginya, together with their subjects' (*Ibid.*: 232).

Kajeguhakwa provided a totally different account: those areas were simply 'natural regions', different from one another by their geomorphology. 80 percent of those regions' traditional rulers, not kings, were Hutu and 'depended directly on the Mwami [Tutsi King] or on the Queen Mother. The blame should be on the coloniser who deposed those rulers during the 1925–1926 administrative reforms that grouped many of those regions into sub-chieftainships and chieftainships (Kajeguhakwa, 2001: 309–311). Thus, while Nahimana's account supports the expansionist thesis according to which Tutsi Kings attacked and annexed former Hutu kingships, Kajeguhakwa's presents a unified Rwanda, victimised by pseudo-reforms by the coloniser.

Nahimana and Kajeguhakwa further diverged on the demographic composition and migratory movements in the north. Kajeguhakwa (2001: 314) maintained that under King Cyilima II Rujugira back in the late-17$^{th}$ century, both the Hutu and Tutsi migrated and settled in the north, as the region offered both fertile soils for farming and prairies for cattle rearing. Nahimana (1993: 235–236) offered a different version: as the Hutu had resisted all the predecessors of Rujugira, the latter decided to opt for a different strategy, namely a peaceful infiltration of cattle breeders in the Buhoma, Bushiru, Bugoyi and other Hutu kingdoms. The pseudo-migrants psychologically and militarily paved the way for the subsequent conquests, as they allowed the troops of Rujugira and his successors to count on local informants and accomplices. Nahimana admitted, however, that some Tutsi cattle breeders had previously migrated to those kingdoms prior to the strategic infiltration. Here again, it is not possible that the two versions can converge or even get close to one another. Nahimana's point was corroborated by Alexis Kagame's account that Rujugira was at war against three powerful neighbours: Burundi in

---

[19] Ferdinand Nahimana was sentenced by the ICTR [International Criminal Tribunal for Rwanda] to 30 years in jail in 2007.

the south, Gisaka in the east, and Ndorwa in the northeast (Kagame, 1969: 190). He could not afford another front in the north and northwest, especially when he knew that his predecessors had failed each time they had attempted to annex that area.

Oral historian Jan Vansina studied the pre-colonial past of Rwanda and claimed to have offered the most original version. He criticised Alexis Kagame for handling oral sources uncritically, and other early European historians and anthropologists for having reproduced the narratives fabricated at, and by, the royal palace. Vansina considered his work as providing 'an image of Rwanda's past that conforms with reality', an interpretation that is 'more correct' (Vansina, 1962: 9). Regarding the migration versus infiltration issue opposing the accounts by Nahimana and Kajeguhakwa, Vansina sided more with Nahimana. He wrote that the Tutsi devised a strategy comprising three phases:

> Firstly, Tutsi nomadic cattle breeders went to occupy regions that were hospitable to cattle amidst Hutu communities. That is how the cattle breeders infiltrated the Mutara region, especially the less fertile plains pushing the Hutu to remain in the more fertile mountains… The two communities lived side by side without having any relations with each other… In the second stage, the regions were raided and plundered, first, sporadically, then more frequently by Rwandan warriors. As the military organisation of the Hutu clans and their kings were not so developed, those incursions were often successful. The last phase was the one of colonisation. In places where the infiltration described above had not taken place, the King of Rwanda decided, after a series of lucrative raids, to impose his authority on the region by sending troops to colonise it (Vansina, 1962: 79).

The point is that when the European colonisers came to Rwanda, they found a situation of domination, which they blessed and somehow codified. African history scholar Gerald Caplan (2007: 20) maintained that the colonisers made the existing structures 'more rigid and ethnically inflexible', and, in doing so, 'institutionalised the split between the two groups', for instance, issuing the identity card. He noted that this card turned into a 'tragic irony, during the genocide', when it enabled Hutu killers to identify the Tutsi who were its original beneficiaries. It would therefore be too simplistic to assert that the colonisers divided to rule, while it appears that the Hutu and Tutsi were already divided. The right accusation, in my view, would rather be that the colonisers maintained, and even deepened divisions to rule.

## 1.2 The 'True Story'

Of the different ways of remembering the past, the one that is proclaimed as national memory in Rwanda depends on the relationship between the leaders in power and the pre-independence system. In other words, the official national memory that is promoted in schools, textbooks, museums, courts of justice, libraries, films, arts, state media, street naming, calendrical celebrations, hero canonisation, etc, is the one relating to the ethnic identity of the leader, while the previously dominant version is reduced to 'falsified history' (Karekezi *et al.*, 2004: 70). Historian Hermann von der Dunk (2005: 215) discussed the so-called 'falsified history' and suggested that it is difficult to present one's own vision of the past as true or untrue because, 'in practice, everyone finds his own version self-evident. That is why one believes in it'. The 'degradation of the past to pre-history' results from the exclusive, one-trace-based exploitation of the past (*Ibid.*). Much earlier, philosopher John Dewey ([1909] 1933: 28) had pointed out the somewhat natural tendency to consider as true what one wishes so, and as false or falsified what is contrary to one's wishes. He maintained: 'We take that to be true which we should like to have so, and ideas that go contrary to our hopes and wishes have difficulty in getting lodgment'. Generalisations and sweeping assertions such as those by Karekezi and colleagues might be understood in this perspective, as the true history in their view is one that corresponds to their hopes and wishes, whilst the falsified history is the one contradicting their wishes.

Rwanda scholar Catherine Newbury (2002: 67–68) termed this situation the 'politics of history'. That concept encompasses the 'competing visions of the past', the ones that have been providing 'the intellectual foundations' for ethnic conflicts. Central to that concept are three key elements: 'the politicisation of ethnic cleavages', 'the generalisation of blame', and 'a corporate perception of ethnicity'. Given the complexity of that 'politics of history', Newbury (2002: 69 & 79) not only suggested that 'there is no single history: rather there are competing histories', but also advised historians and others 'to engage with the competing visions of the past… to go beyond them rather than choose between them… [and keep in mind that] they cannot avoid them'. Newbury's point is in line with historian Carl Becker's reflections on the notion of 'historical fact'. In his article 'What are Historical Facts', Becker (1955: 330) held that the historian cannot deal directly with the events of the past, but rather with statements and affirmations about those events: 'For all practical purposes it is this affirmation about the event that constitutes for us the historical fact'. With this symbolic nature and function, 'It is *dangerous* to say that it is true or false' [Emphasis added].

History is no longer taught in Rwanda [at least at the time of completing this volume in February 2013] 'because there is no agreement on what should be taught as history' (Mamdani, 2001: 267; see also Freedman *et al.*, 2004: 248), given that two versions of the past – the Hutu version and the Tutsi version – have proven impossible to merge. Of course, 'documents for official interpretations of Rwandan history' under the RPF administration exist and tell the official version of the country's history (Longman & Rutagengwa, 2004: 163–164). In this official version, the previous grand narrative promoted by the pre-genocide Hutu regimes, is described as 'shaped by ideological considerations' (*Ibid.*). Longman and Rutagengwa (2004: 168) further noted that a third version of Rwanda's past exists, the one 'offered by most specialists in Rwandan history'. This version, they suggested, 'differs substantially' from both the Hutu and Tutsi versions of Rwanda's past. I would suggest that the major difference between the three versions is that the first two are pure ethnic, cultural memories that include myths and traditions alongside everyday experiences, whilst the latter is historiography or any other scholarly driven endeavour, essentially based on evidence, and, where enough evidence is yet to be found, on hypotheses. Arguing against postmodernist history and its relativism that leaves room to cultural memory narratives in historical discourse, historian Gertrude Himmelfarb (1999: 72–73) did not systematically reject relativism in historical work. She rather stressed that relativism should be 'firmly rooted in reality'.

I would basically agree with Longman and Rutagengwa regarding the existence of the three categories of these versions of the past. I am calling them categories rather than just versions, because within each category – the Hutu version, the Tutsi version, and the specialist version[s] – there is no absolute unanimity. A Tutsi close to the former monarchy, Mukasonga (2006: 45), for instance, whose father was an upper-class civil servant, considered the monarchists' bloody attacks of the 1960s as being an insignificant 'suicidal dash of a hundred poorly armed refugees from Burundi.' Unlike her, Twagilimana, a Tutsi with no obvious connections with the aristocracy under the monarchy and a fervent critic of the 'Hutu Republics', referred to the same wars as 'attacks to force their [Tutsi refugees'] return to power fomenting an already strong anti-Tutsi sentiment in the country' which 'were followed by severe reprisals against the Tutsi living in Rwanda'. These attacks took place while 'the Hutu majority had not yet forgotten the yoke under which it had lived for centuries' (Twagilimana, 2003: 72 & 75).

On the Hutu side, for instance, there is no unitary vision of the Second Republic [1973 – 1994]. During that period, the natives of the central and southern parts of the country were subjected to a silent but visible discrimination in senior public positions, in education, and in the army (Gasana, 2002: 35; Ntisoni, 2007: 36). This situation led to two different attitudes towards the 1990–1994 war. Coming from war devastated Byumba, Umutesi (2000: 34–35) maintained that the southerners had no sympathy for the displaced. The northerners were told that 'they were responsible for their misfortune because they were members of the presidential block parties, but in reality it was because they were from the north'. On their side, the displaced and the northerners suspected the southerners of being RPF's accomplices. Regarding the specialist version, too, there is no single version on which specialists agree. Moreover, there are so many areas of specialisations with regards to Rwanda's past: Cultural History, Oral History, Oral Literature, Memory Studies, Genocide Studies, Legal Studies, Cultural Anthropology, Religious Studies, Ethnology, [Post] Colonial Studies, to mention but a few. They necessitate specific approaches and methodologies, and thus lead to specific results. Finally, as Associated Press' Peter James Spielmann pointed out, within those individual disciplines, there is no unanimity on many issues. There are rather 'disputes among researchers at several highly respected international peace institutes' which are echoed in academic journals and papers and claim 'to shed light on questions that have implications beyond the academic world.'[20] Following Spivak (1990: 34), what is essential to retain is that each version of

---

20 Peter James Spielmann, 'War: Is it getting more hellish, or less?' CBS News, 12 July 2009. http://www.cbsnews.com/stories/2009/07/12/ap/national/main5153528.shtml (Accessed 13 July 2009)

history is a production of narratives none of which can be 'an objective analysis' or 'an end of narrativisation'.

## 1.3 Controlling Memory through Education

Napoleon Bonaparte once said that 'of all our institutions, the most important is public education', because 'all depends on it, the present and the future'.[21] The first Republic President Grégoire Kayibanda [1961–1973], a former teacher and political activist, seemed to know this principle. In 1966, his government – equally composed of former teachers (Erny, 2003: 21) – took a number of measures regarding the educational system in Rwanda. Two of these were [1] that all schools that were ever constructed with state subsidies became state property; and [2] the removal of 'the choice of textbooks and curriculum from the sole jurisdiction of school authorities' (Mamdani, 2001: 136). This is exactly what Napoleon asked his minister of cults to do back in 1804. He had to make a reading list comprising both classic and modern authors so 'to impose to the youth a spirit and opinions that are in conformity with the laws of the Empire'. Moreover, teachers should do all that is in their power 'to avoid any reaction while handling the Revolution'.[22] President Kayibanda's administration also introduced a new course in the primary and secondary education curriculum, namely Civics, to inculcate the new political ideals into pupils' minds. The Hutu Revolution needed to have its own history taught because 'Revolutions have their own relevant past' (Hobsbawm, [1983] 2012: 2). For the Tutsi, the course rather aimed 'to propagate hatred and to preach the Parmehutu[23] ideology to the school-going Hutu youths' (Kajeguhakwa, 2001: 103).

Mahmood Mamdani observed that 'the 1966 law provided an instrument for Hutu-ising control over a Tutsi dominated educational system'. Before that law and just after independence, Kayibanda had appointed himself as Minister of Education besides his functions as president (Erny, 2003: 21). He had been in the Church circuit since his childhood to the Nyakibanda senior seminary and knew that 'a great majority of the clergy and school directors were Tutsi' (*Ibid.*: 27). The above measures show that Kayibanda was willing to have full control over the educational system and its curricula. Doing so required limiting the authority of the Church on them. The 1966 legislation, as Erny (2003: 28) explained, implicitly targeted both the Tutsi pre-eminence and the Church. Despite that law, the Catholic Church remained in control of most private education even in post-genocide Rwanda (Freedman *et al.*, 2004: 251).

The narrative taught in schools as history during the second Republic [1973–1994] was largely fetched from the memories relating to the Hutu ethnic identity: the stress was put on the nation-forming process during which the Tutsi

---

21 Napoléon Bonaparte, *Vues politiques* (Paris: Librairie Arthème Fayard, [1806] 1939), pp. 211–212.
22 *Ibid.*, pp. 232–233.
23 Parmehutu is the Hutu Emancipation Movement led by Grégoire Kayibanda since the late-1950s. With the sympathy and support of the Church and the Colonial Administration, the Parmehutu assumed control of power as state-party from 1961 until 1973.

conquerors invaded Hutu kingships, decapitated their kings, emasculated them, killed their male descendants, before annexing the conquered territories to the Rwanda in making. The events in 1959 were also largely portrayed from the Hutu emancipationist perspective. The 1959 Hutu Revolution appeared as the founding act of new Rwanda, while the Tutsi refugees who ran away during that period emerged as the enemies of democracy. Without openly acknowledging it, the post-genocide Rwanda has reversed the situation, if one agrees that radio, television and public campaigns are other powerful ways to teach history outside conventional school settings. Through these channels, pre-colonial Rwanda is depicted as a land of milk and honey; the 1959 Hutu Revolution emerges as just an *avant goût* of the 1994 genocide and Kayibanda and the Hutu Emancipationists are depicted as criminal despots. The attacks of the Tutsi refugees throughout the 1960s are presented as early attempts to liberate, and bring democracy to, Rwanda, which eventually happened in 1994.

Moreover, even though no particular course is labeled history, memory narratives make it into schools through other disciplines. Primary Social Studies is one such discipline where accounts coloured with ethnic identities and related memories are distilled and channeled to the learners, without necessarily being called history. For instance, one textbook contains a unit titled 'Traditional relationships in our district' (Bamusananire *et al.*, 2006: 81–84) and discusses 'Family relationships', 'Social relationships', 'Cultural relationships', 'Economic relationships', and 'Political relationships'. Apart from the 'Family relationships' and the 'Cultural relationships' sections, all others are pure memory, where a clear Tutsi ethnic bias is perceptible. Under 'Social relationships', pupils learn that 'there are many orphans in our district as a result of the genocide' (*Ibid.*: 81), whilst perhaps a number of the pupils reading that, were orphaned by the RPF. The 1990 – 1994 war, which made hundreds of thousands of Hutu orphans, is tactically avoided for obvious memory purposes. The 'Economic relationships' section is the most memory-tainted part, with a clear ethnic bias. There, the young learners get acquainted with the *Ubuhake* system (see Section 1.1.). This is what they should know about that system:

> Ubuhake was a traditional economic relationship between people who owned cattle and those who did not. People who did not own cattle could work for someone who was rich, and in return could be given a number of favours, including a cow, or plot of land to farm. Sometimes, a farmer will look after cattle belonging to someone else. In return that person will give the farmer a calf (*Ibid.*: 82–83).

With this account, the pupils are expected to long for that era depicted as a golden age, when people were so kind to one another and the rich were keen to help the poor. The relationships between the Hutu and Tutsi ethnic groups within that system are simply camouflaged behind phrases like 'people who owned cattle' and 'people who did not', and no single critical issue is raised about the system. From a Hutu memory perspective, this could be seen as a way of guiding the pupils to a certain understanding of the 1959 events, which appear to them as having had no valid grounds to take place. As for the 'Political relationships' section, it presents the political system in a way that leaves an ethnic-memory biased picture in the minds of the learners. The pupils learn that 'The King came from one family and kingship was hereditary... The King chose the chiefs in each of the country's chieftaincies and sub-chieftaincies and they made the laws for the people' (*Ibid.*: 84). Viewed from the vantage point of the Hutu's memory, the pupils were not told that only the Tutsi from a certain clan [*Abanyiginya*] were eligible for kingship. They were not taught that no single Hutu was ever appointed as Chief until the late-1950s when political change had reached a decisive stage. Once again, this appears as a tactic to trigger a certain thinking among the pupils, with the aim of demonstrating that the Hutu emancipationist movement was not grounded and justified.

## 1.4 Inheriting a Heavy Past

President Kayibanda's father, Léonidas Rwamanywa, was himself a former serf, *Umugaragu*, which contributed to the shaping of Kayibanda's memories and political views about the system and its supporters. In a speech on 10th April 1964, about five months after the attack of the Tutsi refugees close to the *Union Nationale Rwandaise* [UNAR] – a monarchist party –and willing to avenge themselves on the Hutu (Chrétien *et al.*, 1995: 92–93), President Kayibanda repeatedly referred to his *Ubuhake* memories, and the fear that the idea of the return to that system provoked in him and those who shared those memories. He said: 'Some of you [Tutsi rebels] have even recognised that if the Tutsi had won [the Christmas 1963 war], no Hutu would have survived, except those who would have accepted to be ten times tied with the *Ubuhake* chains'.[24] The 'ten times' comparison most likely refers to the 'one chain' that [figuratively] tied his father, and implies that the revenge-seeking Tutsi would tighten the system ten times.

Assmann ([2006] 2008: 213–214) noted that although memories extinguish with the death of the person who bears them, they nonetheless go through a recycling process and manage to make it to the next generation. Assmann contended however, that such embodied memories, i.e., based on lived experiences, 'do not transcend the temporal range of three generations, a span amounting to at most 100 years'. Discussing generational memories and their transmission, Assmann (2006: 24) noted that when the generation that experienced the past has passed away, the younger generation takes over and steps into the older generation's shoes. She called this phenomenon the 'shift from a "generation of experience" to a "generation of confession" who identifies with the experience of their parents and grandparents and tries to transform it into a lasting and respected memory'.

Rwanda scholars Albert-Enéas Gakusi and Frédérique Mouzer authored a book with a memory inspired title: *From the Rwandan Revolution to the Counter-Revolution* (2003). Its front cover is even more memory-evoking as it shows, side by side, the portraits of President Kayibanda in black and white, and of President

---

24  Excerpt from Kayibanda's speech in Jean-Pierre Chrétien (Ed.) *et al., Rwanda : Les médias du génocide* (Paris : Karthala, 1995), pp. 122–123.

Kagame in colour. The title and the cover could easily be interpreted as representing the generations of the 1960s – President Kayibanda and the Revolution, with the black and white portrait sending the viewer to the past – and of the 1990s – President Kagame and the counter Revolution, with a picture in colour sending the reader to the present times. The two authors called the current behaviour of the RPF-dominated regime 'an inter-generational reproduction of the pre-1960 attitude, consisting in denying the abuses that led to the 1959 Revolution-related violence' (Gakusi & Mouzer, 2003: 84). In other words, the current Tutsi leaders, who are mostly the second generation from the one contemporary to Kayibanda (Chrétien *et al.*, 1995: 93), are a generation of confession, identifying itself with, and imitating wholly, or to some extent, the previous generation. Von der Dunk (2005: 218) used the bill metaphor to explain relationships between the old and the young generations. He wrote: 'Each generation inherits a bill [from the previous generation], and leaves its own behind'. Kayibanda's personal notes about his father and his experience as a serf push to think that Kayibanda inherited that unpaid bill from his father:

> … Like 'everybody else', he [Kayibanda's father] had worked for 'customary authorities'… but had never accepted to engage in seeking favours, getting the only leisure allowed by his own labour. While doing everything to get 'the best' out of the situation, he waited for the usual cow without bowing down, and, above all, had refused to have his children involved in the cattle-based clientelism that 'he abhorred' (Paternostre de la Mairieu, 1994: 39–40).

Discussing inheritance and its connections with language, Derrida maintained that it 'always passes from one singularity to another' and implies 'a filiation with language and a singular memory'. More importantly, and this is where Derrida's point joins Assmann's theory on the generation of confession, an 'inheritance is not simply a good I receive; it is an assignation of fidelity, an injunction to responsibility' (Derrida & Stiegler, [1993] 2002: 86 – 87). In other words, as Pierre Lévy (2010: 108) explained, 'a generation finds itself confronted with *one* essential question, which is really a meta question, namely, " what is the essential problem facing us?"' There is no doubt that the most essential issue Kayibanda's father was facing was his status of serf.

As first post-monarchy president, Kayibanda started paying the bill, or taking what he considered to be his responsibility, by bringing radical changes at all levels. All those who shared his ethnic identity and memories found in him their hero, whilst those with opposite memories, those who were fighting for the *status quo*, found in him their enemy. Like the *Ubuhake*, the 1959 Revolution was viewed differently, as the former serfs and their sons finally took power, sending most of their former masters and their sons into exile. President Kagame represents the latter group. His father Deogratius Rutagambwa was 'related to the royal family of Mutara [III] Rudahigwa, and had enjoyed a close association with the king in his early career' (Misser, 1995: 31 & 38). He was also a 'property and cattle owner', which allowed him to lead 'a comfortable life' (*Ibid.*). Paul Kagame added a detail: his father was 'privileged', based on his wealth and on his 'belonging to the [Queen-providing] Bega clan' (*Ibid.*).

His mother Asteria 'was very closely related to the queen[25] and so the family had access to the benefits of a position in traditional Rwandan society' (Waugh, 2004: 8). Waugh quoted President Kagame as saying that his father could have become a chief,[26] but did not like it, preferring to conduct business (*Ibid.*). With this background and in the light of the above-mentioned arguments about ethnic identities and related memories, it would not be astonishing that President Kagame would view the November 1959 Revolution as a mini-genocide,[27] not as a revolutionary change of power that brought those who made his father's fortune to the leading position.[28] Until today, as Buckley-Zistel (2006: 125) noted, 'there is no agreement about the nature of that event', because 'most Tutsi refer to it as "genocide" or "massacres"', while 'for many Hutu it marked the emancipation from Tutsi oppression'. Newbury (2002: 69–70) summarised the way in which two narratives have emerged to represent that crucial event in Rwanda's history as follows:

> One view holds that the changes from 1959 to 1962 in Rwanda were engineered by Belgian colonial authorities and the Catholic Church… From this perspective, manipulation by external forces was the main reason for political violence in Rwanda during the reversal of power relations, and the subsequent exodus of many Tutsi into exile… A contrasting view claims that while some Belgians and leaders in the Catholic Church supported change, it was Hutu leaders and the rural majority in Rwanda who effected the revolution, by reacting to the double colonialism of rule by Tutsi and Belgian authorities. In this view, Hutu counter élite demanded an end to the privileging of Tutsi in employment, education, access to political power, and economic advancement and thereby an end to discrimination against Hutu… As will be evident, the first versions tend to be advanced by those wishing to rationalise rule by Tutsi; the second versions are more characteristic of powerholders in the Hutu dominated governments that ruled from 1961 until 1994 (Newbury, 2002: 69–70).

In late-1998, a group of leading historians from the University of Rwanda proposed yearly seminars on Rwanda's history in an effort to, one day, come out with a unified, consensual version of Rwandan history. Deo Byanafashe, Dean of

---

25  Waugh (2004: 12) and Misser (1995: 39) indicated that Kagame's mother Asteria was the sister of Rosalie Gicanda, the wife of King Mutara III Rudahigwa.
26  King's official representative.
27  The description that Paul Kagame made of his flight from Nyarutovu (Gitarama) gives a clear idea as to the mini-genocidal character that he gives to the 1959 events (Waugh, 2004: 7).
28  In 1957, the future president of the first Republic Grégoire Kayibanda was elected chairman of the managing board of Trafipro, the biggest commercial cooperative of those days (Paternostre de la Mairieu, 1994: 129). According to Waugh (2001: 233), Trafipro was founded by Kagame's father and was the first parastatal organisation opened to non-Tutsi. Waugh's argument is strongly challenged by Mamdani who indicated that Trafipro was rather founded by the Catholic Church in 1956, and that from then on, the cooperative served as 'cells for the development of the Hutu movement' (Mamdani, 2001: 118). This makes any involvement of the Tutsi aristocracy – Kagame's father included – almost unthinkable.

the School of Arts and Letters, noted that 'the historians who lived through these events are now more conscious that there is a big gap between what is written and the reality', and stressed 'the need to correct things, before it goes too far, before the history inspires another genocide'.[29] The October 1999 seminar was dedicated to the hot 1959 events, which, as noted above, are called Revolution or [mini] genocide depending on one's ethnicity. Prominent history professor Gamaliel Mbonimana wished the Hutu and Tutsi were at the same table 'to discuss and come to an agreement', based on hard, 'objective data'.[30] For Byanafashe, 'a revolution is a radical change which is beneficial'. He implied here that the 1959 change was radical but not beneficial, while for former Prime Minister Faustin Twagiramungu, who reacted from abroad, the 1959 events were definitely beneficial, because, 'what people wanted was to get rid of [the] feudal system',[31] which they achieved. While genuine consensus about the long-gone past seems still to be far, a certain 'truth' of the more recent past to be remembered in the future has been engineered, as the next chapter shows.

---

29  Deo Byanafashe speaking in *Hopes on the Horizon* (2001), a documentary by Onyekachi Wambu.
30  Gamaliel Mbonimana speaking in *Hopes on the Horizon* (2001), a documentary by Onyekachi Wambu.
31  Deo Byanafashe and Faustin Twagiramungu speaking in *Hopes on the Horizon* (2001), a documentary by Onyekachi Wambu.

*Chapter 2*

# Parallel Remembrances

Remembering in modern-day Rwanda is a very complicated matter. It can lead to imprisonment, harassment, and even death. The kind of remembering I am discussing here is remembering publicly as opposed to remembering internally without any external manifestation of the act of remembering. In this chapter, I argue that these two forms of remembering are common currency in post-genocide Rwanda, as the dominant narrative of the tragic period between 1990 and 1994 excludes traumatic experiences suffered by the Hutu, whilst promoting equally traumatic experiences suffered by the Tutsi, including the genocide. The remembering exercise becomes even trickier when the legal system is used to intimidate and prosecute those who want to publicly remember other past experiences than those defined by the government. In what follows, I start with a concrete case of parallel remembering, whereby a remembering subject knows the 'right' past that she can safely remember and the one she had better forget to remember. I then analyse this situation as being a form of government-engineered amnesia, which, in turn, has resulted in self-imposed amnesia. Finally, I discuss some ways in which those forms of amnesia are overcome through everyday use of language.

## 2.1 Remember the 'Right' Past

During Christmas 2006 I met, in Brussels, a young Rwandan lady, 25, who survived the 23rd April 1994 massacre that she perceived as counter-genocide by the Rwandese Patriotic Front [RPF]'s rebels in the Byumba soccer stadium. Being from Byumba myself where I spent much of my early childhood, I was highly inquisitive about how the people from that place were killed. I asked her the details of what had happened that day. She painfully told the story, admitting that it was the first time in 12 years she was able to talk about that heart-tearing event, simply because she was unsure if her story would not land into untrustworthy ears. I was lucky to have asked her my questions after reading the first ever written book about the so-called counter-genocide by an insider, former RPF lieutenant and secret agent Abdul Ruzibiza.[32] I was struck by the coincidence of the two stories, one from the victim's side and the other from the killer's side. Unfortunately, the lady, whom I will not name since she still lives in Rwanda, could not go beyond the scene of 'huge black smoke rising from the stadium' taking the souls of those poor peasants to the skies.

---

32 Abdul Ruzibiza, *RWANDA: Histoire secrète* (Paris: Editions du Panama, 2005), pp. 274–276.

Whether 2,500 or so people were butchered and burned or not and by whom and why, is not the subject of the discussion at this moment. My concern is to know how this painful event is [not] remembered, and by whom. The undeniable reality is that the 23$^{rd}$ April 1994 massacre took place in that particular place, but, unlike other similar events, it has not retained the attention of Rwandan authorities, nor has it prompted them to raise a monument in memory of those people, who, until now, have neither been mourned nor have they received any appropriate burial, let alone an official day of remembrance (Brandstetter, 2010: 15–16; Longman & Rutagengwa, 2004: 167).

After minutes of weeping, my interlocutor evacuated much of her pain and asked if I wanted to know more. The 'torture' resumed. I wanted to know how these people had been counted during the 2002 official census of the genocide victims in the city of Byumba, where 'little genocidal violence' took place (Freedman *et al.*, 2004: 249), because the percentage of the Tutsi population there was much smaller. She told me that, 'all the dead in 1994 were genocide victims'. She went on to say that 'the only details we were asked to provide were whether our relatives had been killed by machete, grenade, gun, etc.; or whether the killer was a militiaman, a government soldier or a civilian [neighbour]'. There was, thus, no room for RPF rebels as killers. 'Why should I put myself in problems by evoking the [23 April 1994] massacre?' the lady asked, concluding our talk.

## 2.2 Imposed Amnesia

In his book discussing the *Development of Affect, Perception, Attention, and Memory,* psychologist Ernest Schachtel (1959: 317–318) distinguished three sorts of amnesia: normal amnesia, pathological amnesia, and imposed amnesia. Normal amnesia, which is close to the Freudian dream amnesia, consists of the 'constant forgetting of those parts and aspects of experience which do not fit into the ready patterns of language and culture'. Pathological amnesia refers to the forgetting caused by 'individual traumatic experience' and by 'the stresses and conflicts operative in the culture…' As for imposed amnesia, it is caused by the clichés which cultures impose on experience and memory: 'even within a culture different *groups* may show marked differences in the degree to which conventional schemata of experience and memory prevent the recall of actual experience' [Emphasis added].

In the Rwandan post-genocide context, the third type of amnesia took unprecedented dimensions, especially because politics, rather than culture, is the one that imposes the clichés. Sam Wineburg (2001: 242–243) used the term 'occlusion' rather than 'amnesia' to describe such situations, preferring to use it because it conveys in a clearer manner the notion of certain stories from the past being excluded from the dominant narratives. According to him, 'occlusion' renders better the idea of 'blockage', 'partiality and opacity', while 'amnesia' implies erasure or forgetting:

Collective occlusion is the flip side of collective memory. It speaks to that which is no longer common knowledge, no longer easily retrieved or taken for granted. Collective occlusion asks us to think about the stories, images, and cultural codes that become blocked in the transmission process from one generation to the next. Archived in historical memory and present in lived memory, occluded stories are at risk of being lost in the everyday processes of how societies remember and transmit their pasts to a new generation (*Ibid.*).

The most important point in this regard is that Rwanda's political authorities are forcing part of the population to forget, to purge their memories, or, let's say, to remember events in a different way from how they took place. In his book *History Remembered, Recovered, Invented*, historian Bernard Lewis (1975: 55–56) reminded that remembering is not a fortuitous act but rather a means to an end. One of the purposes of remembering is 'to explain and perhaps to justify the present – a present, some present – on which there may be dispute'. Ricoeur (2004: 85) took the argument further, contending that memory manipulation is used for ideological purposes to justify and legitimate power and domination. The past, as literary critic Walter Benjamin ([1955] 1973: 256–257) observed, has 'a temporal index' which the present generation takes advantage of to endow itself with some Messianic powers. Any image of the past that does not contribute in showing that 'Our coming was expected on earth' is deemed to be filtered out [by those in the dominant position, or 'the ruling classes' as Benjamin ([1955] 1973: 257) called them]. Thus, 'every image of the past that is not recognised by the present as one of its own concerns threatens to disappear irretrievably' (*Ibid.*).

Considered from this angle, remembering is 'a tool for the ruling classes' (*Ibid.*: 257) and serves political, ideological goals and is unmistakably subjective. The lady from Byumba has two parallel remembrances of the 23rd April 1994 killings: the official one, which is the one she learnt from the government that was formed by the victorious rebels, and the true, prohibited, and more intimate one, which she shares with trustworthy people far from public ears. The official narrative, as summarised by President Paul Kagame, RPF Commander in Chief during the 1990 to 1994 war, is:

> … they keep saying that the RPF, too, killed people? Whom did they kill? Millions of people crossed the border after massacring [the Tutsi]! Who was killed by the RPF? The RPF does praiseworthy things only. Maybe were we somewhat careless. But I think the means at our disposal were not enough [during the 1996–1997 invasion of Zaire/DR Congo]. That is why we could not achieve everything the way we should. That is also why I am regretting.[33]

---

33 President Paul Kagame's speech, 7 April 2007 in Murambi, Southern Province: … *ngo na RPF nayo ngo yarishe yishe abantu? Yishe abahe se? Miliyoni zikarinda zambuka zimaze kwica? RPF yishe abahe? RPF igira neza gusa. Cyangwa yararangaye sinzi. Ariko ngirango ni uko ubushobozi bwari buhari butari buhagije. Ngirango ntitwajyaga gukora buri kintu cyose uko gishoboka. Niyo mpamvu nsubira inyuma nkicuza.*

Hearing President Kagame wondering whom the RPF killed and regretting his failure to kill millions who crossed the border, sparks two reflections: first, the lady from Byumba is warned regarding what she must consider as non-events or, alternatively, as praiseworthy acts; second, this statement betrays the president's own ethnic identity, which determines which of his past achievements he forgets and which he remembers as praiseworthy. By proclaiming that the alleged crime was praiseworthy, the President declared that particular event – and all others similar to it – as taboos, and thereby forced the survivors to lock their memories (Assmann, [2006] 2008: 212). Assmann's use of the verb 'to lock' is helpful in explaining the way forced forgetting takes place. Locking is not erasing, but rather rendering something inaccessible to other people. It joins the survival of images discussed by Ricoeur (2004: 433), who contended that the fact of 'Recognising a memory [whether locked or not] is finding it again. And finding it again is assuming that it is, in principle, available, if not accessible'. In other terms, forgetting in this sense becomes pretending not to remember, because 'what we have once seen, heard, experienced or learned is not definitely lost, but survives since we can recall it and recognise it' (*Ibid.*: 434). One way of understanding this, is that complex and conflicting memories like the ones in Rwanda are often 'imbued with moral imperatives' because, as sociologist and cultural memory scholar Iwona Irwin-Zarecka (1994: 8–9) rightly observed, 'some kill because of memory obligations'. President Kagame further justified his armed struggle and all it involved as being part of his rights:

> I am a Rwandese, I had a right, I had the basis for getting involved in the armed struggle to liberate my country from Habyarimana, from the government he was leading; I have been a refugee in ... outside Rwanda for 30 years. .. Well I had the right to fight for my rights![34]

In other words, the 23rd April 1994 killing was part of the struggle 'for my rights', the ones he lost when he was forced to leave the country in 1961 as a result of another ethnic [memory] conflict (Misser, 1995: 31). His memory, thus, serves as a justification for whatever happened and creates what Irwin-Zarecka called memory obligations to kill. Holding the speech on the national radio and knowing that survivors of RPF's praiseworthy acts would hear it, is part of the memory process, comprising both remembering and forgetting. When massacres are described as 'praiseworthy acts', the survivors of those acts draw the conclusion about what they should remember and what they should essentially forget (Zerubavel, 2003: 5). What appears here is that imposed amnesia necessarily implies 'imposed memory' or 'forced memorisation' on the part of the governing body claiming legitimacy (Ricoeur, 2004: 85). The kind of forgetting that is at work here is special, as it involves intimidation on the part of higher powers. In such a situation, as Ricoeur (2004: 448) suggested, 'The resource of narrative

---

34  BBC Hard Talk, Stephen Sackur talks to Rwanda's president, Paul Kagame on 7 December 2006 http://www.bbc.co.uk/newsa/n5ctrl/progs/06/hardtalk/kagame07dec.ram (Accessed 13 April 2009).

[then] becomes a trap', whereby social actors are stripped of their original power to recount their actions themselves.

Contrary to what is observed in other post-conflict situations, where reconciliation efforts pass through confessions and mutual forgiveness [in South Africa and Burundi, for instance], Rwanda has embarked on a 'good-massacres' versus 'bad-massacres' path, which, in the end, creates ethnic supremacy on one hand, and inhibition on the other hand. Referring specifically to this situation, Huyssen (2003: 15) suggested that 'the issues of memory and forgetting... are all-present in Rwanda'. In another speech commemorating the 16$^{th}$ anniversary of the genocide in Kigali, President Kagame explained how one can kill without regretting or otherwise having remorse for it – and thus forget that that was a crime – and asked young generations to follow that lesson:

> While building peace, we should do all we can to achieve that peace. But when there is no peace and when one has to fight for one's rights, there is no need to ask for forgiveness, but rather, one fights wholeheartedly. That is the culture we should be cultivating or fostering, so that our children can acquire it, and our leaders can be guided by it in the future.[35]

As other chapters will show, President Kagame belongs to an ethnic group, the Tutsi, which has a certain identity and corresponding memories, including traumatic and triumphant episodes. Shared by most other Tutsi, these memories constitute a lens through which each event is viewed and interpreted. Longman and Rutagengwa (2004: 177) researched the perceptions of the genocide in Rwanda, and came to the conclusion that

> people continue to relate to society differently depending upon their ethnic background. Certainly, Hutu and Tutsi experienced the violence in 1994 very differently. But the substantial divergence in responses in our research between Hutu and Tutsi, especially the survivors, suggests strongly that the two groups continue to experience the current situation differently.

A number of ways were used to confuse the remembering process by preventing part of the population from having material traces – memory as object – of their past. Ruzibiza (2005: 266), a prime witness [and actor] of the RPF killings asserted that the corpses of the Hutu were mixed with those of Tutsi and are thus remembered as Tutsi genocide victims, forcing the Hutu survivors to never mourn their loved ones. During her field research in Rwanda, Susanne Buckley-Zistel interviewed both Hutu and Tutsi living near the areas of the mass killings. One rural Hutu woman in Nyamata complained that

---

35  President Paul Kagame's speech commemorating the 16th anniversary of the genocide, 7 April 2010.

> ... *we* cannot identify the people they put into the memorial sites. *They* took all bones.[36] And no particular ethnicity died, all Hutu and Tutsi died. The problem is when *they* remember, *they* remember only Tutsi, while during the war RPF killed many Hutu, so *they* should remember also *our* people who died during that period (Buckley-Zistel, 2006: 138. Emphasis added. See also Brandstetter, 2010: 14–15).

The most important point in this peasant's opinion is the meaningful use of 'we/our' and 'they', which refers to ethnicity and translates a state-engineered, memory-based frustration. The opinions of the two women from Byumba and Nyamata who are not allowed to 'lament the killings by the RPA',[37] suggest that 'ethnic group identity is still very significant in Rwanda', and, that the government is responsible for creating 'hierarchies of suffering', by pushing some to remember and forcing others to forget (Buckley-Zistel, 2006: 146). The question is to know why a government dominated by an ethnic community – the Tutsi[38] – that was victimised by the genocide, should force another community – the Hutu – also victimised by another unprecedented massacre to forget their past or assimilate it to the Tutsi's.

Lewis (1975: 55–56) noted that 'where there are conflicting loyalties or clashing interests, each [community] will have its own version of the past, its own presentation of the salient events'. To answer the question of why, that I have just posed, I will borrow Lewis' thought about political authorities in earlier times. These controlled people's remembrances to 'predict and even to control the future' (*Ibid.*). It is also worth noting with Huyssen (2003: 26–27) that national, regional, and local memories are 'a fundamentally political question' with intimate links that include processes of democratisation. Let me add with Derrida, that this 'politics of memory' that consists in representing 'a fraction of the nation, if not a class' or 'something which is not the "integral will" nor often the "general will" of all the citizens of [the] state' (Derrida & Stiegler, [1993] 2002: 62–63), is dangerous and makes the future of Rwanda even gloomier. It is likely to lead to the violent breaking of the 'pact of secrecy' and provoke what Derrida (2002: 23–24) called 'a movement of the liberation of memory'. In the meantime, however,

---

36 Anthropologist Anna-Maria Brandstetter (2010: 14 – 15), who conducted research about genocide memorial sites in Rwanda, noted that although the sites were 'places for the "victims of the Tutsi genocide"', they nonetheless harbor the remains of the Hutu who opposed the previous regime. However, the statement that 'the Tutsi and Hutu are buried together without regard to the circumstances under which they lost their lives', implies that other circumstances than genocide existed. This explains why the relatives of the killed Hutu 'express mixed feelings about the memorials', as they are all referred to as 'victims of the genocide against the Tutsi' (*Ibid.*: 15).
37 The Rwandese Patriotic Army was the armed branch of the Rwandese Patriotic Front.
38 President Paul Kagame's biographer Colin Waugh revealed the ethnic reality within the RPF administration. He wrote that the RPF had skilfully managed to draw on the support of moderate Hutu opposed to the former Kigali regime. The first president of the transitional government, Pasteur Bizimungu, the new regime's second prime minister Pierre-Célestin Rwigema, and Interior Minister Seth Sendashonga were all prominent Hutu and each gave a semblance of multi-ethnicity to the regime... The façade of multi-ethnicity crumbled quickly and Kagame increasingly found himself forced into the stance which he had long sought to avoid: that of an embattled military dictator, maintaining power by force and internal repression, representing the interests of only a minority of the total population he purported to govern (Waugh, 2004: 149).

the amnesia-imposing process has borne its fruits, as Rwandans know by now which version of the past they can safely remember.

## 2.3 Self-Imposed Amnesia

A more worrying issue is self-imposed amnesia, which Buckley-Zistel (2006: 134) called 'chosen amnesia' which is defined as the deliberate inability or unwillingness 'to recall particular aspects of the[ir] past… to avoid antagonisms and to be able to live peacefully'. The question asked by the lady from Byumba – 'why should I put myself in problems by evoking the [23rd April 1994] massacre?' – falls under the notion of chosen amnesia. Mentioning that her family had been killed by the RPA would be a useless provocation, and would bring more trouble. For sure, this situation of unacknowledged and hidden frustration on one hand, and of triumphalism on the other hand, allows peaceful and 'harmonious' relationships amongst the two ethnic groups, at least for a certain amount of time. However, 'it prevents the transformation of the society into one that will render ethnicity-related killings impossible', and, therefore, 'constitutes a time-bomb' (Buckley-Zistel, 2006: 147). During her field interviews, Buckley-Zistel (2006: 132) placed memory at the center of her research and focused 'on the stories people tell to refer to their past'. She noticed the parallel remembrance phenomenon, as she realised that Rwandans have both hidden and public memories:

> Interviewees frequently made their omissions explicit, stating that, despite their public attitude and occasionally even their participation in reconciliation projects, in their hearts it looked different. Although I felt that it was important for my interviewees to communicate this reservation, how it 'really' looked in their hearts was never revealed. Moreover, some of my interviewees, in particular those engaged in reconciliation efforts, cautioned me not to trust my impression of peaceful coexistence; they suggested that people hide their true feelings, especially from an outsider like myself (Buckley-Zistel, 2006: 133).

The study of post-genocide memories among the Hutu is hindered by this [self-] imposed silence that prevents all the pieces of the puzzle from being put together. This makes all future efforts vain, as any meaningful solution should be based on an overall picture of the perception Rwandans have of themselves, their neighbours, and their country in the future. Studying the relationship between enunciation and language, philosopher Michel Foucault (1969: 131–133) stressed that no analysis or study of enunciations would be possible if the latter have no 'material existence', either in the form of voice or other signs giving them shape: 'the enunciation needs that materiality; … It is part of the enunciation itself: any enunciation needs to have substance, a carrier, a space, a date'. Longman and Rutagengwa (2004: 164) made a similar observation during their two-year research in Rwanda. Whilst studying the impact of the RPF-dominated regime's policies on the way the population remembers the past, the two researchers' interviewees were not willing to discuss 'certain politically sensitive topics'. They realised that 'this reluctance [was] most pronounced in Buyoga, where RPF repression was most widely experienced'.

In another instance, Longman and Rutagengwa (2004: 177) were trying to understand a particular former Hutu refugee's perception of ethnic identity. They pointed out a sort of voluntary ambiguity created by the interviewee, in a way that left them with uncertainty as to what conclusion to draw: 'Whether he actually believes that his identity has changed is unclear'. What appeared to be more or less clear to the researchers is that the Hutu have engaged into a double memory game, whereby the rule is not to forget their past as they acquired or experienced it, while making an 'effort to adapt to the message of the regime – at least publicly'. This game, as Longman and Rutagengwa (2004: 177) remarked, 'is common to many of the people we interviewed'.

The two research projects cited above – Buckley-Zistel's and Longman and Rutagengwa's – confirm a Rwandan adage, which, it should be stressed, still serves as a guiding principle, that 'what goes out of one's mouth can hardly be withdrawn' (Erny, 2005: 208). In other words, excuses and apologies do not erase what has been uttered. The uttered words – enunciation – follow the one who uttered them. Therefore, one must be careful about what one says – for instance by being as ambiguous as possible – or simply say nothing at all, which is the conclusion of both projects (Amnesty International, 2010; see further illustration in the next section).

## 2.4 Overcoming Amnesia through Language

In his groundbreaking works on language in the early-20th century, Ferdinand de Saussure, the father of modern linguistics, maintained that that 'scientific study of languages' concerns itself primarily with 'the spoken language' and to a lesser extent with its 'envelop', the written texts. He stressed the connections between linguistics and other sciences, especially psychology and history: 'some borrow information, data from linguistics, and others, on the contrary, provide it with support in its task' (De Saussure, [1916] 1967: 20–21). In his study of Rwandans' perception of the notion of Being – *Etre* – philosopher Alexis Kagame[39] (1956: 22–23) contended that, in the same way western researchers use libraries to fetch information about their cultures, language was his first source for his philosophical inquiry. On his part, Foucault (1969: 20; see also Vansina, 1971: 450) observed that in some respects, history concerns itself with issues covered by other disciplines, namely linguistics, ethnology and others. In the case of Rwanda, a linguistic approach is essential in the study of Rwandans' memories and their manifestations. A close study of the different uses of Kinyarwanda, especially the choice of words, revealed that ethnicity provides guidance for some strategic choices of vocabulary, particularly when one has to speak about sensitive episodes

---

39 Alexis Kagame (1912–1981) is a Roman Catholic priest who extensively published volumes and articles on Rwanda's history, language, culture and traditions, and philosophy. He is not a family member or a relative of President Paul Kagame. Since the two names are recurrent in this book, I have decided to refer to the author as Alexis Kagame, and the statesman as President Kagame or Paul Kagame.

of Rwanda's past. Longman and Rutagengwa highlighted a revealing hide-and-seek game of expressions that pushes one to think that the self-imposed amnesia does not affect so much of everyday language. The two researchers realised that while the Tutsi genocide survivors constantly used the expression *itsemba bwoko* [extermination of an ethnic group], the

> Hutu were more likely to refer to *Intambara,* the war, *ubwicanyi,* the killings, or more vaguely *ibyabaye,* the happenings, or *amahano,* horror or tragedy. They tended to employ *itsemba bwoko,* if at all, only secondarily. Some Hutu mentioned as well *itsemba tsemba,* massacres, implying massacres of Hutu, which very few Tutsi, whether survivors or repatriated Tutsi refugees, mentioned (Longman & Rutagengwa, 2004: 170).

This example could be interpreted as a sign that shows that the choice of words in Rwanda often depends on one's ethnic identity and experience. Postcolonial critic Gayatri Spivak (1990: 36) suggested that 'even speaking "off the cuff" is conditioned by a whole variety of psycho-social, ethno-economic, historical and ideological strands', which Longman and Rutagengwa appear to have exemplified in Rwanda. Each syllable or combination of syllables has a meaning. The difference between the expressions *itsemba bwoko* and *itsemba tsemba* resides only in two syllables replaced by two other syllables. The two expressions should normally mean almost the same thing, and, in principle, should be inter-changeable. [*u-*]*Bwoko* means ethnic group, but in this expression, no specific group is mentioned, which means that the Hutu, too, would normally find their place behind the word [*u*]*bwoko*. Yet, the Hutu [survivors] do not consider their plight as incorporated within that term. As for *tsemba*, it is simply a repetition of the first word – *itsemba* – that stresses the systematic character and the large extent of the massacre. The latter expression does not make any distinction between, or reference to, ethnic groups, hence the preference of the Hutu.

More interestingly, without making any reference to any period of time, but only through daily usage, the vague and all-inclusive expressions preferred by the Hutu encompass the 1990–1994 period, while the specific, exclusive ones preferred by the Tutsi, for the same reasons, refer to the April–July 1994 period. For instance, the choice and the order of words in Marie-Béatrice Umutesi's (2000: 34) autobiography, gives strong indications about her 1990–1994 memories. She wrote that 'the assassination of president Habyarimana, the resumption of war, the massacres, the genocide surprised us…'. In this arrangement of words, each Rwandan finds his or her own place, but some hierarchy is established. As a Hutu from Byumba whose relatives were massacred by the RPF (Umutesi, 2000: 26–29), Umutesi put the memories of her own family members and friends before the rest by putting 'massacre' before 'the genocide'. Scholastique Mukasonga (2006), a Tutsi whose family was decimated during the genocide followed the same logic, but abstained from mentioning even once the massacres of the Hutu by the RPF, which is another way of establishing a memory-driven hierarchy.

These instances confirm theories that were developed in the 1950s by cross-cultural anthropologist Edward Hall. He conceptualised culture as being a form of communication, and language as one of the tools that use 'arbitrary vocal symbols to describe something'. He went on to suggest that 'talking is a highly selective process because of the way in which culture works. No culture has devised a means for talking without highlighting some things at the expense of some other things' (Hall, [1959] 1981: 97–98). The way individuals communicate follows some mental patterns, some laws 'governing changes in meaning when order is altered', or when 'the sequence of words, sentences, and paragraphs' is modified (*Ibid.*: 132). I want to stress the selectivity of both language and culture, and in doing so, I intend to remind the selective character of memory that I discussed in the introduction (Section 0.3). Many authors in various disciplines (Huizinga, 1936: 40–44; Hall, [1959] 1981: 20; Geertz, 1973: 44; Spradley, 1980: 6) have pointed out features that suggest that memory constitutes a great, if not the greatest, part of culture. From this perspective, 'culture' in Hall's quote at the beginning of this paragraph could be replaced by 'memory', to mean, as the example given above shows, that memory has devised means for talking that highlights certain things at the expense of others.

Another expression that has lost its initial 'innocent' meaning due to ethnic identities and related memories is *rubanda nyamwinshi*, that literally means the majority populace or 'the great masses'. The expression has ended up referring to the Hutu in the collective memory (Twagilimana, 2003: 68), and has become a taboo in post-genocide political discourse. Any research about the meaning of democracy in Rwanda would most likely come out with another hide-and-seek game, where the Hutu would conceive it as the rule of *Rubanda nyamwinshi*, a phrase frequently used in the Hutu rhetoric of the late-1950s–early-1960s, whilst the Tutsi would most likely refer to it as the rule of some form of non-ethnic majority. Aimable Twagilimana (2003: xxi), a Rwandan English language scholar also interested in ethnic studies in the African Great Lakes Region, suggested that the phrase 'Hutu majority' summarises the ideology underlying the 1959 Revolution, and is close to 'Hutu solidarity', 'Rwanda as a Hutu country', and 'Hutu Power'. An ambassador of Rwanda in Belgium once maintained that the 'democracy-equals-numeric-majority' equation is a false concept created by the Catholic Church and the colonial administration. He wondered: 'Should power be in the hands of the ethnic group with the numeric majority in the country?' For him and his government, President Kagame's regime has the 'idea-based majority',[40] and that is the true concept of democracy. It is here a question of 'numeric' referring to the Hutu, and 'ideas' referring to the Tutsi. In any case, the Tutsi will not use the expression *rubanda nyamwishi* – except when they want to mock those with different views (see for instance Mukasonga, 2006: 79) – to define democracy because, to use Twagilimana's words, behind that expression lurks 'a very dangerous anti-Tutsi ideology' (Twagilimana, 2003: 73). However, Sebarenzi (2009: 152–153) is the exception to the rule, as his vision of democracy

---

40   Rwanda's ambassador to Belgium quoted by Pierre Péan (2005), p. 443.

in Rwanda turns around 'finding a formula to ensure fair *power-sharing between the minority* [Tutsi: less than 20 percent] *and the majority* [Hutu: at least 80 percent]' [Emphasis added]. One way to prevent deadly struggles for power between the Hutu and Tutsi would be a rotating presidency.

The peculiarity of those hide-and-seek expressions is that not a single mention of ethnicity is made. Yet, no one can be mistaken in choosing their expressions or in detecting the hidden message or ideology. In his theories on discursive regularities, Foucault (1969: 66–67) analysed the relationship between words and the objects they refer to. The signs that make up the discourse do more than just designate objects or things. In the case of the Kinyarwanda language, that meta-language function of words is connected to ethnic identities and related memories. In his masterpiece song *Imparirwakunesha* [The perpetual winner], Hutu folksinger Simon Bikindi chants both the Hutu traumatic and triumphant memories tracing them back to times immemorial and comes to the conclusion that the solution is 'true democracy'.[41] He uses a multiple-meaning but certainly memory-inspired phrase of *Bene Sehabinzi* – The Cultivator's Children, to refer to a community he presents as including the Hutu, the Tutsi, and the Twa:

> The Cultivator's children should know that they have to stand together
> And stick strongly together to defend their interests…
> The Cultivator's children should know that in this move to strengthen true democracy and the Republic,
> The power should emanate from the majority through fair elections…
> Ask therefore for elections
> If a Hutu is elected, let him lead us.
> If a Tutsi is elected, let him lead us.
> If a Twa is elected, let him lead us…
> Rwanda belongs to all three of us.[42]

From a memory point of view, the voluntarily created confusion ends with 'The power should emanate from the majority' – majority here translates *rubanda nyamwishi* – which, as observed above, refers to the Hutu since the 1950s. Examples

---

41  Simon Bikindi was sentenced by the International Criminal Tribunal for Rwanda to 15 years. The Tribunal found him guilty on the count of 'public incitement to commit genocide' but stressed that Bikindi's songs did not 'constitute direct and public incitement to commit genocide per se' (ICTR, THE PROSECUTOR v. Simon BIKINDI. Case No. ICTR-01-72-T. JUDGEMENT , 2 December 2008, p. 104. https://www.unodc.org/tldb/pdf/International_Jurisprudence/Adhoc_Tribunals/ICTR_BIKINDI_Judgement.pdf [Accessed 6 July 2012]).

42  Simon Bikindi, *Imparirwakunesha* (Ballet song).
*Bene Sebahinzi bagomba kumenya ko bagomba kwishyira hamwe
Bakaba impuzamugambi koko kugira ngo inyungu zabo zidahohoterwa…
Bene Sebahinzi bagomba kumenya ko muri iyi nkubiri yo gushamangira
Repubulika na demokarasi isesuye,
Rubanda nyamwinshi aribo batanga ubutegetsi biciye
mu matora azira uburyarya…
Nimusabe amatora rero
Nihatorwa umuhutu twemere atuyobore
Nihatorwe umututsi, twemere atuyobore
Nihatorwe umutwa, twemere atuyobore…
U Rwanda ni urwacu uko turi batatu*

of this kind abound, and include such ordinary terms as 'war' or 'war victims' that implicitly put all the 1990–1994 victims in one basket, regardless of their ethnicity. Popular Hutu solo singer Juvénal Masabo Nyangezi adopted this all-inclusive attitude, especially in his [tragic memory] album – *Inkovu z' ibihe* [Times' Scars], dedicated 'to all tears, whatever tears'.[43] Composed during his 1994–2001 stay in jail on genocide charges, the decision to dedicate the all-inclusive songs 'to all [Hutu and Tutsi] tears' could be considered as a highly risky one. These subtleties of the Kinyarwanda language turn that language into a laboratory where researchers can measure the country's social temperature. Social temperature is best measured from the figurative, non-analytic form of language, rather than from its literal-analytic counterpart. Social and Cultural Studies scholar Paul Willis (2000: 11) distinguished these two forms noting that the literal-analytic 'is more likely to be standardised and instrumental… self sufficient, autonomous in space and time', while figurative, non-analytic, also known as 'metaphoric language'

> is *not standardised* and functions expressively – to *show feeling, emotion and identity* – rather than instrumentally. It *engages* you… You must use *your own experience* of the compared and the referred-to thing in order to make sense… of the relation embedded in the figure… *Metaphoric language always has, or always finds, a location in experience* [Emphasis added].

Given the abundance of such examples in Kinyarwanda, I would argue that that language is much more metaphoric than anything else. The ease with which metaphoric expressions are created from everyday experiences turns ethnic identities and related memories into a well from which Rwandans fetch to verbally express their feelings. The above-mentioned divergence of perceptions and expressions relating to the genocide might explain why the government has decided to leave the ambiguity-rich Kinyarwanda aside and borrow the French term genocide – *jenoside*. This is now used within the Constitution, with a clear specification that not only did it start on 1st October 1990 [war start] but also that it was [exclusively] against the Tutsi. Whilst this seems to have offered a legal solution to the naming and qualification of the latest epoch-marking events, the issue of dual interpretation of the past persists, and has even resulted in collective culpabilisation as the next chapter shows.

---

43   '*Iyi CD nyituye amarira yose, ayariyo yose*' http://www.masabo.tk/ (Accessed 13 July 2009).

*Chapter 3*

# Ethnic Guilt

The court, or any justice system, constitutes a framework in which memory is exercised in the sense that it looks into the past and interprets it in order to ultimately 'sort[ing] out what happened' (Shuman & McCall Smith, 2000: 88). Memory comes into play at many stages of the process: the offence that is being judged took place in the past; testimonies that are delivered during the trial are another form of memory; the judges' exercise to confront and weigh those testimonies against an already known – or assumed so – historical, social, political context, is another way of interpreting the past. In postwar or post-conflict situations, like the one in Rwanda, where a winner emerges and sets out to punish the loser, another dimension of memory appears: the winner determines which past to look into and which lines never to cross. The so-called *Gacaca* courts, the grassroots popular courts set up in 2001 allegedly to speed up genocide trials, was exactly a memory exercise in which a certain past had to be looked into, while another one was declared irrelevant. In this chapter, I argue that *Gacaca* was part of a larger ethnic culpabilisation process, which aimed to cast the net of guilt on more than one million Hutu, while no single Tutsi was worried for the now well-documented mass crimes committed against the Hutu. The focus of this chapter is firstly on a certain pedagogy, the *Gacaca* pedagogy, which could be summarised as aiming at the collective guilt of the Hutu whom the RPF leadership holds responsible for the genocide against the Tutsi, each at his or her own level. I will then discuss collective guilt itself and ways in which ethnic identities and related memories interfere with, and influence, the culpabilisation process, resulting in a phenomenon known as 'scapegoating', whereby an ethnic group constantly becomes a target every time that something goes wrong.

## 3.1 The *Gacaca* Pedagogy

The concept of *Gacaca* is very old and has long served as a way to settle disputes at the community level. The name itself comes from the fact that the community gathering usually took place with people sitting in a *gacaca*, that is, in the grass. In everyday life, *Gacaca* has come to mean settling the dispute among peers, *inter nos*, without taking it to higher authorities – parents, teachers, headmasters, etc. As this short explanation shows, the use of the concept to speed up genocide trials was the other way around, as it was a top-down exercise, with the highest authorities – whom the initial, traditional *Gacaca* avoided to involve – defining not only which disputes *must* be looked into but also which ones *must* be skipped.

This is an illustration of historian Eric Hobsbawm's ([1983] 2012: 6) observation about how ancient materials are used 'to construct invented traditions of *a novel type for quite novel purposes*' [Emphasis added].

As this section shows, the aim of the new type of *Gacaca* was far from the traditional peer-to-peer dispute-settling mechanism, as it appeared to be establishing new social relationships between the two ethnic groups, based on guilt on one hand, and on domination on the other hand. President Kagame was confident that his government's ethnic reconciliation strategy passed through *Gacaca*:

> The *Gacaca* operation is only accessorily repressive, as it is primarily pedagogical. The aim is not to jail tens of thousands of small genocide perpetrators, but to *make them aware of their acts and to push them to repent* [Emphasis added].[44]

Looking at the pedagogical aspect of the *Gacaca* from the Durkheimian perspective, there is no doubt that the *Gacaca* has achieved its goal of making people aware of their acts – even those they deny responsibilities for – and pushing them to repent. Early-20th-century sociologist Emile Durkheim ([1922] 1966: 67) theorised pedagogy, observing that its objective is 'not to describe or explain what is or what has been, but to determine what has to be'. Therefore it turns not to the present nor to the past, but to the future, and – this is interesting for the *Gacaca* pedagogy – proposes 'not to faithfully express given realities, but to decree precepts of conduct'. I should immediately stress that Durkheim's ([1922] 1966: 54–55) approach to pedagogy refers in the first place to the conventional educational settings, where children are naturally in a state of passivity due to their yet-to-be-filled memory that exposes them to 'contagion' and, thus, to the systematic absorption of knowledge taught to them.

One key aspect of the *Gacaca* pedagogy, as it appears in the aforementioned quote of President Kagame, is 'mak[ing] them aware of their acts and to push them to repent'. Far from being the proclaimed truth-and-reconciliation framework on the South African model, the *Gacaca* turned out to be a Confession-and-Repentance-at-all-costs machine. Anne Aghion made a series of documentaries about the *Gacaca* since the inception of that system, and these offer some insight into the *Gacaca* pedagogy. Her 2005 documentary, *In Rwanda We Say*, featured repentant *genocidaire*, Abraham Rwamfizi, who told how he was allowed to leave jail to be judged by his neighbours. The subtitles indicate the following: 'I was told that the only way was for me to confess. So, as I didn't want to make waves, I did. I asked that they write down my admissions'. Since subtitles are meant to render the general idea and are far from being a translation – in the sense of the source-text and the target-text matching each other (Ricoeur, 2006: 7) – I would like to provide my own word-to-word translation, which, in my opinion, provides more details about Rwamfizi's point:

---

44  Paul Kagame speaking to Francois Soudan (20–26 February 2005), p. 43.

> Whether you confess, or reject your guilt, or do whatever you want, [you should know that] that is how things are [must be]. I immediately decided not to defend myself, and I put my confessions on paper. I told people to write them thoroughly!...[45]

The difference between this word-to-word translation and the subtitled message is that in the former it appears more clearly that Rwamfizi was not given a choice [between confessing and defending himself]. Making no waves was the sole option. Once back home, Rwamfizi was supposed to bow down and ask for forgiveness, which he did, even though he was denying many of the charges. Unlike Rwamfizi, Isidore Gahutu, an elderly Hutu genocide suspect featured in Bernard Bellefroid's 2005 documentary, *Les collines parlent* [Hills Speak], attempted to defend himself before the Kagarama *Gacaca* Court of Appeal. He made waves for some time before realising that his fight, alone against all, would lead nowhere. As Gahutu was denying all the charges, the presiding judge read out pieces of evidence, undeniable as he described them, because 'they are written in a book'. The president knew that the old man was illiterate, and, as such, would not dare refute something 'written in a book'. Yet Gahutu kept denying, and, interestingly, reminded the furious judges of one basic principle of justice: 'If anyone would come here and accuse me, I would confess. I would confess because that witness would have seen me, in the presence of other witnesses'.[46] On hearing this bring-the-witness argument, the judges, on their turn, reminded Gahutu that he was just an accused, who could not give orders or lessons to the Court. As the judges were not keen on calling in eye-witnesses whose testimonies were rather 'written in the book', Gahutu stopped making waves and, as the *Gacaca* pedagogy wants him to behave, gave up the fight and repented:

> - GAHUTU: All they say is not true, but I confess.
> - VOICE FROM THE AUDIENCE [thus, a neighbour]: Of all those *untruthful* accusations, those you consider *untruthful*, don't you pick out one and confess to it? [Emphasis added]
> - GAHUTU: I have said that for now it is useless to go on defending my case. I confess.
> - PRESIDING JUDGE: That is contempt of Court... And that is punishable.
> - GAHUTU: I have confessed... Let the law be applied.
> - PRESIDING JUDGE: To which crime have you confessed?

---

45 Anne Aghion, *In Rwanda We Say* [documentary] (2005). Rwamfizi said the following in Kinyarwanda: *Wabyemera, wabihunga, wagira ute ntakundi niko bimeze. Nahise ngira ntya nanga gutera rwaserera, mpita mbyandika. Mbwira abanyandikira baranyandikira neza[aaa!]...*

46 Genocide suspect Isidore Gahutu speaking in June 2005 during a Gacaca hearing, in *Les collines parlent* (2005), a documentary by Bernard Bellefroid: *Ubungubu njye uwamvuga ku kintu njye ncyumva, nshobora kucyemera. Icyatuma ncyemera nacyemezwa n' uko uriya muntu yambonye, kandi akambona ahantu n' abandi bantu bahari.*

- GAHUTU: You told me that all has been said [meaning 'written in the book'], I cannot choose one crime and confess it. I accept to confess to all of them.[47]

Gahutu received 30 years in jail, a sentence aggravated by his obstruction to truth-seeking efforts and his misbehaviour before the Court. Proponents of the *Gacaca* approach would say that these are just two cases, while hundreds of thousands of others have taken place under optimal conditions. This argument is not convincing because the cases presented in the two documentaries are rather presented as a representation of the process. Aghion, for instance, is accompanied by a prosecutor, who, it appears logical, would not select the worst cases knowing that they would harm the image that the government wanted to spread about *Gacaca* courts. In Bellefroid's documentary, the case even appears to be a public relations opportunity for the judges. Before reading one testimony from the 'reference book', the presiding judge asked Gahutu to lend him his ears. When Gahutu said that he would not listen, the judge replied: 'Let me then read for you people and Westerners [white people]…'.

In what ways are these cases relevant to the discussions about ethnic identities and related memories? This is a legitimate question that readers might ask at this level. Ethnic identities and related memories are at stake here, because more than a million Hutu, like Rwamfizi and Gahutu, were forced to erase their relevant memories to replace them with confessions, or feel-good-memories, that the system wanted them to display. In this process there was a past to be interpreted from a certain perspective, in a certain present dominated by some political ideology, with a clear aim to influence future political, social, and economic relationships among ethnic groups. Sociologists Pierre Bourdieu and Jean-Claude Passeron (1977: 5) discussed the concept of pedagogy in political settings and its relationships with authority and power in a way that helps understand the *Gacaca* pedagogy described above. They referred to 'Pedagogic Action' as 'the imposition of a cultural arbitrary by an arbitrary power.' They further suggested:

> In any given social formation, the PA [Pedagogic Action] which is the power relations between the groups or classes making up that social formation put into the dominant position within the system of PAs is the one which most fully, though always indirectly, corresponds to the objective interests (material, symbolic and, in the respect considered here, pedagogic) of the dominant groups or classes, both by its mode of imposition and by its delimitation of

---

47 Genocide suspect Isidore Gahutu speaking in June 2005 during a Gacaca hearing, in *Les collines parlent* (2005), a documentary by Bernard Bellefroid:
-GAHUTU: *Ndavuga ngo barambeshyera ariko nabyemeye.*
VOICE FROM THE AUDIENCE: *Mu byaha byose bakubeshyera, mu byaha byose wivugira ko bakubeshyera, nta nakimwe wemera?*
-GAHUTU: *Njye nabasobanuriye aho bigeze sinirwa nongera kugira icyo mvuga. Nabyemeye.*
-PRESIDING JUDGE: *Usuzuguye urukiko … Ibyo kandi birahanwa nabyo.*
-GAHUTU: *Nabyemeye… Ubu ntegereje amategeko.*
-PRESIDING JUDGE: *Wemeye ikihe cyaha?*
-GAHUTU: *Ubundi mwe muragira muti babivuze byose. Uko babivuze byose, ntakintu mvuga ngo ndagishyira imbere nkemere. Njye nemeye ko byose mbyemeye.*

what and on whom it imposes... It is through the mediation of this effect of domination by the dominant PA that the different PAs carried on within the different groups or classes objectively and indirectly collaborate in the dominance of the dominant classes...' (*Ibid.*: 7).

The above provides an excellent theoretical framework to further analyse the *Gacaca* pedagogy and its memory implications. In another documentary titled *Gacaca: Living Together Again in Rwanda?* (2002) dedicated to the campaign paving the way for *Gacaca*, Aghion shows general prosecutor Jean-Marie Mbarushimana visiting the Ntongwe prison inmates. After giving lessons of Civics to men, the prosecutor went to the women's cell and told them what it meant and implied to be innocent in the *Gacaca* framework. Here is the conversation as rendered by the subtitles:

- GENERAL PROSECUTOR: Even if you neither denounced nor macheted anyone, in prison there are many women who massacred people. They wore militia uniform, like the men.
- WOMAN PRISONER 1: Women who bore children?
- GENERAL PROSECUTOR: Yes. Young girls and children [*toddlers*][48] also killed. It's true. You are old enough; you saw it with your eyes. Whether you approved or not, you saw it.
- WOMAN PRISONER 2: I have a question... We did nothing.
- GENERAL PROSECUTOR: If you are innocent we ask you to say: 'This is what I saw, here are the guilty ones'. Even your own husbands (Aghion, 2002).

The pedagogical message behind the prosecutor's definition and implication of innocence was that innocence had a price: denouncing the guilty. To be innocent was not to prove it but to denounce someone else, be they a spouse or someone else. To be innocent was to have seen something. An innocent who had seen nothing was not innocent. In a recent BBC Great Lakes' broadcast, Colonel Patrick Karegeya, a former RPF officer who headed Rwanda's military intelligence but was forced into exile in South Africa, said that Rwandans have become spies: a husband denounces his wife; a grandmother denounces grandchildren, and so on.[49] This is exactly what prosecutor Mbarushimana told the female inmates, namely that they should not hesitate to denounce their husbands and their children, including those who were toddlers at the time of the genocide.

Here one detects the memory agenda of the *Gacaca* approach: the prosecutor stressed many times that the inmates should search their memories and remember what they saw; and he told them what they should have seen, that is, what the *Gacaca* system expected them to have seen. Moreover, the prosecutor *reminded* them not to *forget* that even toddlers killed. Once again, the subtitles were misleading in rendering the term *abana b' ibitambabuga* with 'children' as if it were just *abana*.

---

48  The term 'children' is rendering *abana b' ibitambambuga* while that expression clearly refers to toddlers.
49  Patrick Karegeya speaking on 29 May 2010 during BBC Great Lakes' *Imvo n' Imvano* Show http://www.bbc.co.uk/greatlakes/meta/tx/nb/greatlakes_0530_au_nb.ram (Accessed 29 May 2010).

There is a palpable long-term goal to strongly push the almost 100 percent Hutu accused into a memory-rooted self-flagellation exercise, meant to keep them quiet about the other side of the traumatic memories of the 1990s. For instance, Rwamfizi's last-minute repentant attitude and the accompanying commitment to helping Tutsi survivors leave at least two unanswered questions: is this offered help mutual assistance or unidirectional? Rwamfizi seemed to be paying for offences he denied, but gave the impression he had no choice. Secondly, when will the chain stop? In other words, if Rwamfizi were to die,[50] would his children inherit that debt? This is likely to be the case, as I explain in the next section.

## 3.2 Collective Guilt

In his 2002 book on *Genocide and Crisis in Central Africa*, genocide scholar Christian Scherrer wrote: 'Anyone looking for evidence of collective guilt will have no trouble finding it in Rwanda' (Scherrer, 2002: 126). He backed this assertion with figures: 60 to 80 percent of educated people in higher professions took part in the genocide, while 'the civil servants were involved to almost 100 percent'. According to Scherrer, 'every fourth person in Rwanda's Hutu population – this includes men, women, and children – was probably directly involved in the genocide, and *millions* rendered themselves indirectly responsible' (*Ibid.* Emphasis added). As mentioned above, it is officially due to these extremely high and extensible figures that the *Gacaca* courts were set up. Basing his conclusions on three months of fieldwork in 2000 in Rwanda, anthropologist Darryl Li (2007: 101) went even further than Scherrer, to assert that '[E]ven Rwandans who did not kill still arranged their activities around and took advantage of the rhythm of "work".'

Combined, the claims of Scherrer and Li are startling: *millions* of Hutu are guilty of genocide and the rest of the Hutu gain comfort from it. These claims are certainly based on [field] research, but do not resist criticism. In a country where amnesia is [self-] imposed (Chapter 2), where confession and self-flagellation are turned into a means of survival, it is not astonishing that researchers come to the conclusion that almost 100 percent of Hutu admit having either killed, stood by, or organised their work around the killings. Why would they put themselves in trouble by saying the opposite? Some authors, however, quantify the number of those who participated in one way or another in the 'tens of thousands' (Brandstetter, 2010: 4).

As the previous section has shown, acceptance of guilt by the Hutu was facilitated by the *Gacaca* system, which ultimately institutionalised the Hutu's collective guilt. Human Rights Watch's Kenneth Roth (2009) described *Gacaca* as a 'tool of repression… run without trained lawyers or judges' and, *ipso facto*, 'open to manipulation'. Knowing this in advance, Rwamfizi, and others in his position, wisely adopted the *mea culpa* attitude, and refrained from making waves, no matter what the popular judges accused them of, even if this involved falsely

---

50  In her another documentary on the *Gacaca* titled *My Neighbor My Killer* (2009), Anne Aghion announced that Abrahim Rwamfizi had died at the time she was making the documentary.

testifying against a father or a brother. On one hand, the regime expressly forbade the *Gacaca* courts from treating cases of crimes allegedly perpetrated against the Hutu by the RPF or its supporters (Des Forges & Longman, 2004: 62; Longman & Rutagengwa, 2004: 167). On the other hand, President Kagame, like some scholars and researchers, hastened to speak of 'millions' of Hutu killers.[51] Probably there were three million killers as his biographer indicated (Waugh: 2003: 97), or four to five million, which is 80 percent of the Hutu, as one official once said (Mamdani, 2001: 266), or simply the entire People – *le peuple* – as Rwandan ambassador to the UN Joseph Nsengimana[52] and some Tutsi survivors maintain (see for instance Mukasonga, 2006: 115–116; Rurangwa, 2006: 77).

The zeal with which numbers of Hutu killers are announced in millions – while Tutsi victims are situated around one million – appears to cause more harm than the quota or ethnic policies of presidents Habyarimana and Kayibanda. *The New Yorker* journalist and writer, Philip Gourevitch (1999: 245) once asked Paul Kagame, Vice-President and Defence Minister at that time, what he intended to do with innocent Hutu in jail. Kagame answered:

> Yeah it's a problem... I would rather address the problem of putting them in prison because that is the best way to do it for the process of justice, and simply because I don't want them out there, because people would actually kill them.

A way to get them 'out there' was found in the *Gacaca* system, when hundreds of thousands of Hutu prisoners – including thus innocents – were released 'in exchange for confession and implication of others' (Des Forges & Longman, 2004: 59). The consequence for those of them who would have pleaded not guilty and who were convinced of their innocence was, indeed, not a physical death, but a psychological death.

Kajeguhakwa (2001: 342) maintained on his part that post-genocide authorities should not be blamed for such a narrow vision of society, because most of those who governed Rwanda had no other experience but war and refugee camp suffering: 'it is not their fault. It is the fault of the architects of [the] 1959 [Revolution]'. Kajeguhakwa's observation implied that political leaders are prisoners of their ethnic identities and corresponding memories, a point which, to some extent, I share. Wars – in the 1960s and then in the 1990s – and refugee camps – since 1959 – and the consequences thereof, greatly shape the political views of Tutsi President Kagame, just like the *Ubuhake* and the injustices associated with it had held Hutu President Kayibanda prisoner.

The situation described above is turning Rwanda into what Mamdani (2001: 282) called 'a simmering volcano' that might blow up yet again, 'this time engulfing the wider region'. Mamdani (2001: 266) identified the key dilemma that needs

---

51  President Paul Kagame's speech, 7 April 2007 in Murambi, Southern Province.
52  Rwandan ambassador to UN and head of the delegation to the 95th meeting of the UN Human Rights Committee in Geneva on 18 March 2009, was quoted as saying: 'The genocide was perpetrated by the People and we needed a way to render justice while fostering reconciliation'. http://www.aidh.org/ONU_GE/Comite_DH/95rwanda01.htm (Accessed 22 April 2009).

to be addressed to prevent that volcano from blowing up again: 'how to build a democracy that can incorporate a *guilty majority* alongside an aggrieved and *fearful minority* in a single political community'. Addressing that issue, Paul Kagame [still Vice-President] stated that Rwanda will never have democracy (Misser, 1995: 134–135), which is perhaps not totally incorrect, given the conditions set for its coming. Here is the Hutu-*culpabilising* dilemma with regards to the difficult-to-achieve democracy from a Tutsi ethnic identity perspective:

> ... political majority can be confounded with ethnic majority under certain conditions. But what sense would democracy have if ethnic majority confounded with political majority would allow itself the right to commit a genocide against the national minority? If that minority manages to govern the majority in order to ensure its survival, what sense, once again, would democracy have with regard to the classic meaning of democracy? (Kajeguhakwa, 2001: 293)

Although exaggerated, this dilemma of a genocide-committing majority and a no-crime-committing minority that has no other way to survive genocide but through taking and controlling power, is serious. This constant fear of a new genocide has created a risk of a permanent state of exception that will last as long as that fear. Keeping that fear alive is keeping that state of exception and keeping power. The result of this loop is that 'the social complicity of the majority, so-called collective guilt... is part of that domain about which questions are never asked and is part and parcel of harsh social normality' (Scherrer, 2002: 10–11). In other words, since that situation has become part of normality, it is meant to last.

### 3.3 Some Are Guiltier Than Others

Former RPF intelligence officer Ruzibiza (2005: 330–332) elaborated on the general Tutsi perception of the guilty Hutu majority and distinguished five categories of guilt levels: [1] those who enrolled in militias and actually killed with the help of the security forces; [2] those who were initially reluctant but later assimilated and executed the government's orders; [3] those who offered shelter and protection to Tutsi but also engaged in their killings elsewhere; [4] those who hated Tutsi but never engaged in killings, even though they raped Tutsi women and looted their properties; and [5] those – constituting the largest category – who offered shelter to Tutsi, refrained from killing but, when threatened, revealed the Tutsi's hide-outs to the killers.

Ruzibiza added a sixth category, the tiniest, composed of the heroes, those who challenged the government and risked their lives to rescue a maximum of Tutsi. He noted, however, that almost all those who took these risks paid it with their lives, as their heads were 'smashed into pieces with a used hoe' by RPF's secret services whenever surviving Tutsi were found (*Ibid.*: 332). This particular example would most likely push the Hutu to evoke this old memory-proverb: 'when you heal the teeth of a Tutsi, he bites you as soon as he gets fit' (Erny, 2005: 76). The most known Tutsi rescuer, Paul Rusesabagina, a Hutu whose genocide experience inspired Terry George's film *Hotel Rwanda* (2004), seems to confirm the claim of that memory-proverb. Replying to my question about whether he was afraid for his life, he said:

> Definitely! President Kagame himself has harassed me in his own words. He went even as far as calling me a thief, calling me a swindler, calling me a negationist… If the president himself has been attacking me for the last three years… Even he went as far as calling me a Hollywood-made hero in front of my wife. If the president is saying this, what will his small employees do?[53]

This systematic categorisation of the collective guilt of the Hutu reminds of Jean de la Fontaine's fable 'The Wolf and the Lamb'. According to President Kagame, the number of genocidaires is open-ended as the content of each *Gacaca* hearing and each confession was likely to generate new indictments.[54] The talk of general prosecutor Mbarushimana at Ntongwe communal prison also showed how denunciation – even of toddlers – was given a high price (Aghion, 2002). This policy of forcing and forging new indictments from confessions resulted in the impossibility to close the *Gacaca* on the initially planned dates. On 30 June 2009, the additional six months given to the *Gacaca* to close were expiring. Speaking on that date, Ben Simbikesha, a senior staff of the *Gacaca* supervisory body, said that numbers estimated initially had increased following special investigations in areas like Kabgayi and Bisesero. The special investigation was still underway and Simbikesha could not say how many people were to be indicted.[55] The *Gacaca* era finally came to an end on 18th June 2012. According to an official report, 1,958,634 cases were tried, 1,681,648 [86 percent] resulted in conviction and 277,066 [14 percent] in acquittal.[56]

Ironically, though, another serious and perhaps ethnic identity-motivated issue arose: about 40,000 of those previously considered irreproachable or 'people of good integrity' [*Inyangamugayo*] and who had served as *Gacaca* judges had to face Justice on their turn, as they, too, had played a part in the genocide.[57] Those Hutu grassroots judges had enjoyed the status of being irreproachable, apparently to give some credibility to the system. However, the system reminded them that they, too, were somewhere in one of the categories described above. The system's principle is finally simple to grasp. As Twagilimana (2003: 181) wrote, the Hutu should know:

---

53 Olivier Nyirubugara, Interview with Paul Rusesabagina [Video interview] (26 April 2008) http://www.olny.nl/RWANDA/Videos/Hague_Peace_Conference_26_April_2008.html (Accessed 22 April 2009).
54 Paul Kagame speaking to Francois Soudan (20-26 February 2005), pp. 42–43.
55 BBC Great Lakes, 30 June 2009.
56 Inkiko Gacaca, *Gacaca Report Summary*. http://inkiko-gacaca.gov.rw/English/wp-content/uploads/2012/06/Gacaca-Report-Summary.pdf (Accessed 9 July 2012).
57 Florence Muhongerwa, 'Inyangamugayo 40.000 za gacaca ziraregwa kugira uruhare muri Jenoside', *Izuba Rirashe*, 13 July 2010. http://www.izuba.org.rw/i-419-a-15592.izuba (Accessed 9 July 2012).

that the genocide was planned by a small group of people *in the name of all the Hutu*, and it was mostly carried out by ordinary Hutu. The majority of Hutu did not share the genocide ideology, but *they were eventually convinced or forced to kill* [Emphasis added].

Tutsi survivors on their part took an even more extremist position. For instance, Révérien Rurangwa (2006: 79–80), the sole survivor of his family, believes that 'each Hutu family is involved, closely or from afar, through the participation of one of its members – if it's not ten! – in the massacre. Everyone has dirty and blood-tainted hands'. This statement fits perfectly in the official policy voiced by President Kagame, that 'genocidaires' children, fed with a genocidal ideology, are potentially as dangerous as their parents' and should be subjected to prevention measures'.[58] Here again, one sees ethnic identity and related memories at work. The future has to be sealed here and now, using the memories of the past. Genocidal ideology, and by extension, guilt, is declared a hereditary disease among the Hutu, which implies that the net can catch not just those who were toddlers at the time of genocide, but even their posterity. Asked by CNN's Becky Anderson about a comment sent in by a Hutu viewer prior to his interview, President Kagame answered that even those who were not involved in the genocide [due to their low age] are under the influence of those who committed it:

BECKY ANDERSON: You've got a lot of powerful viewer comments asking about the accusations of genocide by your own government in neighboring Congo. I want to read out just what one of our viewers has written. Ru... mihigo [not well pronounced. Probably Rugenzamihigo or Rukezamihigo] has written: 'I am a Rwandan who grew up as an orphan in exile after my parents were massacred by your army in Remera [Kigali neighborhood]. All Hutus from there, hundreds of them, were massacred. I survived by miracle and they were killed simply because they were Hutu intellectuals. Is that not genocide?' What is your response?

PAUL KAGAME: Well. If, if, if it happened, if it ever happened, that would be a problem. But as far as I am concerned, and as I know, and *as many Rwandans know, that did not happen*. But these stories or accusations come from sections of people who are actually linked in one way or another, surprisingly even those who were very young and certainly did not participate, come under the influence either of their parents or relatives or others who were part of it. And the argument has been to try and create an equivalence. They have been trying to say: 'now actually there is no no... There are two genocides. There is one genocide of Tutsis and there is another genocide of Hutus'. This has been the issue underlying this whole argument about, you know, the RPF, or you know, the Tutsis also having committed a genocide, and so on. This is, this is nonsense. This is absurd [Emphasis added].[59]

---

58  Paul Kagame speaking to François Soudan (20–26 February 2005), p. 43.
59  Becky Anderson, 'Connector of the Day: Paul Kagame', *CNN*, 16 September 2010. http://videos.wittysparks.com/id/36028863582739599 (Accessed 16 September 2010)

Note this part of the answer – '… and as many Rwandans know, that did not happen' – which, in my view, perfectly falls under the self- or officially-imposed-amnesia approach to ethnic identities discussed in Chapter 2. The message behind this statement is: 'what I ordered/forced Rwandans to know/remember, is that that did not happen'. One prevention measure taken against the children who happen to know what they are not supposed to know – like the one who sent a comment to CNN – is their placement in rehabilitation camps, where they are brainwashed (Soudan, 2008: 31). At the political elite level the same rule applies. Pierre Celestin Rwigema, initially a 'moderate' Hutu and Prime Minister under the RPF regime from 1995 to 2000, turned 'extremist' after his dismissal as Prime Minister. From his exile in the United States, he said that being in the opposition leads to two sorts of consequences depending on the opponent's ethnicity: 'A Hutu is a killer' while 'a Tutsi is a thief'. In the latter case, he was referring to Kajeguhakwa, the self-assigned defender of the Tutsi rights since the mid-1960s, whom President Kagame was accusing of stealing money from the bank in which he owned the majority of the shares. Kajeguhakwa fled the country and was arrested in the United States, in August 2004.[60] In the meantime, Rwigema returned to Rwanda in 2011.

## 3.4 Scapegoating

Since the 1959 Revolution, Rwanda's leadership has been successively marked by state-promoted collective guilt targeting the ethnic group of the ousted leaders (Newbury, 2002: 74). In this respect, 'all the Tutsi came to be portrayed as *monarchistes*' in 1959 and during Kayibanda's administration; the same occurred in 1994 when 'all Tutsi were labeled as agents of an "evil" Rwandan Patriotic Front' (*Ibid.*). The post-genocide government fell in the same trap, as 'all Hutu became portrayed as *génocidaires*' (*Ibid.*). Despite their divergence in political views and ideological orientations, the three most epoch-marking presidents of Rwanda – Grégoire Kayibanda, Juvénal Habyarimana, and Paul Kagame – seem to have engaged in a dangerous copy-paste game. One instance of this game is what Newbury (2002: 76) called 'the pattern of scapegoating'. In the 1960s, thousands of rural Tutsi residents 'were punished as scapegoats' following the attacks of Tutsi monarchist rebels. After the 1963 attacks, President Kayibanda had warned the Tutsi refugees in particular and all the Tutsi in general, and had asked them to reflect on the consequences of a Tutsi military victory:

> Suppose, by any unthinkable chance, that you managed to assault and capture Kigali. Do you measure the chaos that would victimise you in the first place…? You certainly say it to one another: 'it would be a total and precocious end of the Tutsi race'.[61]

---

60 Elizabeth Wendt-Kellar, 'Family's hopes of staying in U.S. dwindling', *Naples News*, 25 July 2005. http://www.naplesnews.com/news/2005/jul/25/ndn_family_s_hopes_of_staying_in_u_s__dwindling/ (Accessed 1 July 2009).
61 Grégoire Kayibanda's letter to Tutsi refugees in 1964. Object: '*Salut fraternel*' [Brotherly greetings]. Quoted in Ntisoni, (2007), pp. 24–25.

It is obvious here that there was no distinction between the assailants and the Tutsi living in the country, and that the latter's extermination could be a national defense strategy. In the 1990s, following the attacks of Tutsi-dominated RPF, thousands of internal Tutsi were targeted again and suffered arbitrary arrests and massacres. Like in the 1960s, the Tutsi, especially the educated ones, were considered as 'natural allies of the Tutsi rebellion' (Umutesi, 2000: 22). It is however interesting to note how some Tutsi have been trapped into the tragic memories of scapegoating in the 1960s and the early 1970s to the extent of identifying themselves with the attacking rebels. On hearing the rumors that a Tutsi rebellion was about to attack Rwanda in 1990, Joseph Sebarenzi (2009: 47) – who served a few years as Speaker of the transitional national assembly in post-genocide Rwanda – spontaneously reacted to his friend's news saying: 'If the Tutsi refugees attack… it will only mean reprisal killings of Tutsi living in Rwanda'. Then his friend added: 'But *we* have to fight…' to trigger another response that '*We* cannot win…'. This identification of the larger group to the smaller attacking force – which is the reverse of scapegoating – could be attributed to memory. In the first place, the attacking refugees and those who stayed in Rwanda enjoyed the same privileges before the Hutu took over; secondly, many had suffered the same discriminations under the Hutu administrations, with the sole difference that some had fled, while others had accepted to live in Habyarimana's 'cosmetic peace' (*Ibid.*: 44) whereby they 'were physically safe… [though] still discriminated' (*Ibid.*: 43).

It should be noted here that ethnically-coloured massacres during the 1990 – 1994 war were taking place on either side of the frontline, probably more so on the RPF side than on the Hutu government side. For example, in Muvumba in the early 1990s, RFP chief Paul Kagame ordered his troops to systematically kill 'recalcitrant Hutu populations' who broke the cover of the rebels with the help of dogs. The survivors were forced to run away (Ruzibiza, 2005: 150). Once on the other side of the frontline, the traumatised displaced would tell their apocalyptic stories, increasing tensions (Umutesi, 2000: 26–27), and eventually provoking sentiments and scenes of revenge. For the attacking forces, the principle seemed to be: 'if it is impossible to capture the *Interahamwe*, it is acceptable to liquidate civilians assumed to be associated with them' (Newbury, 2002: 76–77). This echoes Kayibanda's warning to the Tutsi back in the 1960s that a victory of the rebels would mean 'a total and precocious end of the Tutsi race'. In other words, Kayibanda meant that 'if we can't kill the fighters, we will kill their Tutsi brothers and sisters'. In a similar vein, Caplan (2007: 29–30) pointed out that when the Hutu rebels launched incursions into Rwanda from Eastern DR Congo in the late-1990s

> The government, *suspicious of all Hutu* [emphasis added], responded with brute force, frequently failing to distinguish between *genocidaires* [emphasis in original], and ordinary peasants. The latter, in turn, were reinforced in their belief that the RPF government was not theirs.

However, Caplan did not put this statement side by side with his other contention, namely that when the RPF invaded Rwanda in 1990, 'All Tutsi, both citizens and RPF soldiers, were portrayed as alien invaders' (*Ibid.*: 22). Putting these two ethnic scapegoating examples together would only confirm the memory-inspired copy-paste argument I am making here. Communication Scholar Jean-Marie Vianney Higiro (2007: 88) held that just like the Hutu elites turned the original acronym of *Inyenzi*[62] into cockroaches to label all Tutsi, the RPF use[d] the terms *genocidaires* and *ibipinga* – those who reject what another person says – to label all the Hutu.

Memory-motivated ethnic scapegoating in post-genocide Rwanda becomes more worrying when it is considered side by side with the already mentioned and equally worrying statement by President Kagame, that *genocidaires'* children are potentially as dangerous as their parents. Caplan (2007: 36; see also Kinzer, 2010) was right when he maintained that the RPF government was uncertain about the loyalty of 85 percent of the population [the Hutu], and, more worryingly, that President Kagame was determined to take necessary steps to keep his country secure and his government in power.

## Summary

In this part I have discussed dual interpretation of the past, saying that this duality follows ethnic lines. On one hand, the Tutsi perceive pre-colonial Rwanda and its *Ubuhake* system as close to the ideal Rwanda, as the Hutu and Tutsi allegedly lived in peace and harmony without any deadly confrontations. On the other hand, the Hutu consider all those centuries prior to independence as characterised by Tutsi domination and exploitation through the *Ubuhake* system. There are many other subjects and experiences the interpretations of which radically divide Rwandans along ethnic lines. The result is that at least two versions are in circulation, the dominant one [Tutsi] and the repressed one [Hutu], to which expert narratives should be added. The two first versions are all memory narratives and the one that assumes the status of history is the one of the winner of the latest confrontation. To make sure that the school-going generation is fed with the 'appropriate' memory material, the winner's administration does all in its power to control education, purge it of the previous dominant memory-inspired curriculum before introducing the newly-proclaimed history, which is nothing but the memories related to the winner's ethnic identity.

---

62  Jean-Marie Vianney Higiro (2007: 84–85) explained that contrary to what many authors (Chrétien *et al*, 1995; Mukasonga, 2006; and others) have suggested, the name *Inyenzi* was not an invention of the Hutu who aimed to dehumanize the Tutsi. Referring to a 2003 BBC interview with Joseph Ngurumbe, he explained that *Inyenzi* originally meant, *Ingangurarugo yiyemeje kuba Ingenzi*. *Ingangurarugo* were an army division of King Rwabugiri – the same who called himself *Inkotanyi cyane* or Redoubtable Fighter. Thus, *Inyenzi* meant the troublemaker 'who has committed himself to bravery'. The meaning shifted to cockroaches during the 1960s, when '*Inyenzi* would attack at night and kill innocent civilians. They would then rapidly vanish in the countryside or vanish into neighbouring countries'. Because of this, Higiro went on, 'the population associated the attackers with cockroaches instead of bravery', because they behaved like cockroaches, which are 'annoying insects that disappear when somebody turns on the light'.

I have also highlighted the ways in which Rwandans [are forced to] remember their past, even the one they witnessed. I pointed out that the remembering process in Rwanda comprises of at least two major steps: firstly, weighing the past or the remembered experience with one's own ethnic identity, that is the one conveyed naturally and spontaneously from one generation to another; and secondly, gauging that very past or experience with the officially proclaimed and promoted memory conveyed through official channels such as schools, media, and commemorations. The latter has more authority than the former, as the safety, and even the life of the remembering subjects are tied to it. I have maintained that most Rwandans have at least two versions of the past and have always had to judge the circumstances and their audience before deciding which version to display or communicate. Rwanda scholars have called this attitude – which is a calculated lie – 'a national sport' in Rwanda (Erny, 2005: 214), as 'truth… varies according to the listener, to its beneficiary or to the one who risks to suffer its consequences'.[63] I have mentioned that even field research does not manage to get out the true feelings of Rwandans, as answers vary based on both the interviewee's and the interviewer's [or his/her translator's] ethnicity.

This situation has resulted in a new memory reflex especially among the Hutu in post-genocide Rwanda: self-imposed amnesia. Resulting from state-imposed amnesia, self-imposed amnesia implies that the remembering subjects know off by heart which part of the recent or long-gone past they have to lock. Their survival depends on this. Despite this, everyday use of language offers a way to free oneself from amnesia, though in a very limited way. Choice of terms and the formulation of sentences often betray which parts of the past the remembering subjects have been forced to forget.

In this part, I also touched upon ethnic, collective guilt in post-genocide Rwanda, especially the use of the traditional grassroots *Gacaca* courts to achieve that purpose. Ideally, that system was meant to speed up genocide trials that were in the hundreds of thousands. However, it immediately appeared that its premises were wrong, biased, and contrary to equal justice for both the Hutu and the Tutsi: only the Hutu should appear for the crimes committed against the Tutsi, while the Tutsi who committed crimes against the Hutu should go unpunished. Another wrong and ethnic-guilt-reinforcing principle of the *Gacaca* was the obsession for confession and denunciation, which appeared to be at the heart of the system's pedagogic approach. The direct effect of this was that every Hutu had, from then on, to live with guilt and fear.

I have observed that since 1994, the Hutu have been subjected to categorisation and sub-categorisations that all aim to determine the level of their guilt. The ones who did not kill helped by denouncing the Tutsi; the ones, who did none of them, stood by and watched; the ones who were not there had bad intentions which they had no occasion to put into practice. In any case, no Hutu could be innocent, because, to quote a Rwandan prosecutor, 'even toddlers killed'. However, this collectivisation of guilt is not an invention of the post-genocide regime. Its

---

63  Charles Ntampaka, quoted in Erny (2005), p. 214.

predecessors had almost done the same by putting the Tutsi in the same basket during the attacks of Tutsi refugees in the 1960s and in the 1990s: they were natural accomplices of the rebels, whether they wanted it or not. Known as scapegoating, this phenomenon is one of the deadliest traps of ethnic identities and related memories. The dominant group has to make sure that the group associated with the defeated one is so weak that it prevents any return to the previous situation when the dominated were dominant. It also sends a strong and clear message to whoever would attempt to dream of a change of power control. It appears to play both a punitive role and a preventive role. In this part I have focused on the various manifestations of ethnic identities and related memories and the political manoeuvres that police it. In the next part I discuss some channels through which the memories connected to ethnic identities are mediated into the present.

# Part Two

Memory Transmission

*Chapter 4*

# Oral Traditions and the Representation of the Past

In one of the previous chapters I pointed out the diverging interpretation of pre-colonial Rwanda depending on one's ethnicity. For the Tutsi it was not such a bad system, as everyone lived in peace, without any ethnic confrontation. For the Hutu, that peace was far from being accepted, but rather imposed by the powerful Tutsi who benefited from Hutu free labour within the *Ubuhake* system. There is no [written] documentary or material evidence that could tell, in a more palpable way, what social relationships were like before colonisation, as Rwanda was an essentially oral society until even after the coming of the colonisers. Moreover, no deeper archeological research has been conducted to that end. The sole memory texts that tell something about social relationships among the Hutu and the Tutsi are myths, legends, tales,[64] proverbs, dynastic poems, and the like. I am calling them 'memory texts' in the sense that was described in the introduction, to stress that they are subjected to the various needs, concerns, and pressures of the various 'present times' they have gone through – including the current present time –, and to the various 'futures' that were projected at different moments in time. According to Vansina (1971: 444), oral tradition – which is the generic name for oral memory texts – is oral testimony transmitted verbally, from one generation to the next one or more. This excludes accounts by eyewitnesses which are oral data. It excludes rumor which is oral but is not transmitted from one generation to the next, since rumor is gossip and 'hot news,' soon to be forgotten. But on occasion rumor can be transmitted and thus become a source for tradition... Oral tradition is presented as the respected lore of the past; it has a tradition, whether it purports to tell specifically what happened in the past (historical traditions) or merely to take delight in the performance of oral wisdom, wit, or beauty of the past (literary traditions). Thus religious hymns, proverbs, and animal stories are just as much oral tradition as are lists of kings or royal chronicles.

---

64 Historical tales have emerged as a generic term that 'applies to all historical narratives irrespective of style, origins in social terms (whether from the Nyiginya court or local), or period of contents' (Vansina, 2000: 378). The Kinyarwanda term *–Ibitekerezo* – literally means 'reflection, thought', which infers that the storyteller – always a man – 'aims as much to offer one's thoughts to the auditors as to narrate events of the past' (*Ibid.*). In a strict sense, *ibitekerezo* 'are rather long and complex, are told in the refined flowery language of the court, stem from that milieu, and deal with earlier times, not with contemporary or subactual happenings'.

However distorted or corrupt they might have been,[65] nonetheless they keep an element in them that gives clues as to what the situation was like at the time of their first utterance. If they survived all those centuries, one should assume, it is because they were relevant and referred to something concrete within society (see Kagame, 1959:7). What is more, it is easy to detect those that originated from the Hutu and those that originated from the Tutsi. My aim in this chapter is to analyse ways in which those oral memory texts convey memories related to ethnic identities, especially those of pre-colonial Rwanda. I do that by first understanding the memory value of myths – which is often neglected – and then by focusing on the clue-providing character of those oral memory texts, before zooming in on how they throw light on pre-colonial Rwanda and ethnic relationships at that time.

## 4.1 Myths Are not Just Myths

Once again, I want to make a detour to another country and culture to discuss ways in which myths and legends intermingle with reality and help come closer to the understanding of certain past situations. In November 2007, Franco Rutelli, Italy's Minister of Culture at the time, announced an unprecedented archaeological finding that not only marveled the entire world, but also and above all, opened a new page in the ways legends and myths are considered. Rutelli announced the discovery of 'the legendary cave where the she-wolf allegedly suckled Romulus and Remus and rescued them from death', which served as 'the beginning of the myth of foundation of Rome.'[66] Italian archaeologist Andrea Carandini directed the excavation and was almost certain that the discovered cave was the fabled Lupercale sanctuary (Hooper, 2007). This discovery has at least one major merit: taking legend from the realm of mythology to the one of historical facts. The story that the finding confirmed was, until recently, considered as a pure myth mediated by numerous works by Roman authors.

Titus Livius [59 B.C.–17 A.D.] is considered to be one of the greatest historical authors of Ancient Rome, for his famous and groundbreaking *Ab Urbe Condita Libri* [Books about the city's Foundation, or simply History of Rome since its foundation]. Based on *Aeneid* – a legend taken up by Virgilius [70 – 19 B.C.] and inspired by Homer's *Iliad* and *Odyssey* – this work tells the 'History' of Rome, including its foundation by the two wolf-suckled twins Romulus and Remus, sons of Mars, The God of War. This [Hi]story of Rome is thus a mixture of facts, mythology and legends, all of which are components of the city's collective memory. The question is now to know how far this kind of discovery can change or confirm Rome's mythology-inspired history, or whether it should even be considered as mythology-inspired at all.

---

65 Vansina (2000: 375) noted that tales are often subjected to arbitrary erasure and dismissal of 'the bits and the variants that do not conform to one's preferred version'.
66 RTL4, '*Grot Romulus en Remus gevonden*' (20 November 2007).
http://www.rtl.nl/(vm=/actueel/rtlnieuws/)/system/video/html/components/actueel/rtlnieuws/miMedia/2007/week47/di_1930_romulus.avi_plain.xml (Accessed 21 November 2007).

Cicero, another remarkable Roman author, adopted an attitude worth mentioning with regard to the foundation of Rome. Putting his thoughts in Scipio Africanus' mouth, Cicero repeated Livius' narrative, signaling to the reader where fables stopped and where facts started. Regarding the birth of Romulus and Remus, 'we may grant that much to the popular tradition.' Then further, after discussing their suckling by 'a wild beast from the forest', he paused momentarily 'to turn now from fable to fact.'[67] He alternately used phrases such as 'we are told' for fabled narratives, and 'we are informed that' for what he held to be factual narratives.[68] Cicero went on to comment on the choice of the site of Rome, its naming after Romulus, the latter's wisdom, the war against neighbouring Sabines, etc., as being facts. Obviously, Cicero did not consider the foundation of Rome as entirely legend-based. He argued that during Romulus' lifetime, 'learned men already existed and the age itself was one of culture', where 'there was very little opportunity for the invention of fables,' as 'the age of Romulus… was quick to mock at and reject with scorn that which could not possibly have happened'.[69] The writings of Cicero, Livius, and Horatius and of other celebrated authors have most likely played a certain role in the archaeological discovery mentioned above. In his book about the methods of Field Archaeology, early-20th-century archaeologist Leonard Woolley considered literary sources as the second most important clue-provider after surface traces. He wondered: 'Why do you dig just where you do?' His answer was:

> Burial does not always mean obliteration, and there are generally some surface signs to guide the digger. In the Near East no one could possibly mistake the great mounds or 'tells' which rose above the plain to mark the sites of ancient cities; very often, if the place was an important one, it can be identified from literary sources even before excavation begins; the difficulty is rather which point of attack to choose in so great an area (Woolley, [1930] 1954: 27).

Archaeologist Howard Williams (2003: 10) suggested that social memories 'are rarely a simple narrative', as they involve 'complex, frequently biographical and multi layered histories that are constructed through and with material culture'. In this respect, Herodotus' writings about his visit to Egypt in the 5th century B.C. and his description of local temples' architecture gave 'a very obvious clue' during the early-20th century excavations in Egypt (Woolley, [1930] 1954: 27).

I have chosen to discuss the contribution of myths and legend to the [scientific] knowledge of ancient times using a non-Rwandan, widely known case, to stress that the point I want to make is not specific to Rwanda. What is specific to Rwanda is the almost consensual refusal on the part of the post-genocide Rwandan leaders and many scholars to glean some clues from those oral memory texts, the sole ones that are likely to shed some light to that chapter of Rwanda's past.

---

67   Cicero, *De Republica* (Cambridge: Harvard University Press, [54 & 51 BC] 1970), pp. 113 & 115.
68   *Ibid.*, p. 115
69   *Ibid.*, pp. 127 & 129.

## 4.2 Clue-Providers

My point in this section is that Rwandans acquaint themselves with the past mainly through orality, including tales, legends, myths, proverbs, riddles, some everyday use of language [swear, curses, etc.] and so on. Prefacing Cyprien Rugamba's compilation of Rwandan tales, Luc Bouquiaux (1981: 6–7) held that tales constitute 'cultural heritage' [*un patrimoine culturel*], which plays the role of written documents and monuments in western civilisations:

> In the absence of written monuments and monumental sites, orality-based civilisations, through oral traditions, leave us the heritage containing a picture of their own functioning, and enlighten their own past. While archaeological excavations cost much money, and many other sites have been identified for future excavations, one could be astonished to realise that the interest in these other mental monuments, so fragile as they are, has been felt so late.

Rwandan proverbs, sayings, tales and other oral memory texts are sources for historians and researchers in related fields, as they often provide 'interesting details for the country's history', although they present certain limitations that require recourse to other data and sources (Vansina, 1962: 36; see also Vansina, 1971: 442–443; Vansina, 2000: 375 & 377; Ki-Zerbo, 2008: 40). Vansina (2000: 382) even considered historical tales, which need to be studied with due precaution, as 'constitut[ing] an *indispensable source for our knowledge about the more remote past*' [Emphasis added]. Burkinabe historian and thinker Joseph Ki-Zerbo (2008: 24) maintained that oral texts are profoundly rich in information about the society that produced them, even though they also contain some lacunae. Ki-Zerbo even praised orality for its capacity to give life and warmth to those texts, which writing would rather petrify. He wrote: 'Maybe oral culture produces a less rigorous, less precise man, but this man is better skilled to communicate and exteriorize emotions'. In the same vein, Alexis Kagame (1959: 6–7) rejected the prejudice that automatically disqualifies all non-written or immaterial sources as historical sources. He maintained that oral cultures, like that of ancient Rwanda, are capable of keeping and transmitting accounts of past events.

In this perspective, a proverb is not an exact report of a past event, but rather, as Benjamin ([1955] 1973: 108–109) asserted, 'a ruin which stands on the site of an old story and in which a moral twines about *a happening* like ivy around a wall' [Emphasis added]. The proverb, therefore, does not appear *ex nihilo*, but from *a happening*. Like other types of 'invented traditions', Rwandan oral memory texts 'are important symptoms and therefore indicators of problems which might not otherwise be recognised... they are evidence' (Hobsbawm, [1983] 2012: 12). Moreover, since 'Each society expresses its beliefs, values, and ideals in its [oral] literature and stereo types', it follows that 'From the corpus of traditions it is easy to deduce which ideals, which virtues, and which vices are exemplified by different heroes in the narratives' (Vansina, 1971: 457). Alexis Kagame (1956: 23) went a step further to maintain that those 'institutionalised documents', namely proverbs, fables, tales, and all sorts of poems 'contain in themselves assertions that are philosophical in nature'. For those reasons, those who invented those philosophically-loaded memory texts can be called, in a way, 'intuitive philosophers', as they 'managed to penetrate deep into fundamental issues of the concept of Being [*l' Etre*], devised adequate terminology for it, even though they were not aware of the role [of philosopher] they were playing' (*Ibid.*: 37–38). Ki-Zerbo (2008: 25 & 39) took this philosophical character of oral texts inherent to many Sub-Saharan African cultures to argue that what Descartes' *cogito ergo sum* is to the West, is what *I speak, therefore I am* is to those African cultures.

It is also worth mentioning that proverbs and sayings occupied a very important role in ancient Greece rhetoric and philosophy: like in Rwanda, they served as guiding references. In Plato's *Symposium* for instance, the various orators, among whom Socrates, attending Agathon's party kept referring to the ancient proverbs and sayings either to support or to illustrate their arguments. Socrates asked uninvited Aristomedus to accompany him to 'prove the proverb wrong, and make it say: "Good men go uninvited to *good* men's banquets"'. On his side, Alcibiades warned Agathon not to fall into Socrates' trap, to avoid, 'as the proverb puts it, be[ing] the fool who only learns by his own suffering' (Plato, ca 385 BC) 1999: 3–4 & 78). It might then be concluded that proverbs, perhaps more in Rwanda than anywhere else, reflect society's perception of itself. Discussing 'Poetry and Imagination' and the relationship between the two, 19th-century philosopher Ralph Waldo Emerson equated proverbs, which are the product of both poetry and imagination, with [social] truth: 'One man sees a spark or shimmer of the truth and reports it, and his saying becomes a legend or golden proverb for ages…' *(*Emerson [1872] 2010: 42*)*.

Based on field research and interviews she conducted in Rwanda, Buckley-Zistel (2006: 141) observed ways in which Rwandans refrain – following state-imposed or self-imposed amnesia – from 'remember[ing] the social and economic cleavages that marked their society', but which they kept remembering without noticing it through everyday sayings. One recurring saying referred to 'a rich person' as being 'a Tutsi' and another one – 'I am not your Hutu'– is still widely used 'to fend off exploitation'. This example suggests that the memories and the traces of the *Ubuhake* system have been removed from the promoted, public memory, but have remained in popular culture, where people engage in a perpetual remembering process without even noticing it. In the expression *I am not your Hutu*, 'Hutu' is used as a synonym of 'servant' (Twagilimana, 2003: 39). Everyday cultural practices, including everyday use of language, play a crucial role in the meaning-making process in Rwanda, though mostly in non-calculated ways. Those practices, as Willis (2000: xv) put, 'are unselfconscious and take the normal life world of everyday culture as their working context'. From the points raised by Willis and Buckley-Zistel, it appears that everyday culture or use of language is not always under one's control, and might unselfconsciously bring out the innermost thoughts of remembering subjects.

Rwanda's everyday culture and use of language are reservoirs containing oral memory texts that mediate certain social realities (Erny, 2005: 292). Even today, the use of proverbs and adages is still valued and constitute a sign of a good command of language and oratory skills. The proverbs below, which are still in use today, though often in private settings, reflect the almost eternal mistrust between the Hutu and the Tutsi:

1. When you lodge a Tutsi in your house, he chases you out of your bed (*Ibid.*: 76).
1. When you heal the teeth of a Tutsi he bites you as soon as he gets fit (*Ibid.*).
2. What is in the heart of a Tutsi is known only to God and to himself (*Ibid.*).
3. If one chooses Hutu as messengers, one better sends many (Twagilimana, 2003: 39).
4. A Hutu is not thanked twice (*Ibid.*).
5. If you teach a Hutu to shoot a bow; he'll shoot an Arrow into your stomach (*Ibid.*).

Rwanda customary law scholar Charles Ntampaka (1997: 7–18) contended that popular sayings, proverbs, and adages are like articles of the Rwandan customary law. They define the role of men and woman, the relationships within the family, society, and the state apparatus. Ntampaka suggested that based on them, but especially on their adaptation to modernity and the rejection of obsolete ones, Rwanda can become a democratic nation, where justice prevails. Besides their organisational role, these oral memory texts serve as conveyors of ethnic ideologies, and, for some of them, indicate the ethnic group that use it against the other (Twagilimana, 2003: 39). In other words, the proverbs where the Hutu are depicted as forgetful [4], ungrateful [6], unable to complete good actions [5] are 'said by the Tutsi', while those in which the Tutsi are depicted as unpredictably wicked [1 & 3] and almost always ill-intended [2] are 'said by the Hutu' (*Ibid.*). Vansina (1985: xii) extensively studied these oral traditions in Africa, including in Rwanda, and remarked that they constituted 'important sources for the historian', as they are crucial to the understanding of the people's present and the past whose traditions are under consideration:

> Yes, oral traditions are documents of the present, because they are told in the present. Yet, they also embody a message from the past, so they are expressions of the past at the same time. They are the representation of the past in the present. One cannot deny either the past or the present in them… Traditions must always be understood as reflecting both past and present in a single breath (*Ibid.*).

Alexis Kagame (1956: 23 & 27) went a step further to not only call oral memory texts 'institutionalised documents', but also and most importantly, to qualify them as 'independent' and immune of any manipulations caused by Westerners [through religion, education, etc.]:

> I can be mistaken in my interpretation, but someone else can contradict me or correct my interpretation. In any case, the document remains perpetually intact. The current generation might evolve as it pleases, but the sources of my references will not suffer from it (*Ibid.*: 27).

The proverbs mentioned above were invented both by Hutu and Tutsi who were trying to describe the relationships prevailing between the two groups. No study has so far focused on dating and explaining the exact origin and the history of those proverbs. The situation is different for popular sayings and adages about which much more is known and has been put into writing. In 1980, Benedigito Mulihano, then working for the Ministry of Primary and Secondary Education, published a compilation of the 100 most popular sayings and adages titled *Ibirari by' Insigamigani*, translated as 'the traces of sayings' or 'the stories behind sayings'. One adage he explored is *Ntabyera ngo de!* – No situation is 100 percent perfect. It *certainly* dates back to around 1730, as it initially referred to King Cyilima Rujugira's famous remark that his enthronement would have been perfect if his beloved wife – whom the royal tradition keepers had poisoned – had attended it (Mulihano [1980] 2005: 92–98). Studying thousands of them seems a Herculean task in advance.

Despite the missing dating, it might be argued that most proverbs, if not all, antedate the coming of the colonisers, and thus, for that very reason, constitute documents of the past, useful for the cultural scientist interested in Rwanda's memories. In the early 1960s, language and oral tradition researchers André Coupez and Thomas Kamanzi (1962: 6) dedicated a study to what they termed 'historical tales' – *récits historiques*. The deeper they proceeded in oral traditions, the more they were convinced that they would be relevant for the historian and the ethnologist, as they would allow them to make their first critical analysis of the facts. Having prepared the ground by stressing the historical value of myths and the clue-providing character of oral memory texts, I want to proceed now to a few concrete instances of the relationship between those texts and some social realities in Rwanda.

## 4.3 Mapping Ancient Rwanda

In his 1951 study of the dynastic poems, Alexis Kagame presented those oral memory texts as the carriers of Rwanda's collective memory and, based on them, distinguished three major periods in Rwanda's past: the mythological era comprising the kings called *Ibimanuka* [those who fell from the skies]; the conquest era in which the founding fathers called *Abami b'umushumi* [the Kings who tightened their belt, that is, who suffered considerably] who, starting from Gihanga, endured hardships to build a nation and laid the basis of future Rwanda; and finally the post-Ruganzu I Bwimba era corresponding to *Abami b' ibitekerezo* ['historical' kings], starting approximately in 1400 A.D.. Dynastic poems shed light on the last era for which considerable amount of certitude exists (Kagame, 1951: 31; Kagame, 1959: 20–27; see also Coupez & Kamanzi, 1962: 58). The first two periods are comparable to what Cicero called 'fabled narratives', whilst the last one corresponds to what he termed 'factual narratives'. In another study, Alexis Kagame discussed the social structures in ancient Rwanda, including a chapter with the title 'Three races' (Kagame, 1954: 37–61). In the part dedicated to the Tutsi, he considered one myth according to which many Tutsi clans [the *Abasindi*,

*Abashambo*, *Abahondogo* and *Abega*] originated from heaven and were, for that reason, superior. With such a background, the *Abasindi* sub-clan of *Abanyiginya* could justify their monopoly in giving the monarch for over five centuries and the rest in giving the monarchs' wives.

It was not a question of sharing power amongst cattle breeders and cultivators but rather of sharing power amongst the members of the former group. Whereas the celestial origins could not be taken for historical truth, the fact that the monarch was always a Tutsi from the *Abasindi* clan, precisely from the *Nyiginya* sub-clan, is an historical fact, which dates back to long before the coming of the colonisers. I can argue with Walter Lippmann ([1922] 1997: 80–81) that this myth contains both truths and errors, and that its sole problem is that it lacks 'the critical power to separate its truths from its errors', which is common to all myths. Lippmann suggested that 'If it [the myth] has affected human conduct a long time, it is almost certain to contain much that is profoundly and importantly true', which is obviously the case for the myth mentioned above. Moreover, following the same mythic logic, about 70 percent of all administrative positions were in the hands of Nyiginya people, the rest going to other Tutsi clans (Gakusi & Mouzer, 2003: 24).

Studying the period around 1900, Maquet (1961: 105–106) interviewed over 300 people, mostly Tutsi, who were adult at that time. From their interviews, it appeared that only three names of Hutu land-chiefs were mentioned – Ndarwubatse, Kanyonyomba, and Segore. This pushed him to conclude that 'the share of the Hutu in political power was probably symbolic rather than quantitatively great', while 'a Twa could be neither a land-chief nor a cattle-chief, unless he was ennobled'.[70] Unlike Maquet, who cited a symbolic participation of the Hutu, Scherrer (2002: 19; see also Sebarenzi, 2009: 13) concluded that 'the Hutu (but not the Twa) were part of the ruling classes', without mentioning how significant their involvement was. Vansina (1985: 7) suggested that such physical impossibilities as celestial origins should not be summarily dismissed as useless embellishments: 'their survival in tradition means something in terms of historical consciousness and of contemporary mentalities and ideologies'. In other words, the heavenly embellishments reflect a certain social situation that needed an explanation. The myth provided that explanation, and by providing it, determined the organising principles of the Rwandan society and justified their bases (White, 2000: 54; Vansina, 1985: 23). Furthermore, as Vansina (1971: 453–455) observed, oral traditions have three levels of meaning: the literal, the intended, and the symbolic. The literal meaning is based on the use of language itself – archaisms, esoterism, foreign expressions etc.; while the intended meaning 'corresponds to its internal structure', that is, 'literary devices, including playing with words'. As for the symbolic meaning – under which level I place the embellishments mentioned above –

---

70 Discussing the political organisation of pre-colonial Rwanda, Alexis Kagame (1952: 117) presented a different portrait: 'as far as the civil administration was concerned, the Hutu and Tutsi were treated on equal footing', but generally the Hutu were appointed as land-chiefs while the Tutsi were generally appointed as cattle-chiefs. As for the Twa, they could occupy lower positions like local sub-chiefs but never be appointed as land or cattle chiefs unless they were ennobled.

it consists of 'the unconscious message concealed in all texts' reflecting 'the fundamental values cherished by that particular society'.

Linguistic anthropologist Michael Agar ([1980] 1996: 54) maintained that the most important aspect of any myth is not its truthfulness or its falsehood: 'It tells us *something important* about the group that generated it' [Emphasis added]. Politically, the Tutsi sub-clan of *Abasindi* could legitimately claim the throne, and other clans the privilege to give kings' wives. This is an undeniable historical reality grounded in a myth, and pushing to agree with Huyssen (2003: 15–16) that 'the fault line between mythic past and real past is not always easy to draw... The real can be mythologised, just as the mythic may engender strong reality effects'.

Another example of how myths and tales justify a prevailing social phenomenon can be found in the following tale about of the *Abanyiginya* sub-clan. The tale is about two brothers – Mututsi and Sabizeze, the latter born from a bull's heart – and their sister, who all ran away from home to the Umubari kingdom, where King Kabeja, of the *Abazigaba* clan warmly welcomed them and helped them settle. This friendship led to frequent intermarriages between the migrants and the Umubari natives. The tale concludes:

> That is how that custom was born, that was its origin. That is the reason why reciprocal marriages between the Abanyiginya and the Abazigaba repeat themselves... That custom started at that time, it still goes on today, it was never stopped until today (Coupez & Kamanzi, 1962: 65).

This tale makes it clear that the teller is talking about a current social phenomenon that binds together young men and women from both clans. As mass communication scholar John Mirrill (2006: 49–50) points out, these kinds of mythic tales 'help us believe what we cannot understand... simplify the complex and romanticise the puzzling aspects of life' by translating them into 'believable pictures in our minds'. As such, therefore, 'Myths contain considerable truth'. Another media scholar, Michael Schudson (1995: 163), added that the truths conveyed by myths 'necessarily have multiple meanings' because, besides telling 'a culture's simple truths', they also 'explore its central dilemmas'. Any effort striving to understand the relationships between the *Abanyiginya* and the *Abazigaba* clans could not ignore the mythic tale mentioned above, which rather serves as society's memory-keeping mechanism. Therefore, as Twagilimana (2003: 36) suggested, myths and tales are not 'mere fiction, but an attempt to imagine a reality enacted in the unwritten law of the Rwandan society.' Being part of any community's memories and providing a 'believable' and understandable picture of human life and relationships, myths cannot be ignored or be disqualified as relevant clue-providing sources.

By discussing myths and tales and connecting them to concrete social realities, I intend to call for an in-depth analysis of the roots of the deadly memory traps in which Rwandans have been stuck. I also want to dismiss the widespread belief that colonialists are the sole culprits in the Hutu-Tutsi conflictual relationship. I therefore agree with Newbury's (2002: 78) point that while reassessing Rwanda's history, one should not be blinded by the changes made by the Europeans and neglect to consider 'those aspects in which Rwandans themselves were involved'. Myths, legends, proverbs, adages and other oral memory texts are the creations of Rwandans themselves. The same Rwandans channel them from one generation to the next, adapting them to the new situations. They do/did so not because the colonialists encouraged them to do so, but because, as Twagilimana (2003: 40) contended, 'the different myths are cultural realities shaping social relations and regulating interactions'. It is even stronger than that: 'just as the Christians believe in the Bible and the Muslims in the Koran, these myths were part of the daily fabric of Rwandan life' (*Ibid.*). With such power, one can now understand the role myths and other oral memory texts have played in the past and are playing in the present. The greatest power of myths resides in their ability to appeal personally to individuals (Fontaine, 1991: 13), and in their capacity to 'assume the dimensions of reality in the sense, [and] to the extent, that people believe in them' (Strath: 2000: 25).

## 4.4 Myths as Source of Divergence

One interesting point is how Rwandan society navigates between myth and reality, and how today's realities have mythical origins and/or justifications. The former are visible and palpable, while the latter are speculative and thus debatable. Historian P.F.M. Fontaine (1991: 12) conceptualised the relationship between myth and reality, suggesting that 'we need myths to explain reality', as they make our lives easy to live. It could be argued that indeed the mythical tales about Tutsi's celestial origins explained and justified a certain reality – the monopoly of power and their dominant position within the *Ubuhake* system – and made life easier, as no one could dare challenge such a supra-natural phenomenon. For this reason, any study of the Rwandan genocide, and how its ideology was propagated should necessarily consider the pre-colonial period if it aspires to be complete and comprehensive. It should go beyond, and actually question, the cliché circulated by the RPF-dominated regime that portrays a united, harmonious pre-colonial Rwanda (Brandstetter, 2010: 12). What genocide scholar Ugur Ungor (2004: 343) termed Hutu's antipathy against the Tutsi should be considered not only in post-colonial Rwanda or during colonisation, but also in pre-colonial Rwanda, since it could be argued that it was a continuation of an existing antipathy.

As I will discuss in more depth in the next chapter, the major issues opposing the two groups in the late-1950s to the early-1960s were memory related, rather than diverging political agendas. Interestingly, as Vansina (1985: 65) pointed out, both the Hutu and the Tutsi elites, each on their side, used the same myth to back their political claims. However, the interpretations were totally different. In the Hutu interpretation, also reflected in the 1957 *Manifeste des Bahutu*, or *Hutu Manifesto*, 'Kanyarwanda had several sons, including Gatutsi and Gahutu, who were ancestors of the Tutsi and Hutu'. The Hutu and the Tutsi were therefore 'brothers'. In the Tutsi version, the Nyiginya [Tutsi] ancestor Kigwa's [The one who landed from heavens] posterity conquered the Hutu kingdoms, cut their monarchs' genitals, and thus never had any brotherly relations with the Hutu. For this reason, the Hutu had no basis whatsoever to claim more rights and a role in public affairs.[71]

Kajeguhakwa (2001: 341) claimed to have spoken to the Tutsi nobles who rejected power-sharing with the Hutu in the late-1950s. Their views did not reflect the Tutsi version, as the old, illiterate noblemen lived as parasites at the royal palace. For them, sharing power with the Hutu would mean having no daily bread any more. However, Kajeguhakwa did not explain why King Rudahigwa and his literate staff and advisors did not distance themselves from those fire-lighting statements emanating from within the royal palace. This could be interpreted as a *qui tacentur approbant* silence. Not fighting it meant approving and sharing it. Vansina, who directed the recording and preservation of more than 1,000 historical tales at the Institute for Scientific Research in Central Africa [IRSAC] between 1958 and 1962, regretted that scholars had shown no interest to that 'bedrock of the history of the [Rwanda] kingdom' (Vansina, 2000: 376), while they could greatly help them 'to document perceptions in the 1950s of the range of then current meanings of the words Hutu and Tuutsi' (*Ibid.* 2000: 382. Tutsi is with double *uu* in the original). To Vansina,

> The whole corpus of these narratives constitutes first and foremost an *irreplaceable record about the historical consciousness of Rwandan men* in the first half of the twentieth century. It also documents many of their customs, as well as *their attitudes and opinions about many cultural and social issues of their time*. By their concrete descriptions of settings, the tales show how material culture was integrated in the then current social, intellectual, and emotional life (Ibid.) [Emphasis added].

As it appears in the example mentioned above, the Tutsi establishment used a mythic narrative to remind the Hutu emancipationists of the celestially-justified reality, which, once again, brought Rwandan society at the meeting point of myth and reality. I should say realities, as each reality depends on the group that believes in it. René Lemarchand (2004: 310) nicely described myths as being both 'polymorphous and polysemic', as 'operating in ambiguity', and as evoking 'the sacred and the profane, tradition and modernity, the imaginary and the real, legitimacy and contestation, the past and the present'. Although polysemic, 'there are myths that foster conciliation, peace, and those generating the worst atrocities' (*Ibid.*: 316). In this respect, I should say that the Hutu version was fostering brotherhood, thus conciliation, while the Tutsi establishment's version was calling for exclusion, therefore leading to atrocities.

At this level, the power of orality appears as one important aspect that deserves a few lines in this section. Although the country has shown fast development in its educational and literacy policies since independence, it largely remained a profoundly oral society, where talks are preferred to the use of books. The past – not necessarily the long-gone past – is orally transmitted from one generation

---

71  This letter was published in Nkundabagenzi (1961), pp. 35–36.

to another. This past is first of all personal, then family-related, and then village, or region-related. Each Rwandan has a story to tell about their years in exile, their suffering in the displaced camps, the atrocious killings of their loved ones, the survival experience, the missing of a relative, the crossing of the forests and rivers in the Democratic Republic of the Congo, etc. Each tries to find the [political, ideological] reasons why they found themselves in that situation and by doing so, they share their experience and thoughts with their children, towards whom they have the parental duty of transmitting the family's past. Whatever political teachings are prevailing, parents make sure they have some private time to tell their 'truths' to their posterity. To make sense of those experiences, myths, proverbs, and other oral memory texts are often used to back and justify the teller's interpretation. In this respect, then, oral memory texts appear not only as memory reminders, but also as memory-backers and memory-clarifiers. The next chapter focuses on one specific memory reminder – the royal dynastic drum – that, in and by itself, was imposed as a memory reference.

*Chapter 5*

# The Reminders

In the late-1950s – early-1960s, Rwanda was in its most intense political period. Both the Hutu and the Tutsi elites were fighting using different ideologies and contradictory arguments. What appeared to be the most intriguing or impasse-causing aspect was not the type of government system that would be put in place, but rather the place and significance of the *Kalinga*, the dynastic drum, the supreme and sacred symbol of the kingdom of Rwanda. Actually, the drum summarised the social and political relationship between the Hutu and the Tutsi and was maintained to serve as a perpetual reminder. In what follows, I will show how heated discussions led to a political impasse in the late-1950s that culminated in the change of power and of the political system. I then discuss in more depth the symbolic significance of that drum, which, for part of some Rwandans [Tutsi] represented the golden age, while for others [Hutu] it symbolised bondage and oppression. Finally, I connect the drum to the ethnic-identity-shaping process that was kept until today.

## 5.1 The Drum Impasse

The first important measure the Hutu revolutionaries took after ousting the Tutsi monarch in 1961 was the banning of the Kalinga royal drum and its replacement by a national flag. Whilst almost all political parties backed the measure unconditionally, monarchist UNAR, the *Union Nationale Rwandaise*, suggested that such a measure would only be accepted after a referendum on the issue (Nkundabagenzi, 1961: 199–201). Why was it so crucial for the Hutu emancipationists to have the Kalinga banned before any further discussion could take place? Simply because of the traumatic memories it embodied, at least from the memory perspective of the Hutu. Reflecting on the Hutu-Tutsi memory conflict, prominent Hutu emancipationist leader Joseph Gitera[72] maintained that the Tutsi kings had violently conquered the Hutu masses, marching on the corpses of their kings and using women as traps (Nahimana, 2007: 83). One excerpt from

---

[72] Until 1960, Joseph Gitera was the most prominent Hutu leader known especially for his outspokenness. He led the November 1959 revolt that turned into a social revolution. He headed the Hutu delegation that met King Mutara III Rudahigwa in 1958. He was later marginalised due to his lack of political stability and his lack of nationwide political basis.

the dynasty's esoteric code *–Ubwiru* – a sort of unwritten but well-memorised [by selected Tutsi families] and thoroughly followed constitution under the monarchy,[73] refers to Kalinga in these terms:

> Our Drum bears you [the Kings]
> It's always adorned with the Hutu kings [meaning their testicles]
> The Abanyiginya clan provides it with the bull [the King]
> While the Abega clan provides it with the mother-cow [The Queen].[74]

Regarding the testicles of the Hutu kings still adorning Kalinga, Gitera mentioned his visit to King Mutara III Rudahigwa in 1958:

> As a reconciliation protocol, we demanded that the venerable corpses of our ancestors that hung on the Kalinga to symbolise the ignominious bondage forever, and the immortal trophies, be removed and officially and honourably buried. Astounded and furious, Rudahigwa and his entourage responded: 'There is no Hutu-Tutsi problem in Rwanda, as there is no brotherly relationship between Tutsi and Hutu in Rwanda. They have nothing in common but 'domination and bondage' (Nahimana, 2007: 83; see also Waugh, 2004: 233).

At this stage, the political debate was dominated not by diverging political agendas, but just by diverging visions of a common past. Whilst the Tutsi monarchy was proud of the Kalinga, its ornament and its history, the Hutu felt humiliated by it. A similar request was addressed in 1960 to Rudahigwa's successor Kigeri V Ndahindurwa, by the Special Provisional Council,[75] a body created by the Belgian colonial administration after the November 1959 Revolution. The strongly weakened new monarch responded in a written statement:

> That issue relating to the dynasty and to Rwandan society is crucial and fundamental. It cannot be dealt with so summarily by a Provisional Council that is not representative. It should be considered by a more representative organ, especially one in charge of drafting the Constitution (Nkundabagenzi, 1961: 199 – 202; see also Kagame, 1956: 19–20).

The drum had become the central issue in those years. Why? King Ndahindurwa provided an answer: because it was crucial to the [Nyiginya-Tutsi] dynasty and to the Rwandans. Why, then, was it so crucial to the dynasty and to the Rwandans? The answer is in memory. Writing about the introduction of Kalinga by King Ruganzu II Ndori around 1580, Alexis Kagame presented the story of Rwoga

---

73 Alexis Kagame (1959: 10–14) provided an extensive explanation of the Ubwiru, its content and its central role in the ways in which the Kingdom was run, the succession was organised, etc.
74 The original Kinyarwanda text reads:
*Irabahetse ingoma yacu,*
*Ihora yambaye abahinza,*
*Abanyiginya bayibyarira imfizi,*
*Abega bakayibyarira insumba* (Nkurunziza, 2004).
75 The Special Provisional Council comprised Rwandan counsellors, the Special Resident, and the leaders of the four main parties [Parmehutu, Aprosoma, UNAR, and RADER] (Nkundabagenzi, 1961: 199–201).

– Kalinga's predecessor – which the Banyabungo[76] had seized after defeating King Ndahiro II Cyamatare. During the 11 years that separated Ruganzu's return from Karagwe [West of current Tanzania] and the death of his father Cyamatare, Rwanda had no royal drum and the situation was dramatic. A popular legend about this period has entered Rwanda's collective memory:

> The legend[77] speculates about that period of 'widowhood'. According to it, there were no births among men and beasts, there was such a severe drought that smoke came out of cattle's horns… all these misfortunes were due to the absence of the legitimate king on Rwanda's throne! The enthronisation of Ruganzu II Ndori instantly changed the situation which became normal… He inaugurated the new royal drum Kalinga to succeed the taken Rwoga (Kagame, 1951: 39).

The Kalinga drum symbolised not only the Banyiginya's power and supremacy over the rest of Rwanda's populations, but also and above all, substantiated the long blood-tainted history of the Rwanda-in-making process. With the introduction of Kalinga, the Banyiginya – a Tutsi clan – started adorning it with the testicles of the defeated [and assassinated] Hutu kings to symbolise their definitive political extinction. Before this memory-keeping gesture, the King had to make sure that the slain Hutu king left no male descendants. For instance, King Ruganzu II Ndori not only killed, in the 17th century, Bugara Hutu King Nzira, son of Muramira, but also decimated all his male descendants (Nahimana, 1993: 9).

Zither player Sebatunzi sang a seven-minute tune[78] about this sad episode of the Hutu's memories – triumphant in the Tutsi memories. He tells the story of Tutsi King Ruganzu Ndori kneeling down before Nzira and asking to work for him as a firewood splitter. Against the advice of his mother, Nyiranzira, Nzira hired Ndori's services and the latter quickly became his most trusted servant. The first thing Ndori did was to cut down a huge tree that joined the two banks of the nearby lake, where his troops would pass for the attack. One day, on Ndori's advice, Nzira organised festivities and gave rest to his fighters. That day, Ndori's troops surprisingly attacked Nzira's royal residence and decimated all those present. Ndori himself stabbed Nzira and took away all his servants.

A similar story is one about the King of Nduga, Mashira, who was enticed into a 'marriage trap' set by Tutsi King Mibambwe I Sekarongoro I Mutabazi I, who later personally put him to the sword together with all his male descendants (Nahimana, 1993: 9). The sexual organs of Nzira, and other Hutu kings served as an adornment for the royal drum, making the pride of the victorious kings and their descendants. Newbury (2002: 72) admitted that 'pre-colonial Rwanda was a state with serious inequalities', where 'assassination of individuals was part of the political process.' However, she rejected the contention that 'mass murders of

---

76 The Bunyabungo region is across Lake Kivu in the current Democratic Republic of the Congo.
77 See one full-length historical tale about the end of Rwoga and the coming of Kalinga in Coupez & Kamanzi (1962), pp. 204 – 221.
78 Known as *inanga*, this type of tunes are invaluable oral memory texts that tell a great deal about the past. Alexis Kagame (1959: 34) maintained that they were sponsored by the court and were the musical version of existing historical tales.

people on the grounds of ethnic category' occurred. It wasn't until the late-1950s – early-1960s that the Hutu elite realised that they could not be politically at ease with the testicles of their forefathers still adorning the Kalinga.

The above, then, explains why the ban of that drum was so essential for the Hutu emancipationists. As Mamdani (2001: 119) remarked, the Hutu's focus at that time was on that prime symbol of Tutsi power because it signified 'a permanent vision of Hutu inferiority'. King Ndahindurwa's point, that the drum was crucial to the dynasty and Rwanda, should be understood in this memory-keeping perspective. The drum was supposed to maintain his dynasty and ethnic group in an eternally superior position. Removing it would mean ending that superiority that had been reached after centuries of fighting and conquests, each step of which was represented by Kalinga.

## 5.2 The Drum as a Symbol of the Golden Age

The royal drum in the memories that related to the Tutsi ethnic identity summarised the golden age, as, by just viewing it and its adornments, each and every one recalled those perilous conditions under which the courageous forefathers had fought to expand the kingdom and maintain the Banyiginya dynasty on power. Kalinga was thus a golden age reminder and an essential element of ethnic identity, as the Hutu and the Tutsi both needed to position themselves in regards to it. There exists an extensive literature on the notions of memory, golden age, and identity (e.g., Huizinga, 1936: 26–27; Vivanti, 1986: 216–217; Ingimundarson, 2007: 96). Lowenthal (1985: 248–249), for instance, explained that the emblems of history and memory – Kalinga falls under this category – as well as tangible relics – think of the adornments of Kalinga – also symbolise identity. Gitera's request to King Rudahigwa clearly shows that he and his fellow emancipationists identified themselves with the relics.

Adolf Hitler himself identified himself with a certain golden age and had his own idols, namely Bismarck and Frederick the Great for whom 'he was an admirer' (Heiden, [1935] 1971: 59). For his 50th birthday, Hitler received a 'specially designed' and 'handsomely bound facsimile of letters by Frederick the Great' (Ryback, 2009: xvi). The memory process being 'the articulation of public and private interests, values and aspirations', it is quite normal that 'contradictions of identities' appear where those interests and values diverge (Misztal, 2003: 120). Historian Valur Ingimundarson (2007: 96) observed that the notion of a golden age is central to the formation of national identities. This was also the case in 16th-century France, especially with Etienne Pasquier's *Les Recherches* (1560), whose aim was to affirm the French identity by presenting the Gauls with their bravery and virtuous actions as the ancestors of the French. Pasquier defined his objective as follows: 'We will bring the golden age back to life' (Vivanti, 1986: 216–217).

It appears here that from some physical relics, a certain golden age which people identify with in some ways emerges. One important way of establishing a visible link with the long-gone and idealised golden age is to raise a monument that aims to remind of it. In this respect, Kalinga was a memory monument *par excellence*.

Like other monuments it 'reminded people what to believe and how to behave' as most of them 'were exhortations to imitate the virtues they commemorate' (Lowenthal, 1985: 322). This is to say that the way commemorations on a World War I monument or in a cemetery bring back the deeds and accomplishments of those to whom the monument is dedicated, the same way Kalinga brought to the surface the high deeds on the Tutsi side, and the extermination and submission of the ancestors on the Hutu side. Names, which I will discuss in length in the next three chapters, are another way of resurrecting the golden age in the present. Kajeguhakwa systematically called his children after himself and his long-deceased ancestors who lived under a better social, political atmosphere than the one in which he and the children lived (Kajeguhakwa: 2001: 120; 147; 177 & 185). This move could be interpreted as a way of bringing back a paradise lost – represented by the selected ancestor – into the present.

## 5.3 Memory Reminders in Independent Rwanda

As discussed in the previous section, the most significant measure taken by the new Hutu leaders after the abolition of the Tutsi monarchy was to abolish all those Tutsi golden-age monuments and reminders, including in the first place Kalinga, to replace them with a flag, a national coat of arms, and a national anthem. One huge monument remained, that is the name of Rwanda itself, but this will be discussed in length in the next chapter. Confirming the ethnic character of the national symbols, the new RPF-dominated administration, whose connection with the pre-independence monarchy is obvious, removed in 2001 all the symbols that had replaced the monarchic ones, 'claiming that the old national symbols had associations with the genocide and that new symbols could mark a break with the past' (Longman & Rutagengwa, 2004: 166).

While the previous coat of arms showed a machete – strongly associated with the genocide – and a hoe, which historians and anthropologists often associate with the Hutu agricultural traditions (Maquet, 1961: 11 & 15), the new ones show a shield which could be interpreted as representing what Foster and colleagues (2000: 117) called the Tutsi martial tradition. This is the one that led not only to their forefathers' victories over the Hutu kings, but also to the recent recovery of power by arms. The two national anthems could also be interpreted as loaded with memories relating to ethnic identities. The 'Hutu Republics' anthem, if I would call it that way to imply that it was accepted and acceptable as long as the Hutu were in power, used to a certain degree, the hide-and-seek language that characterises ethnic identities in Rwanda (see Chapter 2). Like Kalinga was the symbol of Tutsi's triumphalism, that anthem, too, carried a strong Hutu triumphalistic ideology. The title itself *Rwanda Rwacu* – Our Rwanda – although having 'nothing of ethnic partisanship', referred to the Parmehutu's proclamation 'that Rwanda was a Hutu nation' (Twagilimana, 2003: 74). Also, the praised *abarwanashyaka* – militants – in the first stanza were no one else but the Parmehutu emancipationists (*Ibid.*). The observation about the title is reinforced by the claims of one of the most popular pro-Parmehutu songs *Jya mbere Rwanda* – Go Forward Rwanda – especially the following stanza:

> How was Rwanda before [Independence]?
> The White Man and the Tutsi had swallowed it
> Pushing back the Hutu
> Whereas Rwanda was theirs [meaning Hutu's. Hence *Rwanda Rwacu* – Our Rwanda].[79]

A similar interpretation could be made with the new 'RPF Republic' anthem, where references to Tutsi ethnic identity and related memories can be detected.[80] While the title has changed from *Our Rwanda* to *Beautiful Rwanda* [Rwanda Nziza], it does not take long before the same *Our* comes back, pushing to wonder to whom it refers, and especially, if it is not another hide-and-seek game. The very first line goes like this: *Rwanda nziza gihugu cyacu*, which I would translate as '*Our* beautiful country Rwanda' or 'Rwanda *our* beautiful country'. Even though the first stanza attempts to explain whom 'our' represents, indicating that the country brings together 'all of us' indicating the Rwandese to whom it gave birth – which the previous did as well. The third stanza raises serious suspicions of Tutsi memory references to the Kalinga-embodied golden age. The stanza goes like this:

> Our brave ancestors
> Gave themselves bodies and souls
> As far as making you a big nation
> …[81]

These three lines show how difficult it has become to get out of the memory trap even after the genocide. A combination of 'ancestors' with making Rwanda big, that is expanding it, brings to mind the same memories that Kalinga represented, hence bringing back the question about who is hiding behind 'Our'. These three lines are like a summary of Alexis Kagame's 1943 pamphlet *Inganji Kalinga* [Ode to Kalinga], which, too, emphasised the expansion aspect and the bravery of the ancestors as well as the bloody character of that process. The following excerpt is revealing:

> This pamphlet is going to remind you of who *we* are! So that *we* keep in mind *our* own roots and *our* own heritage when *we* embrace the West's customs! It is going to remind *us* that *we* are not wanderers whom God threw out into nature. It is going to show *us* that Rwanda is a nation with deep roots, with

---

79  Original Kinyarwanda Text:
    *U Rwanda rwari rute?*
    *Kazungu na Gatutsi bari bararumize*
    *Basubiza inyuma Gahutu ari nyirarwo.*
80  Republic of Rwanda, 'National Symbols'. http://www.gov.rw/National-Symbols (Accessed 14 July 2012).
81  Original Kinyarwanda text:
    *Abakurambere b'intwari*
    *Bitanze batizigama*
    *Baraguhanga uvamo ubukombe*

a long *ancestry*; it is going to show us that we have had ancestors who created this nation for us and its customs which *we* inherited! In short it is telling *us*: 'See carefully what your *ancestors* have accomplished! They created Rwanda by *extending* it in its size! *Now peace has returned: there is no war any more to expand the nation in its size*! [Emphasis added][82]

It is important to note the following elements: the repetitive use of the first person in plural – us, our, we –; the connection between 'us, our, we' with *ancestry* or *ancestors*; the ancestors' bravery implied by the hugeness of what they have accomplished, namely making Rwanda a big nation. With this in the back of the mind, who might be hidden behind 'Our' in the new Rwandan national anthem? The connection to Kalinga goes even further. Since the anthem praised the expansion of Rwanda, which the pamphlet did as well, it is worth exploring what that expansion implied. The phrases 'by extending it in its size' and 'there is no war any more to expand the nation' in the pamphlet clearly signal that the process was not a peaceful one, but a multiple-phase war. As already discussed, each war that was won, ended not only with the killings of all males descendants, but also with rituals that consisted of cutting the slain kings' testicles to adorn Kalinga. Yet this appears to be a pride-provoking past worth chanting in post-genocide Rwanda.

While this chapter was concerned with memory transmission through reminders either in the physical, textual or oral forms, and how finally they all intermingled in some interesting ways, the next three chapters explore the transmission process through naming. The name is first presented as a memory keeper that in most cases archives personal, family, and collective memories (chapter 6); then the name is described as often having a powerful mission-assigning force that is believed to seal and unseal one's fate (chapter 7); finally, the name is discussed as a form of political, social, and inter-personal dialogue (chapter 8). What all these aspects seem to have in common is their potential to keep individuals, families, and even political organisations trapped in their ethnic identities and related memories.

---

82  Alexis Kagame, *Inganji Kalinga* (1943), quoted in Ferdinand Nahimana (1993), pp. 199–200:
    *Iki gitabo rero kigiye kubibutsa icyo tuli cyo! Kugira ngo nitujya kwenda ibya kizungu, tubyende tuzi ishingiro lyacu, tuzi icyo tugiye guhahiraho! Kigiye kutwibutsa ko tutali intarasi Mungu yapfuye kujugunya aho. Kizatwereka ko u Rwanda ari igihugu gishinze imizi, gifite amasekuruza maremare; kizatwereka ko twagize abasekuruza baturemeye iki gihugu, bakarema imico basize batwigishije! Mbese rwose kiratubwira kiti: "Witegereze ibyo abasekuruza bawe bakoze! Baremye u Rwanda barwagura mu bugali! Ubu amahoro yaraje: nta mirwano ikiliho yo kurwagura mu bugali!..."*

## Chapter 6

# Name as a Memory Keeper

Most non-informed foreigners keep asking questions about the names of Rwandans: Why are they so long and complicated to pronounce [and even to understand]? Why do brothers and sisters have different names while they were born to the same parents? The reason is that Rwandans have their own concept of the name, to which they assign a number of key functions. These functions can be divided into two main categories: identification-related functions on one hand, and social, memory functions on the other hand. The names in Rwanda, like elsewhere in the world, help individuals identify and distinguish themselves from one another. At the same time, and this is a peculiar feature to the Rwandan name, the name identifies the bearer's gender. On the other hand, the name tells in some sophisticated ways a certain story about the bearer and his or her family or community at the time of his or her birth. It also sometimes refers to the prevailing world views and perceptions. Since each person is unique, born under unique circumstances, to a specific family that has specific world views, beliefs, and perceptions, it is quite normal that the names resulting from all that will be unique in their own way. In the west and in some African countries,[83] the naming system follows a different pattern and serves different purposes,[84] compared to Rwanda and neighbouring countries.[85] In this chapter, I explore the social and cultural record-keeping function of the name, starting with the way in which it defines the bearer, sums up his or her past, selects certain events from the past as

---

83 Among the Tio of Brazzaville in the Republic of the Congo, people 'believe that if one knows the name of a person one has knowledge of the essence of that person and can bewitch him. What is in a name? To these people, everything' (Vansina, 1971: 442).

84 In the Netherlands, for instance, the name's function is to indicate to which family one belongs, and the family meant here is very often the one on the father's side (*Netwerk naamkunde*: '*De familienaam, ook wel achternaam of geslachtsnaam, geeft aan tot welke familie een persoon behoort. Doorgaans gaat het daarbij om de familie in de mannelijke lijn*'.
http://www.naamkunde.net/index.php?option=com_content&task=view&id=18&Itemid=28 [Accessed 6 January 2009]).

85 The memory-keeping function of the name is also common in neighbouring Congo. For instance King Ndatabaye Pierre Weza II, speaking of the Ngweshe kingdom in the Bushi region, explained that he was given the name Weza on his birth in 1943, because a famine was ravaging the kingdom: 'the name was meant to conjure the lot so that prosperity and fecundity could return to the country' (Ngangura, 1994). Weza in the local Mashi language – close to Kinyarwanda – means 'make crops grow'. Similarly, in some tribes in Kenya, the naming of newborn takes into account the prevailing atmosphere. In February 2008 for instance, 68 newborn babies were named after former UN Secretary General Kofi Annan who was heading the mediation team assigned to put an end to post electoral violence. This is a way to mark and remind future generations of that unrest that left over 1,000 people dead (http://www.africanews.com/site/list_message/11056 [Accessed 17 May 2009]).

being relevant to the child's memory and future, and how it relates to collective memory. By discussing these subjects, I want to show how names naturally become part of memory traps, to which they contribute in certain ways.

## 6.1 Name Is Man

While I was conducting some field research in April 2010, at the Baarnsch Lyceum, in the Dutch city of Baarn, I saw a booklet lying on a table in the teachers' room and took it to just browse through without any particular purpose. It was the school's magazine, with a title written in huge red letters on a white cover. Its five-line title was:

*Alle*
*Naam*
*Is*
*Maar*
*Onzin*

I was intrigued by this title. I asked one teacher who explained that the title was *De Animo*, and that the five-line wording was provided by a pupil after the editorial team had asked all the pupils to find a good wording for *Animo*. I asked what it meant: 'Nothing', said the teacher. In the corridors, I met a young pupil whom I asked what it meant: 'Nothing', he answered. I used a different strategy and asked how he would translate this title into English. He said: 'All names are just crap'. I thanked him and moved away to another pupil. I asked him to translate the title into English. His translation was: 'All names are but bullshit'. My interpretation of this wording of the school magazine's title, and the fact that it was chosen and accepted, is that actually it is a serious one that reflects a certain [shared and accepted, though latently] view about the name. The meaning – through translation – that the pupils spontaneously provided is that the name has very little social function.

The philosophy is different in Rwanda. A saying conveys the opposite of the extended *Animo* mentioned above: 'name is man' [thus, name is far from crap or bullshit] or 'such name, such man' [*izina ni ryo muntu*]. Another one completes it: 'receiving a bad name from your father does not mean that he hates you' [*so ntakwanga akwita nabi*]. In fact, the name is part of any family's collective memory as it relates a portion of the past of that very family. Before changing his name for the reasons I will mention in the next section, Lambertus Ntisoni (2007: 28–29) was called Ntirugirisoni, meaning – Death-has-no-shame. The bearer was not happy about that name, yet the name meant that his two older sisters had died before him, and that the father was telling Death that it should be ashamed of that. Ethnologist Pierre Erny studied cultural and traditional practices in Rwanda and described the sophisticated ways in which Rwandans choose their children's names:

> ... as each birth took place under different circumstances, it was possible to create a name fitting each situation perfectly, and through which the name-giver expressed himself very personally... The names were [are] always loaded with meaning. They were preferably enigmatic, allusive, undecipherable, and full of insinuations. Each situation was likely to serve as a source of inspiration. They could fetch from personal memory, family memory, or collective memory; evoke circumstances surrounding birth, public events, the preoccupations of that moment, beliefs and economic activities (Erny, 2005: 156).

For them to be as meaningful as the father wishes, they can be long, composed, and even be full sentences (*Ibid.*). The preoccupation of the father is not to have a sexy or good-sounding name but a meaningful one, even if its meaning is hurtful. Traditionally speaking, any child born of a married woman is the child of the mother's husband, not of the biological genitor (Maquet, 1961: 84). This means that the mother's husband will assume his paternity and give a name. Very often, that name describes that hurtful episode, and the father somehow avenges himself by calling the child Mbwayahandi [The-dog- (born) from-outside], for instance, or Jyamubandi [Join-the-other-(legitimate) children].

Mukasonga (2006: 11–12) wrote that her sister Alexia was born whilst her father was serving a jail sentence. This situation, which prevented him from rejoicing with the family, inspired the 'strange', full-sentence name of Ntabyerangode, meaning 'nothing-is-ever-completely-perfect'. The father meant that he rejoiced, but not to the extent he had wished. Kajeguhakwa's stepbrother was born as the family had just moved to a new red-brick house with an iron-sheet roof. He was called Majyambere, the-one-born-in-a-progressist-environment (Kajeguhakwa, 2001: 94). Let me consider a family of three children called 'I-live-among-enemies' [Ndimubanzi], 'He-is-braver-than-fugitives' [Murutampunzi], and 'The-savior/rescuer' [Mutabazi]. These names describe a certain situation that one specific generation went through. By interpreting these names over 10 or 20 generations, one has the story of one's whole ancestry, which does not necessitate written records or a library.

As it appears from the foregoing, naming in Rwanda is a memory act *par excellence*, that is, a 'meaning-making activity' by individuals (Zelizer 1995: 228). To the meaning-giving function of the memory process, I should add the one of 'giving order' to the past (Irwin-Zarecka, 1994: 145). As the circumstances surrounding birth are multiple and scattered, taking them together indiscriminately would yield no intelligible sense of the time of birth. The family and the region might be suffering simultaneously from an epidemic, [resulting from] a war, and drought. However, at the M-minute when the baby saw the light of the day, it started raining. This salutary and long-awaited rain most likely will retain the father's attention and push him to raise a monument that best reflects and immortalises the end of the tunnel in the memory of the family and of the region. This means that the father has weighed the various events and experiences – epidemics, war, drought, rain – against one another before putting a certain order to them. Ordering is deciding which element comes first, which one follows, which one is relevant or not, and so on. By putting rain in first position, the father signaled that drought was the most preoccupying issue of that moment, at least from his perspective. The rain-inspired name could also be interpreted as the father's willingness to emphasise positivity rather than negativity, or as a way to push the bearer's future and fate into positivity (see section 7.1). In a way thus, and as the next shows, the name sums up one's memory in a few syllables.

## 6.2 Memory in a Nutshell

There is a question that has so far not been discussed with regards to the memory-keeping function of the name: Why do Rwandans code their memories in names, which are meant to last for generations? One answer could be that they want to give the bearer a mission based on the lessons of the past (see Section 7.1); another answer could be that they want to foster the remembering process on a permanent basis, connect the bearer, and to some extent his or her contemporaries, to a certain past. Yet another reason could be put forward. By pronouncing one's name, one tells, in one word, one's story, where one comes from, which battles one's ancestors took part in, and thus who one's friends and enemies are, amongst other things. That is most likely why the Rwandan tradition required the visitor to say who he was before crossing the *Irembo,* the main entrance of the compound, by confirming his identity. The visitor cited his name, his father's name and the clan he belonged to amongst the 18 existing in Rwanda (Kajeguhakwa, 2001: 27–28).

One's name, together with the name of one's father and the clan were enough to identify a person by placing him or her in time, space, and memory, just like a modern-day identity card which leads the police or any other authorised official to a database containing all the details that are required. The self-introduction formality described above is most likely meant to reassure the host by providing a short background on the visitor. I should say that even today, whether in Rwanda or abroad, the old generation still asks the younger ones: 'who is your father?' [*Uri mwene nde?*] In many other instances, the younger ones are referred to as 'the [grand] son or [grand] daughter of...'. At the administrative level, official documents including visa application forms and court documents meant for the public still mention entries like: son of... and... , where the names of the father, mother and even the spouse are mentioned.[86] It is even a tradition for job seekers to mention the names of their parents and wives on their résumé, to allow more clarity about their background – their past.

---

86  The 15 November 2010 Military High Court's summon of former army Chief of Staff, Faustin Nyamwasa and other co-accused, is a good illustration. On the one hand, the MHC identified the accused [all in exile abroad] with their own names, those of their fathers, those of their mothers, and those of their wives, together with the places and dates of birth. On the other hand, the MHC ordered the summon to be made public, including in the pro-government newspaper, *The New Times.* http://www.newtimes.co.rw/index.php?issue=14455&advertorial&id=146 (Accessed 25 November 2010).

Using a fake name, which does occur and has occurred in the past, means not only cheating one's memory, but also the community for some mischievous purpose. King Ruganzu Ndori [early 17th century] could not use his true name when he went to offer his free services to the Bugara King, Nzira, son of Muramira (See Section 5.1). He used Cyambarantama, the-sheep-skin-clothed-man, to confuse the King that he would later assassinate (see Kagame, 1951: 39; Nahimana, 1993: 9). If he had said that he was Ruganzu Ndori, son of Ndahiro II Cyamatare, of the Abasindi clan, then Nzira would have easily traced him, because his own troops, the *Abakongoro*, had allied themselves with the *Abanyabungo* of King Nsibura Nyebunga, to attack Rwanda. They had killed Ndori's father and they certainly knew that Ndori had been sent into exile for safety (Kagame, 1951: 38; Nahimana, 1993: 227). The usual self-introduction formality in this case would have been fatal to him, as it would have thrown all the war-memories into Nzira's face.

Far from Rwanda, specifically in The Gambia, West Africa, similar memory-based naming traditions existed, especially in the 17th century. In his attempt to dig up his African origins in the 1960s, American writer Alex Haley went to a village he named Juffure in The Gambia, where a *griot* – a man serving as 'living, walking archives of oral history' (Haley, 1977: 674; 678–679 & 686) – told him the story of the birth and name-giving ceremony of his seventh great-great-grand father, Kunta Kinte:

> By ancient custom, for the next seven days, there was but a single task with which [Kunta Kinte's father] Omoro would seriously occupy himself: the selection of a name for his firstborn son. It would have to be a name rich with history and with promise, for the people of his tribe – the Mandinkas – believed that a child would develop seven of the characteristics of whomever or whatever he was named for… 'The first child of Omoro and Binta Kinte is named Kunta!' cried Brima Cesay. As everyone knew, it was the middle name of the child's late grandfather, Kairaba Kunta Kinte, who had come from his native Mauretania into The Gambia, where he had saved people of Juffure from a famine, married Grandma Yaisa, and then served Juffure honorably till his death as the village's holy man (*Ibid.*: 2–3).

This quote from Haley's *Roots* brings to light another important function of the name: it gives a sort of past-inspired mission for the future. By naming his son after a hero who saved the tribe from a famine, Omoro was assigning his son the task of repeating the ancestor's honourable actions. This explains why Kunta Kinte, once deported to America and auctioned as a slave, refused to renounce his name, preferring multiple whipping rather than the imposed, memory-empty name of Toby. It should be stressed that 17-year-old Kunta Kinte was more haunted by the strange new name than by his new slave condition, as 'all he could think of was the name "To-by" he had been given' (*Ibid.*: 217).

It is important to note that the art of coding memory into a name is not limited to the Kinyarwanda language. It is much more the philosophy behind it that gives it its peculiarity. Ntisoni, a Hutu who was a junior officer in the former Rwandan army, and who had not yet recovered from an injury caused by a bomb blast, survived thanks to the French *Operation Turquoise*. Sent in the last months of the genocide to create a humanitarian zone in the West of Rwanda bordering Zaire – now DR. Congo – the rescue operation 'prevented the Inkotanyi [RPF rebels] from forcing the Hutu fugitives into the Lake Kivu' (Ntisoni, 2007: 74–75). It is with his rescue by a French corporal in the back of the mind that Ntisoni called his first daughter, born in the refugee camp in Zaire, Miserere France-Tanvîr (*Ibid.*). Although in Latin, French, and Hindu, the name of that Rwandan child is a family memory keeper: *Miserere* – have mercy; *France* – the country that sent the *Operation Turquoise,* a visible sign of that mercy for Ntisoni and the Hutu; *Tanvîr* – a true, unexpected miracle that allowed the father to survive (*Ibid.:* 9). Though not in Kinyarwanda, the child's name is a memory book not only for his family but also for all those who went through the same traumatic situations – war, refugee camps. Her mission is to know that past, and convey it to her own children, which makes the name a mission-giving mechanism. Needless to mention that there is an aspect of Hutu ethnic identity and related memories behind this combination of names.

In a similar way, Sebarenzi named his first son – born eight months before the RPF 1st October 1990 attack – Respect, for obvious reasons relating to Tutsi ethnic identity and corresponding memory:

> How small he was. How could something so small bring with him so much hope – hope for a better future, for a life freely lived, for peace? I named him Respect as part of that hope. Tutsi had been treated without respect for so many years. In giving him the name of that which Tutsi had been denied, I hoped he would embody it – respect for others, respect for himself (Sebarenzi, 2009: 64).

Sebarenzi's family had survived many Tutsi-targeting pogroms in the 1960s and the 1970s. He had been denied access to secondary school and had decided to cross Lake Kivu into Zaire [DR. Congo], where he completed both secondary and higher education before returning to Rwanda in 1989. From this background and the memories associated with it, the name Respect received a special meaning, because of the memories it refers to. The same can be said with Respect's brother, born while in exile in Burundi and at the time when war was raging in Rwanda. He was named Pacifique – the Peaceful (*Ibid.*: 71). From the above, naming appears as a one-word or one-sentence memory process that is far from being all-inclusive. Of all that was going on at the time he was heading westwards to Zaire, Ntisoni selected the mercy which he enjoyed from a French soldier; on his part, Sebarenzi picked out a lack of respect towards the Tutsi as the name-inspiring factor, and left the rest out.

## 6.3 The Selective Character of the Name

The name, like memory, is a sense- and meaning-making process that combines two seemingly contradictory aspects: remembering and forgetting. Memory is not only remembering but also forgetting, and, as Lowenthal (1985: 204) suggested, for it 'to have meaning we must forget most of what we have seen'. Although opposites at first sight, these processes that make the name are not mutually exclusive, but are rather 'two sides of one process' – the memory process (Brockmeier, 2002: 21). Anyway, one omits or forgets what he has retained in the first place. Thus, the memory process is a matter of absorption and indigestions (Michaux, 1974: 9). Naming, then, is the process of remembering haunted by forgetting (Huyssen, 2000: 38), which it encompasses rather than opposes (Nora, 1984a: VIII).

Let me go back to the three names I mentioned above – 'I-live-among-enemies' [Ndimubanzi], 'He-is-braver-than-fugitives' [Murutampunzi], and 'The-rescuer' [Mutabazi] – and suppose that many children were born in the same period as the bearers of the three names. The name of Mr. 'I-live-among-enemies' [Ndimubanzi] supposes other people in the community and a misunderstanding or conflict. While this name emphasises prudence and caution and somehow ignores, forgets, excludes, and neglects possibility for reconciliation, the other side could pretend to forget that enmity and call their child 'hear/know-it-but-don't-pay-attention-to-it' [Byumvuhore]. The latter name stresses a form of reconciliation, or at least invites the bearer to be tolerant, to work on better relations with enemies. In other words, the bearer is requested to remember any positive, uniting sign and forget any dividing development. As for the name 'He-is-braver-than-fugitives' [Murutampunzi], it implies that other children were born in exile. In the latter case, a name like 'The-traveler' [Serugendo or Mugenzi], will be given to the child, if the father prefers to remember the distance he walked to reach his place of exile, and to forget the reason why he left his home country. Lastly, the name 'The-rescuer/rescuer' [Mutabazi] puts emphasis on the act of saving, forgetting the nature of the catastrophe. A child born during that catastrophe, or after it has ended, could be called 'I-am-in-trouble' [Ndimukaga].

In Kenya, where similar naming habits exist, at least in some tribes, the same remembering-and-forgetting pattern applies. In February 2008 for instance, it was reported that 68 newborn babies were named after former UN Secretary General Kofi Annan, who was leading the mediation team that were striving to put an end to post electoral violence. [87] This was a way to mark and remind future generations of the unrest that left more than 1,000 people dead. It could be argued that, by choosing the peacemaker's name, the parents wanted to look at the situation with optimism, and to let the bearer remember that traumatic past with optimism. In other words, there was violence and bloodshed, but this was not the most important message to let the bearer and his children remember. They should remember the thirst for peace that prevailed among many Kenyans at the time of their birth. No detailed study has yet shown how other children were named, especially in the areas most affected by violence like the Rift Valley. It would not be astonishing to find traumatic memory names, that is, names given by parents who looked at the events with pessimism.

---

87   Dennis Itumbi, 'Kenya: 68 newborn babies named after Annan', *AfricaNews* (13 February 2008) http://www.africanews.com/site/list_message/11056 (Accessed 17 May 2009).

While discussing the selective character of the memories behind names, it is important to try and understand why the father is the one giving the name, and the one the child would mention to identify himself to a stranger. The first answer could be that Rwandan society is strongly patrilineal. Only the paternal side of the ancestry is considered as relevant. This is mostly due to the belief that 'man's participation in conception was more important than the woman's' (Maquet, 1961: 29). The analogy behind it was that the man provides the seed 'to be buried in the soil', and that 'strength and vitality are unquestionably in the seed rather than in the passive soil' (*Ibid.*: 83). It could be deduced that this philosophy gave the father the right and the power to choose a name, which, as noted above, immortalised a given experience, or assigned a mission to the bearer, or sealed his or her fate. As it appears, the name is personal but it refers at the same time to the memories beyond the name bearer and even sometimes beyond the family and the region. It is personal but yet it refers to collective memories.

## 6.4 Personal Name and Collective Memory

The above brings to light one important point, namely the frameworks of collective memory. Naming takes place in quite a private setting, as the father exclusively decides what the name will be. The reasoning that the name is given to an individual, not to a community, could lead to the wrong conclusion that names equal private memory. While no one disputes that individuals 'always use social frameworks when they remember' (Halbwachs, [1925] 1992: 40), there is still divergence of views as to who, between the individual and the collectivity, is the prime remembering subject. On the one hand, it is suggested that remembering is an interactive process, and can thus not be just individual,[88] since it 'is determined through a supra-individual cultural construction' (Misztal, 2003: 82), while on the other hand, memory is said to be 'inherently' and 'uniquely' personal, which condemns it to ultimate extinction at every death (Lowenthal, 1985: 195–196). The examples provided above show that though naming is the father's exclusive prerogative, it has 'a social quality', because it is 'interactively constructed, and, therefore, always connected with the memories of others' (Assmann, 2006: 10–11). In this respect, the name is part of collective memory, not only because it involves at least two individuals, the child and the father, but also because these two individuals live in society, which inspires the name and is the ultimate addressee.

Kajeguhakwa authored a story similar to Haley's *Roots*, as he dove into his family's memory back to the 10$^{th}$ century (Kajeguhakwa, 2001: 9). Around 1873, his father, named Rugagaza by his own father, received a nickname from the vulnerable community members who were hiding in a cave to escape a ravaging

---

[88] Communication scholar James Carey was categorical about the publicness of thought – remembrance being understood as one form of thinking (Collingwood, [1946] 1994: 307). Thought is predominantly public and social for a number of reasons: firstly, 'it depends on a publicly available stock of symbols'; secondly, 'it consists of building maps of environments' in which other people, including ancestors, perform a role (Carey, [1989] 2009: 22–23).

war. They nicknamed him Ruhunyenzi – The-one-who-winks-his-eyes [-due-to-overwhelming-light]. The newborn baby was winking his eyes when the fugitives went out of the cave. That community-given nickname overpowered the initial father-given name for the remainder of his life (Kajeguhakwa, 2001: 15), most likely because the community memory it conveyed was so strong. This leads to the deduction that the name is a communication tool by using language to encode the perceptions of the time of birth. As such, like any other communication process, the name supposes the 'other'. Philosopher Georges Gusdorf (1991a: 154) maintained that 'speech, even within personal identity, introduces the presence of the other, the absent-present other', who shares the same discursive universe and cultural patrimony. In this respect, like the private diary written in French which potentially 'exposes a message to the entire *francophonie*', the Rwandan name exposes its message to all Kinyarwanda-speaking people.

Another way to consider the collectiveness of personal names is to look at people involved in the story behind the name. It is not just the bearer, the father, and the mother. Let's consider the name Kajeguhakwa and what the bearer tells us about its meaning. The name means 'The-young-one-who-came-to-offer-free-services'. This was initially a nickname given to him by his young mother, who got married to 67 year old Ruhunyenzi in 1940, when she was not yet 20 years old (Kajeguhakwa, 2001: 24). At the time of birth, the very thing or experience his mother was thinking about, thus remembering, was that 'the difference of age between her and her husband made her not a spouse in the household, but a servant who came to offer free services to her old master' (*Ibid.:* 27). There were other situations to remember but that one was prominent in her mind at the time of her child's birth. Like the father's community-given nickname, Kajeguhakwa finally became the name of the future businessman.

In this story, one sees the father, the mother, and the baby, but also indirectly the mother's parents who were implicitly blamed to have married their young daughter to an elderly man. Through this tacit complaint, a finger is pointed at entire society, as the prevailing cultural practices allowed such situations to happen. Therefore, that personal name is like a picture of that particular epoch, its world views, and its cultural practices. As it emerges here, in a few cases, the mother's chosen [nick]name can gain more prominence than that given by the father. At this point, naming appears as a cultural way at the disposal of individuals, families, and communities to bring the past in the present. The next chapter adds another dimension: the future. The name is the past viewed from the present perspective, but is in most cases meant to serve as a reminder in the future.

*Chapter 7*

# Name as Mission Statement

The mission-assigning function of the name stems from its memory-keeping dimension and is one of the most intriguing aspects of names in Rwanda. It sometimes leads to superstitions and to fear, but in many cases, future realities and experiences show astonishing connections with the name and its message. Let me consider the names that have already been used above to illustrate this point. The name: 'I-live-among-enemies' [Ndimubanzi] later draws the bearer's curiosity as to who those enemies are or were. If the father has decided to anchor or durably archive that enmity in a name, it means that that enmity is meant to be hereditary for generations. And it often is. The bearer is invited to remain vigilant, not to eat or drink anywhere or anything, as he is surrounded by enemies. As for Mr. 'He-is-braver-than-fugitives' [Murutampunzi], he is told by his father to never run away, that is, to fight or die. Finally, Mr. 'The-rescuer' [Mutabazi], like Kunta Kinte, is expected to prevent catastrophes or, when they take place, to never 'entertain the thought of giving up' (Haley, 1977: 216). In a way, the name seals and unseals one's fate, bridges one's past and one's future, leading to the conclusion that one's name is oneself.

## 7.1 Sealing and Unsealing Fate

Mukasonga (2006: 71) noted that one of her childhood friends in the late 1960s had a father called Ngoboka, a name meaning 'Rescue-me' or 'Help-me' with a strong stress on timeliness. Ngoboka, as his name indicates, would always be there, on time, with his feared axe, when the Hutu militiamen would attack the two Tutsi girls, Mukasonga and her friend. Here one can see the opposite of naming in John Bunyan's 17th century literary work *The Pilgrim's Progress* (1678). In this allegoric piece, Bunyan wanted to highlight some virtues and slam some vices and chose characters' names that reflected those virtues and vices. Here, actions and behaviour precede the name and the name stems from the assigned actions and expected behaviour. In this respect, Evangelist, Christian, and Faithful behave in a way that reflects the virtues of their name; similarly, Ignorance, Hypocrisy, Talkative, and the Flatterer were named so because the author wanted them to behave in a certain way. In Rwanda, it seems to be the other way around: the name comes first and actions and behaviour follow and confirm the name to some extent. Ki-Zerbo (2008: 28–29) observed that the name has some power in some other cultures in Africa, where 'it not only signifies, but also *operates*' [emphasis added].

There is a general belief that the name stimulates the qualities it evokes. The name Bugabo – courage – will stimulate its bearer to be courageous, whilst the name Ntwali – the brave – will push one to be brave.[89] However, the process is not a mathematical equation, that is, the mission-giving aspect of the name has no absolute and inescapable grab on one's life. For instance, Révérien Rurangwa (2006: 40), a miraculous survivor of the Tutsi genocide, was intrigued by the contrast between the name of local governor of Gitarama, Mr. Ukurikirayezu – The-one-who-follows-Jesus – and the intention to exterminate the Tutsi he attributed to him. However, Rurangwa mentioned another striking but heart-tearing instance of a name that literally 'followed' someone until her last breath. After powerlessly watching the cold-blooded butchering of his 43-member family by Hutu neighbours, and requesting in vain a quick and immediate death rather than one *à petit feu* coupled with mockery, Rurangwa – who was by then heavily mutilated – was speaking to his dying mother, when, suddenly, her sister Byukusenge – Wake-up-and-pray/ask – woke up from the deceased bodies and prayed to her now-deceased mother to give her food and water. Receiving neither, she died the next day (Rurangwa, 2006: 52).

Many other examples exist to suggest that this fate-sealing power of the name should be seriously considered. Sebarenzi (2009: 97) did not believe he could once become Speaker of the Rwandan parliament: 'I didn't feel qualified to be deputy speaker, much less speaker', he wrote, before finally saying to himself 'Maybe I could be speaker. Maybe this is God's plan for me'. Sebarenzi interpreted his new position from the perspective of his religious faith, but the interpretation from the perspective of the name should not be ignored. This is what Sebarenzi (2009: 26) wrote about his name and the reasons why it was chosen:

> Sebarenzi was the name my father chose for me. It was his grandfather's name and means *chief shepherd*. I never asked my father why he named me Sebarenzi, but I know he admired his grandfather, and I also think it reflected *his aspirations for me*: that I would be a chief shepherd – a good leader [Emphasis added].

And a leader, he became. Since the name seems to be a sort of permanent mission order for the bearer, the latter becomes confused when the name changes. Reflecting on his new name, Kunta Kinte wondered 'if he would ever grow up to be a man like Omoro' (Haley, 1977: 217). He was implying that the name was serving as a signpost or as a navigational tool assisting him on his way to a certain destiny and destination – manhood. Kunta Kinte failed to decipher the mission assigned to him by the new name, even after consulting, in dream, the holy-man after whom he had been previously named (*Ibid.*: 225). Ntisoni explained how he managed to change his destiny just by slightly modifying his name. Although the change is slight in form, it is huge in meaning as the initial Ntirugirisoni – Death-has-no-shame – looks similiar to the current Ntisoni – I-reject-shame. The latter name is the former minus – rugiri – which makes death, here represented by

---

[89] Laurent Nkusi, quoted in Kayumba, *La poésie héroïque rwandaise 'ibyîivugo'* (Butare : IRST, 2005), p. 6.

–*ru[-pfu]* disappear from his name and, therefore, from his destiny. In fact, his father was desperate when he gave him this name: two of his daughters had died of malaria one after the other, prior to Nti[rugiri]soni's birth:

> My parents had not yet recovered from that double loss when they gave me birth. When I was eight days old, obsessed by the idea that I could join my sisters in the other world, my father gave me the name that I hate. After traditional ceremonies, my father had taken his responsibility as father by giving me the name NTIRUGIRISONI… I did not want to be called that detestable name… (Ntisoni, 2007: 29).

By giving that memory and death-warding name, the father made and immortalised the hopeless remark that death had no shame at all, as it took two of his children. It might be assumed that the personified Death would finally be ashamed and let at least Lambertus live longer than his deceased sisters. The change apparently worked as Nti[rugiri]soni survived a deadly bomb blast in May 1994 – the blast only took a few fingers off his hand and damaged his legs (*Ibid.*: 64) – and managed to cross the Congo's 'rivers of blood' where Death was the absolute master. So far, two aspects of the name as a memory mechanism can be distinguished: firstly as a record keeping tool, the name is by nature presentist, as it is shaped by the present vision and intentions of the father or name-giver; and secondly as a mission-assigning mechanism, it is futuristic, since assigned tasks can only be accomplished when the child has grown into an adult.

Whilst introducing the previous chapter, I suggested [in a footnote] that the name in the western name-giving pattern identifies much more the family than the individual, and tells us nothing about his or her past, except that other people of the same name and same blood existed before them. However, one special case, falling under this pattern is revealed with regard to the fate-un/sealing powers of the name. In his autobiography *L' avenir dure longtemps*, Marxist philosopher Louis Althusser attributed most of his psychiatric troubles to his name. He wrote: 'When I was born, I was baptised Louis… a name that literally horrified me for a long time'. The name horrified him because it was the name of his mother's first husband, his father's brother [thus his uncle] killed in Verdun during World War I. The name Louis, referred to, and sounded like *lui* – him – the killed uncle whom the mother kept loving even after his death: '*Lui, c' était Louis*' (Althusser, [1985] 1992: 33–34). One sees memory at work through the name in a totally different way. However, the most interesting aspect in this example is the impact of that name on its bearer:

> … it was not really me that she [my mother] loved or looked at… When she looked at me, it was certainly not me that she saw, but, in my back, in an imaginary sky marked forever by death, *another*, that *other* Louis whose name I bore, but who I was not, that man dead in the skies above Verdun… One can philosophise at will about death: death, which circulates everywhere in social reality… is not present under the same forms in reality and in fantasy. In my case, this death was the death of a man whom my mother loved more

than anyone else, beyond me. In her 'love' for me, something terrified and marked me quite from my early childhood, *sealing for a long time what was going to be my destiny* (Althusser, [1985] 1992: 48. Emphasis added).

I am reaching here the most interesting point that pushed me to mention this example: a name sealing someone's fate. Throughout the book, Althusser kept on reminding that the name Louis had turned him into a 'living dead' (e.g., *Ibid.*: 53 & 83) ; and that all his life, he had been mourning his own death because of that death inscribed in his name from his birth (*Ibid.*: 270). The deduction he came to was that the death-marked fate was culminated in the assassination [by him] of his wife, Hélène in 1980.

The foregoing is not suggesting that Rwandans are prisoners of their names. It is rather suggesting that names influence in some not-always-perceptible ways their behaviour, actions, and worldviews. One different but related cultural practice I want to discuss in the next section is *icyivugo*, literally meaning a 'self-introductory poem', which very often serves like the name's extension both literally and figuratively.

## 7.2 I Am My Past

Close to the naming mechanism is war or heroic poetry, known as *Icyivugo* [Plural: *ibyivugo*]. *Icyivugo* means 'a piece in which one speaks of himself' (Coupez & Kamanzi, 1962: 9; see also Kagame, 1969: 15), brandishing one's spear and roaring strongly as if one wants to impress an enemy. While reciting the *icyivugo*, one utters as many syllables as possible in one breath, and ignores the limits of the sentences (Coupez & Kamanzi, 1962: 9; see also Kayumba, 2005: 17). According to Charles Kayumba (2005: 5) of the Institute for Scientific and Technological Research of Rwanda, that genre was initially meant to stimulate other warriors or potential warriors. It did so by proclaiming the bravery of one of them who fought to defend or to expand the country.[90] That age-long genre has metamorphosed to adapt to new peaceful situations, and is still popular even in modern Rwanda, while the two other genres – dynastic poetry and pastoral poetry – have almost completely disappeared. Why is the only-for-man *icyivugo* relevant in the discussion about names and memories behind them? Simply because the first word, or combination of words – often full sentences turned into proper names – of *icyivugo* generally constitutes the nick*name* or war *name* of the author, who, by the way, is very often referred to with the use of that nick*name*. In other words, *icyivugo* is a new self-given name, based on some real or fictitious past. The self-assigned name can replace the father-given counterpart (Coupez & Kamanzi, 1962: 9).

---

90  It should be noted that the *ibyivugo* are not a specificity of Rwanda. In other places in the region, like in Ankole, a former kingdom in southern Uganda, the same tradition exists. In that area – where a similar political and social system existed before indipendence – the *ebyevugo* [note how this is close to the Kinyarwanda name *ibyivugo*], 'The praise poems… being delivered without pause for breath' (Morris, 1964: 19) persist.

The *icyivugo*, then, is about experience-inspired self-perception. Like the name, it uniquely identifies the author and distinguishes him from other people. For instance, Kampayana son of Nyantaba was also known under his war name or nickname of *Rutajabukwanimitima*, which is the starting sentence of his *icyivugo*: '*Rutajabukwanimitima ingamba zimisha imituku*', which means 'The one who is not disheartened when there is bloodshed on the battle field' (Kayumba, 2005: 18). More recently – to illustrate the above-mentioned metamorphosis and the *icyivugo*-name relationship – former president Juvénal Habyarimana pronounced his own war poem in 1992 during his party's congress. The poem went: '*Ndi Ikinani cyananiye abagome n' abagambanyi*' to mean: 'I am the invincible who resisted the wicked and the traitors'. From that moment on, Habyarimana was more referred to in media, political discourse, and in everyday language as *Ikinani* or Kinani than by his own name. The *icyivugo* reflects the qualities and values the person cherishes. By repeatedly proclaiming them publicly, the person assigns himself the mission to achieve them.[91] As observed above, some names contain the qualities that the father wants his child to cherish in the future. With the *icyivugo*, the author is free to decide on his own, though the large cultural, social, and political context has already established a set of values that he should pick from.

The more one studies and analyses the *icyivugo*, the more one wonders if they have not ended up turning 'killing' into something banal. In most *ibyivugo*, one praises oneself for having violently and spectacularly killed and warns any challenger to behave himself or die. The *icyivugo* often describes its author as inhumane, as someone who fears nothing, who is ready to shed blood and who is thirsty of blood. Very dangerously, that violence-conveying tradition is taught in primary schools, since the idea is to keep the tradition alive. One popular child *icyivugo* that the average Rwandan child can recite goes like this:

> While standing on a roof,
> I flexed my muscles,
> Shot arrows one after another,
> Harangued my companions,
> My *name* is No-Worry [Emphasis added].[92]

This child[ish] war poem not only encourages the use of violence [shooting arrows] but also invites children to be proud of it and to have no worries about it. The last verse – My *name* is No-Worry – is important. As already pointed out, Name is Man. Name is oneself. By repeating this over and over again, the implicit message is that as long as one is oneself, one is not supposed to worry about, but rather to be proud of, shooting arrows one after another, which means nothing

---

91  J. Nsengimana (1988: 28), quoted in Kayumba (2005: 6).
92  Aloys Bigirumwami, *Ibitekerezo: Indirimbo-imbyino-ibihozo-inanga-ibyivugo-ibigwi-imyato-amahamba n' amazina y' inka* (Nyundo, 1971), p. 129. Original Kinyarwanda text:
*Nagiye ku rusenge*
*Ibitugu ndabitigisa*
*Imyambi ndayisukiranya*
*Abo twari kumwe ndabacyaha*
*Nitwa Cyaradamaraye.*

but killing. That violence is to be seen in its raw and brutal form in the adult's war poems, where one is proud of his blood-shedding deeds, fictional or real. Kampayana's war poem, which I referred to above, is one good illustration:

> The one who is not disheartened
> When there is bloodshed on the battlefield
> I belong to the subjects of the King of Mbilima
> I am the bravest whom the Redoubtable Fighter has distinguished
> He ordered me to command troops in a blood-shedding battle
> He *called* me: '[You!] *The Formidable*'
> I replied: '[Here am I!] *The spear-propelling expert*'
> I entertain hatred against the enemies
> And when I encounter them I become furious [Emphasis added].[93]

In this war poem, blood-shedding, hatred, fury, spear-propelling are all praised. More interestingly, those 'values' and 'virtues' are turned into *names* as the italicised phrases show. The warrior introduces himself as an example of bravery that should be followed by the youth. It is therefore no surprise that child war poems follow that model by turning violent, blood-shedding situations into socially acceptable ones. One other popular child *icyivugo* that many children learn quite early on goes like this:

> While standing on the top of the hill
> A girl saw me shoot an arrow and said:
> 'This boy shows so well that he deserves to marry me'.[94]

Through this war poem, boys are told that shooting [killing] well is a criterion for one to be admired and appreciated by girls, in particular, and by society in general. This situation brings to mind Jean-Jacques Rousseau's treatise on education, in which he fought the idea of teaching young children about La Fontaine's fables. Rousseau's (, [1768] 1966: 143–144) point was that children would always identify themselves with the smartest – the fox that managed to get possession of the raven's cheese; the strongest – the lion for instance. It is quite natural to choose the good role, the winning role, but the consequence of this is damaging to good social behaviour: whenever the child, who naturally idealises the strong and feared lion, is in charge of sharing among his age mates,

---

93   Kagame (1969), pp. 18–19:
    *Rutajabukwa n'imitima*
    *ingamba zimisha imituku*
    *rwa Nyili-Mbilima*
    *ndi intwali Inkotanyi yamenye*
    5. *Yashinze urugamba rukora amaraso*
    *ati: "Rwampingane!"*
    *Nti: "rukaraga-ndekwe*
    *nangana n'ababisha*
    *iyo duhuye ndarakara!"*

94   Ibid. p. 129:
    *Nahagaze mu mpinga*
    *Ndasa umwambi umukobwa arambona, ati:*
    *Uno muhungu yarasa neza arakandongora.*

he will imitate the lion and take all for himself. It could be argued that the ease and the zeal with which Rwandans have been killing each other is partly to be blamed on the above-mentioned repeated and encouraged culture of violence that is inculcated into young minds.

Rousseau ([1768] 1966: 128) suggested that the only moral lesson suitable for childhood – which is also the most important of all ages – is to never harm anyone. It is obvious that these poems convey moral lessons different from those Rousseau advocated. Harm seems to be a measure of manhood, a value. Repeated over and over again at school, at home, during festivities, the cliché of the man as a skillful killer ends up conquering the mind and, as mentioned above, turns death and killing into something banal, something normal. Through this repetition and the importance society accords to it, a 'pseudo-environment' is created in the child's mind, whose consequences take place in the 'real environment' (Lippmann, [1922] 1997: 10).

Finally, the *icyivugo* offered and still offers a practical solution to the married woman who could never pronounce the name of her father-in-law and of all the family members with the same status as him, and all other names with the same radical as his name. She has to find figurative ways to designate these people, and one easy way is to refer to those highly respected members of the family-in-law using their nicknames as they appear in their war poems (Kagame, 1954: 168–170). In other words, these people are not called by their names, but by their glorious, often fictitious and exaggerated past. Whilst this and the previous section have considered names borne by individuals, the next section explores the country's name, Rwanda, the memories it conveys, and the fate it seems to have sealed for the country.

## 7.3 The Name 'Rwanda'

As suggested above, the name is a summary of a certain representation of the past. It bridges the past and the future and, as such, presents two major aspects: on one hand 'remembering', and, on the other, 'projecting' past experiences (Van Dijck, 2007: 8 & 21). While remembering takes place in the present and directs the remembering subject or the name-giver to the past, projecting, which equally takes place in the present, turns the remembering subject to the future. The starting point for the naming/memory process, therefore, lies in the present, which emerges as the meeting point of two eternities – the past and the future (Thoreau, [1854], 1983: 59). Philosophising about the past-future bridging by archives – names being a form of archive – Derrida (1996: 33–34) stressed that instead of, and 'more than a thing of the past... the archive should call into question the coming of the future'. He went on to add that the 'question of the archive is not... a question of the past... It is a question of the future... of a promise and responsibility for tomorrow' (*Ibid.*: 36). In what follows, I explore the memory-keeping, and mission-assigning functions of the name 'Rwanda'.

In his study about the emergence of the Rwandan state, Nahimana (1993: 289–319) researched the period that stretched from the 16th century to the early 20th century and claimed that Rwanda became what it is now in only 1931, when all previously independent Hutu kingdoms in the north and the northwest finally fell under the control of the Tutsi-Nyiginya monarch, owing to the military support of German and Belgian colonisers. The name 'Rwanda' comes from an ancient Kinyarwanda verb *kwanda*, which means 'to expand' (Nkurunziza, 2004). The name itself implies a process, something in the making. That is exactly the idea the ancestors of the Banyiginya clan had when they settled in Binaga, in the ancient Kingdom of Mubari, where King Kabeja had warmly welcomed them. However, as Binaga was too small for them, they started to envisage settling in a larger place. Determined to expand the territory, 'that group... chose from the local language the word which is also their motto: RWANDA, that is: great expansion' (Nahimana, 1993: 153). Thus, the Banyiginya expansion process began with *Rwanda rwa Binaga* 'to indicate that from that place [Rwanda located in Binaga] they would launch their expansion in all directions and would enlarge their territory' (*Ibid.*).

From victory to victory, the Banyiginya conquerors imposed the name 'Rwanda' on the conquered places. After conquering the Gasabo hill, King Ruganzu I Bwimba gave the place the name of *Rwanda rwa Gasabo*.[95] Then when the territories beyond River Nyabarongo were annexed, the Banyiginya established the royal residence in Kamonyi and named the place *Rwanda rwa Kamonyi* (*Ibid.*). Rwanda's oral traditions abound with examples of Rwanda-expanding expeditions that were successful, but also of those that were not. In the latter case, subterfuges were used to trap the resistant kings. King Nzira, son of Muramira (see Section 5.1.) is one example. Another example is one about Tutsi King Yuhi II Gahima [*circa* 1520] who failed to conquer Hutu King Samukende's kingdom militarily and preferred to trap him with his own wife, who let herself be impregnated by Samukende when he was drunk. Realising that, as the historical tale goes (see summary in Vansina, 2000: 384), Samukende committed suicide, leaving the throne to his wife Nyagakecuru. Born from that sexual trap, Binama headed the expedition that finally conquered the Hutu kingdom of Bungwe, after a herd of goats had been sent as gift to browse all the thorny vegetations surrounding the royal palace and hindered the attack. It is after that the Bungwe kingdom became part of Rwanda. It is probably when the list of *Rwandas* had become long, that is, when the Banyiginya territory had considerably expanded, that they simply called the new entity Rwanda. According to Nahimana (1993: 289–319), it is only between 1924 and 1931 that the Kingdoms of Bushiru, Bugoyi, Cyingogo, Bugamba-Kiganda, and many others, joined the Kingdom of Rwanda after bloodshed, and with the coloniser's involvement.

---

95   Kagame (1951: 30–50) estimated that King Ruganzu Bwimba reigned around 1400 A.D.. He was the first of the historic kings, that is, those with more or less detailed records in the dynastic poems.

This Rwanda-in-making process shows that Rwanda was far from being just a name. It was, and perhaps still is, given the recent developments in the region, a permanent assignment-giving motto.[96] Very important to know are the memories hidden behind that motto-name. Expansion very often meant war and extermination of the dynasties of the conquered kingdoms. As chapter 5 (sections 5.1 & 5.2) showed, the vanquished were not only killed but also, for memory reasons, their genitals were cut and hung on the Kalinga royal drum. Each *Rwanda rwa...* meant a new set of testicles on the Kalinga, leading to the Kalinga=Rwanda equation: the former symbolised and embodied the making process of the latter. The 1943 pamphlet *Inganji Kalinga* mentioned in Sections 5.1 & 5.2 together with the new national anthem equally discussed in chapter 6, emphasised the idea of Rwanda resulting from an expansion process. While *Inganji Kalinga* specified that the process involved war, the anthem text prefers to refer to the bravery of the expanders, which both lead to the same meaning and memories. One would ask why Kayibanda and other Hutu emancipationists who protested against Kalinga – because of its ornaments and the memories they kept alive – never thought of the Kalinga=Rwanda equation. Both referred to the same traumatic memories for the ethnic group they claimed to emancipate, and one could not have been banned without the other.

This chapter has shown that the name is not a mere compilation of letters and syllables. Name has emerged as having some occult powers that influence one's future in some real ways. I have also discussed one way in which names are extended or supplemented by war poems – *icyivugo* – that tell much about how people perceive themselves and want to be named. However, this practice that has survived until now seems to have taken with it ancient Rwanda world views and values that encouraged and praised violent conduct. It has also appeared in this chapter that names and their memory functions are not an exclusivity of individuals. The nation itself was named after the process that is believed to have led to its blood-tainted birth. The next chapter tackles a different function of the name, namely one of mediating interpersonal, social, and even political dialogue.

---

96  I am referring here to the recurrent incursions of the Rwandan army into neighbouring DR Congo, especially the regions that were previously annexed by Rwanda's kings.

Chapter 8

# Names as a Form of Dialogue

Given the memory functions of the name as discussed in the previous chapters, it goes without saying that it plays an essential role in the shaping of personal and collective identities and identification. Identification has been defined as a dynamic 'process of creating, maintaining, and breaking links' that connect an individual in social contexts (WRR, 2007: 30 & 37). This is to say that Mr. 'I-live-among-enemies' [Ndimubanzi] identifies himself with his region or country through the small community in which he was born when there were some misunderstandings. This is one amongst many other ways in which he identifies himself with his ancestors (Citron, 1987: 175). Philosopher Thoreau opposed any form of identification with past experiences or figures. His reason was: 'Old deeds for old people, and new deeds for new'. The past has no lessons or advice to give to the present (Thoreau, [1854], 1983: 51). From this perspective, society and its structures as well as memory have a rather corruptive and enslaving influence, and individuals should free themselves from their grip. Thoreau's contemporary and fellow philosopher John Stuart Mill ([1831] 1963: 3) shared this view and wondered why people should be 'perpetually exhorted to judge of the present by the past, when the present alone affords a fund of materials for judging'. In this chapter, I argue that the situation in Rwanda is the opposite of what Thoreau and Mill were advocating. It aims to look at how memories are coded into names and how meta-dialogues take place as names call for counter-names, equally coded with memory messages. The Kinyarwanda language facilitates these coding and decoding processes, as it allows multiple-meanings and other subtleties.

## 8.1 Coding the Message

The name, as already pointed out, is a coded message conveying the name-giver's personal feelings about a given prevailing situation. The latter might be directed towards someone else or another family, who, in turn, might retaliate using a similar naming mechanism. Through this name-and-counter-name game, a true dialogue is conducted, sometimes amongst people within the family and social circle, or even between them and the invisible world, to the extent of turning the process into a hide-and-seek game around the family secrets (Erny, 2005: 157).

In the early-1990s, that hide-and-seek naming game left the family settings and took political connotations as it expanded to the entire Nation. The 1990–1994 period corresponds to the so-called October war, and should be extended to the creation and development of the Rwandese Patriotic Front [RPF], a Tutsi-diaspora-dominated movement based in Uganda. The first significant political organisation of the Tutsi refugees dates back to 1979 with the creation of RANU, the Rwandese Alliance for National Unity (Waugh, 2004: 16; Misser, 1995: 43). Any alert observer immediately associates this organisation with UNAR [*Union Nationale Rwandaise*] for three major and obvious reasons: firstly, the founders and supporters of the monarchist UNAR party in the late-1950s – the early-1960s had all fled to neighbouring countries, including Uganda, and had kept their ideology for which they militarily fought until the late-1960s. Secondly, RANU is UNAR read from right to left, which suggests that the new English name kept the core UNARist ideology alive while camouflaging its external appearance. Tito Rutaremara, who joined RANU months after its creation, and who is referred to as 'the patriarch of the RPF' (Sebarenzi, 2009: 95), denied this obvious link (Misser, 1995: 153). His after-victory denial could be interpreted as an attempt to lessen the fears among the Hutu masses, for whom the RPF meant the return to pre-1959 Tutsi domination. The third reason is more cultural and anthropological, namely that 'one could use the name of a dead family member to give him life again, to adopt him as patron' (Erny, 2005: 156).

It is this movement that changed the name in 1987 to become RPF (Waugh, 2004: 39), and which Kajeguhakwa called 'the young generation [that] shared the burden I had been carrying since 1965' (Kajeguhakwa, 2001: 220). This sentence could have gone even further to add 'when the old generation lost momentum', without changing its meaning. The point here is that 'the young generation', or the second generation of Tutsi exiles as Chrétien *et al.* (1995: 92–93) called them, took over the old generation, the UNAR, and laid down a different strategy: 'contrary to the youths of the 1960s, they [the youths of the new generation] had thoroughly refined their revolutionary project between 1979 and 1987' (Kajeguhakwa, 2001: 225), the year in which RANU became RPF. UNAR in the memories relating to Hutu ethnic identity represents the monarchy, a system that killed Hutu kings and their male descendants and kept survivors in bondage for centuries. Former RPF commander and current president Kagame also denied connections with UNAR. Nonetheless, he acknowledged close family relationships with the royal dynasty and accompanying privileges that his family had. Yet, he denied any influence of that past on his political ideals.

Beside this UNAR connection, the RPF added another memory-loaded name of *Inkotanyi*, which, once again, is viewed differently depending on one's ethnic identity. Like the other kings with Kigeri[97] as a royal name, Kigeri IV Rwabugiri [1853–1895],[98] who nicknamed himself *Inkotanyi cyane* [the Redoubtable Fighter], was the most feared warlike monarch in Rwanda's history. According to Alexis Kagame (1951: 46),

---

97 The royal names of Kigeri and Mibambwe gave the bearer the mission to expand Rwanda by war (Nkurunziza, 2004).
98 This Rwabugiri's reign period (1853–1897) is provided by Alexis Kagame (1951: 30–50), who stressed that it was almost certain. It is however different from the period (1860–1895) indicated by Mahmood Mamdani (2001: 69).

> That prince, the last warlike King, was a tireless combatant, like his homonymous predecessors. All the regions bordering Rwanda, expect Karagwe, were targeted by his innumerable expeditions to which he almost always took part. One can say that he was the pest of autochthon princes whose territories lied within his reach. His ravages were mostly noticeable in the west, in the eastern regions of the Congo and in the princedoms of the current protectorate of Uganda, an area that usually served as reserve from where Rwanda used to get cattle supplies.

After one of his triumphant victories in the second half of the 19th century, Rwabugiri is said to have introduced a system based on forced labour in which the Hutu in conquered areas were obliged to work for a local noble two days a week (Erny, 2005: 59). Like Alexis Kagame, Nahimana (1993: 242), too, depicted Rwabugiri as the one who ended the peaceful cohabitation between the Tutsi kingdom of Rwanda and the neighbouring Hutu kingdoms in the north and northwest. He not only sought to impose himself militarily, but he also obliged local Hutu armies to join his own army:

> That situation resulted in tensions between Rwabugiri and the [Hutu] kings of the kingdoms in the north and northwest who were realising that their independence was finally in jeopardy. Here and there, there were armed confrontations between Rwabugiri's fighters and the populations in the north and northwest (Nahimana, 1993: 243).

Mamdani (2001: 69 & 117) perceived Rwabugiri's move in the north and northwest as an effort to reform the state structure by centralising it and expanding it to the Hutu through their [non-obligatory] participation to the army. However, Mamdani (2001: 268–269) admitted that those reforms gave birth to the Tutsi Power[99] and marked the starting point for the 'degradation of the Hutu and the genesis of Tutsi privilege'. Before the RPF attack in October 1990, the name *Inkotanyi* had been immortalised in Rwandan popular memory by a tune by Twa zither player Rujindiri. The song about Rwabugiri's outstanding deeds goes as follows:

> The Redoubtable Fighter
> Had an impeccable youth time
> The Blood-Shedder had an impeccable youth
> He grew up with no single vice

---

99 Mamdani (2001: 271) defined the 'Tutsi Power' as the ideology according to which the control of power by the Tutsi is the minimal condition for their survival: 'Tutsi will only be protected if they have a state of their own'. The same point that the Tutsi minority needs to govern the Hutu majority to ensure its survival is raised by Kajeguhakwa (2001: 293).

He grew up without provoking any reproach
...
He grew up fearless
During his youth he killed [King] Nsibura...[100]

It is worth noting here that, aware of the role that the past played by serving as 'a model to be imitated and even surpassed by the current generation', King Rwabugiri 'insisted that his exploits be chanted' (Kagame, 1947: 46). He would warn composers long in advance to come out with appropriate tunes and urge dynastic bards to retain them faithfully in order to transmit them to future generations (*Ibid.*). Rujindiri's tune, then, might be understood in this framework, as each verse seems to contain, or relate to, Rwabugiri's exploits. Also, a number of war poems, *ibyivugo*, by the contemporaries of Rwabugiri repeatedly refer to him as *Inkotanyi*, but these are less popular than Rujindiri's tune, as they are only known to oral tradition or cultural researchers and the inquisitive ones among the old generation. For instance, the war poem by the famous warrior Nyiringango, son of Nyagahinga mentions this: ' ... I had bet with the Inkotanyi [The Redoubtable Fighter]... '.[101] The one by Kamhayana [modern spelling: Kampayana] son of Nyantaba of the Ingangurarugo [forefront fighters] militia, which I discussed in Section 7.2., mentions the Inkotanyi in this way: 'I am the bravest whom the Redoubtable Fighter [Inkotanyi] has distinguished'.[102]

Choosing *Inkotanyi* to nickname a Tutsi-dominated modern rebel movement was a strong memory message, an indication not only as to the connection of the present and the past, but also as to the intentions, plans, and methods of the new Rwabugiri-idolising rebel movement. I should mention that Chrétien *et al.* (1995: 127) considered *inkotanyi* [not with capital *I*] not through its historical, memory significance, but rather through its primary meaning of '*bagarreurs*', which I render as 'Redoubtable Fighters'. The authors failed to explain why that name has no connections with the above-mentioned 19th century background. In a footnote, they unconvincingly blamed that interpretation on the Hutu regime. The next shows that the message was received and deciphered on the Hutu side.

---

100 *Inkotanyi cyane* by Rujindiri (Author's archive):
*Inkotanyi Cyane*
*Yabyirutse neza*
*Iya Rugina Yabyirutse neza*
*Abyirutse atagira inenge*
*Kandi ngo atagira amakemwa*

*Abyirutse atagira amakemwa*
*Kandi ngo atagira ubwoba*
*Mu mabyiruka ko yishe Nsibura*
*Mu mabyiruka ko yishe Nsibura*
*Mu mabyiruka ko yishe Nsibura*
...

101 Kayumba (2005), p. 9: '...*Nari nagambiriye n' Inkotanyi...*'
102 Alexis Kagame, *Introduction aux grands genres lyriques de l' ancien Rwanda* (Butare: Editions Universitaires du Rwanda, 1969), pp. 18–19: '... *ndi intwali Inkotanyi yamenye...*'

## 8.2 Decoding and Responding to the Message

In his works on the analysis of psychological products, Sigmund Freud suggested that man is incapable of perceiving strange signs or unknown terms, without thinking of already known terms resembling the new term the most, and without being tempted to associate both with each other (Freud, [1900] 1925: 76). This seems to have happened on the Hutu leaders' side. The RPF attackers nicknaming themselves *Inkotanyi* – an already known term – were quickly perceived as the 'revolutionary chickens returning home' (Mamdani, 2001: 36, see also Gakusi & Mouzer, 2003: 11; Newbury, 2002: 75; Chrétien *et al.*, 1995: 113). The responses were equally coded memory messages disguised as names. The names for political parties and groups were seriously thought out to try and connect the past and the present, which, as mentioned above, turned the whole naming process into a coded political dialogue. At the time when the re-born UNAR attacked Rwanda in 1990 with Rwabugiri as their patron saint, a multiparty system was being put in place in Rwanda.

One of the parties that emerged from the Hutu opposition was the MDR – the *Mouvement Démocratique Républicain* – a name that Kayibanda's emancipationist movement Parmehutu gave itself in 1960 to mark its new *republican* – as opposed to monarchist – ambitions and orientations. At that time, it had become clear that King Ndahindurwa was not yielding to their democratisation demands. That party could be called the re-born, or, to use Kajeguhakwa's (2001: 283) words, the resurrected Hutu *Mouvement Démocratique Républicain* not only due to that clearly memory-inspired name, but also to the fact that it was dominated by Kayibanda's sons-in-law – Faustin Twagiramungu, its chairman, and Emmanuel Gapyisi, one of its leading figures – with a strong bastion in Gitarama, Kayibanda's home province. Twagilimana, who was at that time busy collaborating with other opposition leaders to set up another party, the *Parti Social Démoracte* [PSD] (Twagilimana, 2003: xi), noted another important clue-giving detail: the use of the expression 'rubanda nyamwinshi' [majority populace or the great masses][103] in MDR's founding texts, and the exaltation of the work of Grégoire Kayibanda, the original founder of MDR-Parmehutu (*Ibid.*: 102), and thus patron saint of the new MDR. For those reasons, and despite the announced renovations, 'the Tutsi held that party responsible for the massacres committed against them since 1959' (Umutesi, 2000: 39).

Although MDR leaders did not literally follow Kayibanda's Parmehutuist lines towards UNAR and the Tutsi in general, the name served like a marketing tool in conquering Hutu masses throughout Rwanda. During the 1993 leadership crisis within the MDR, the party split into two factions, one known as MDR-Power, and a 'microscopic' one called MDR-Twagiramungu (Gasana, 2005: 222–223). While the former started gradually identifying itself more openly with Parmehutu, the latter adopted a position closer to the RPF. In a tactical hide-and-seek, name-based move that could be perceived as an attempt at reconciliation

---

103  See Section 2.4 (pp. 56–57) for the memory meaning of this expression.

with the humiliated First Republic leaders,[104] the former ruling and state-party, the *Mouvement Révolutionnaire National pour le Développement* [MRND],[105] chose the name *Interahamwe* [Those who work together, those who have the same objective] for its youth organisation that later turned into a deadly militia. In Hutu memories of the late-1950s – early-1960s, that name refers to the Parmehutus, i.e., Kayibanda's supporters during the Hutu emancipationist movement. It was anchored in the memories relating to the Hutu ethnic identity by a famous song by the Abanyuramatwi, a Parmehutu glory-singing choir.[106] Titled *Jya Mbere Rwanda* [Go forward Rwanda], the song goes as follows:

> Go forward Rwanda
> *Your supporters have the same objective* [Interahamwe]
> The Parmehutu leaders were elected by the people
> With a strong government
> Go forward in every sector
> …[107]

The name *Interahamwe* was, thus, initially like a blow to the Parmehutu-idolising MDR, who, in turn, chose *Inkuba* as the name for their youth organ. At first sight, *Inkuba* would mean 'thunder'. However, knowing that the Kinyarwanda language turns confusions and double/multiple meanings into a hide-and-seek game, it is always interesting to look for other possible meanings. For instance, from a memory perspective, there is no reason why this name would have no direct connection with the Hutu hero, Nkuba, son [or father depending on authors] of Mashira [*circa* 1490], the last Hutu king of Nduga, a kingdom that covered the region where Kayibanda was to be born four centuries later. On Mashira's assassination by his Tutsi father-in-law Mibambwe I Sekarongoro I Mutabazi I, Nkuba, the single male survivor of the massacre reportedly fled northward to the Bukonya region – another MDR Parmehutu stronghold in the late-1950s

---

104 Grégoire Kayibanda and his close collaborators from the Centre and South of Rwanda were arrested following the 5 July 1973 coup by Juvénal Habyarimana from the North. Many of them died while in detention, either assassinated or for lack of appropriate medical care. This heralded a conflict between the Centre-South block and the North. More details in Gasana's *Rwanda : du parti-Etat à l'Etat-Garnison* (2002).
105 The meaning of the acronym MRND later changed into *Mouvement Républicain National pour le Développement et la Démocratie*.
106 The Abanyuramatwi choir's songs were exclusively about the 'long walk' to the First Republic and the early years of that Republic from the Hutu perspective. Their songs are a short musical summary of the memories relating to the Hutu perspective of the late-1950s – early-1960s emancipationist movement and the subsequent Republic.
107 *Jya mbere Rwanda*, by Abanyuramatwi:
Jya mbere Rwanda
Ushyigikiwe n'abagabo b'interahamwe
Abaparmehutu batowe n'abaturage
Na Leta yarwo ihamye
Rwanda jya mbere muri byose.

– early-1960s period.[108] The 'survival' idea behind the memories of Nkuba could be interpreted further in two ways. Firstly, the MDR wanted to create a link between its youths – threatened by a Tutsi war – and Nkuba, another Hutu who struggled to survive a Tutsi massacre a few centuries before. Secondly, the same message could have been meant for Habyarimana who had not given any chance of survival to Kayibanda and some other Parmehutu leaders. Considering themselves as heirs of the slain leaders – mostly coming from Nduga like Nkuba – they might have wanted to position themselves as survivors vis-à-vis president Habyarimana and his party. Although the stories of Nkuba and Rwabugiri belong to the oral tradition, it is essential to note that they are not myths or epics. However, they might have gone through some processes of manipulation and adaptation that are inherent to any oral memory text.

What emerges from the above is that the choice of names was highly tactical: with the name *Inkotanyi*, the RPF sent the following memory-inspired message: remember what King Rwabugiri did and how he did it in the north and northwest. That's what we're coming to repeat. Kayibanda's ideological heirs responded by identifying themselves with the latest victors of the Tutsi monarchy and subsequent rebellions. They called themselves MDR, and later named their youth Inkuba, probably to remind the Tutsi that they cannot all die. Taken slightly off-guard, the ruling MRND party borrowed the name *Interahamwe* from the 1960s to formulate its response: Good and fine. Come and fight like the Great Inkotanyi – Rwabugiri – who imposed his authority on the Hutu [ancestors]; we will fight like the [Parmehutu's] Interahamwe and we will see! The MRND meant that those who defeated UNAR monarchists – the RPF's ancestors – in the 1960s would *put their forces together* again to repeat their forefathers' exploit. In a way, though opposed to one another, the MDR and MRND responses were similar: they identified themselves with the latest victor of the Tutsi, while the RPF had done the same by identifying themselves with the latest Tutsi king who imposed absolute Tutsi dominance over the Hutu. Of course the above interpretations could be rejected by anyone, because the Kinyarwanda language allows more than one meaning as the next section briefly shows.

## 8.3 Language Subtleties

My claim here is that ethnic identities and related memories in Rwanda take great advantage of the subtleties of the Kinyarwanda language. One means something without saying it. The name *Interahamwe* is one instance of a word that can mean almost everything, depending on the context, the user, and many other factors. It is a nominalised full-sentence construction with a subject '*I*' – those who –; a verb '*tera*' which I explain separately below; and a complement '*hamwe*' – together

---

108 Responding to my query about eventual connection between the MDR's Inkuba and Nkuba, the surviving hero, Twagiramungu said there was no link whatsoever, as the name rather referred to thunder (Author's interview with Faustin Twagiramungu, 16 March 2008). http://www.olny.nl/RWANDA/Videos/Nahimana_book_conference_15_march_2008.html#faustin (Accessed 30 May 2009).

or in the same place. The verb [*gu-*]*tera* is the one that gives rise to multiple interpretations. It might mean [1] *throw* or *propel* [a stone, a spear, etc.]; [2] *sing* [give the tone]; [3] *stub* [with a knife or sword]; [4] *attack* [a country, or another place]; [5] *provoke* or *cause* [fear, shame, disease, disorder, etc]; [6] *go in the same line of thought* or action; [7] *kick* [the ball]; [8] *tell* [a joke]; [9] *impregnate* [a woman]; [10] *climb up* [a hill]; etc. The list is long and can hardly be exhausted. It is like the verb 'to get' or 'to do' in English or *faire* in French, which could mean practically everything depending on the context in which it is used.

The Tutsi – who had traumatic memories and experiences with the initial *Interahamwe* of the 1960s and, to a much greater extent, with those of the 1990s, tend to render the name *Interahamwe* as 'Those who *attack* [the Tutsi] together' (Twagilimana, 2003: 107. Emphasis added), which is not wrong from a grammatical and memory perspective. The Hutu – who are mostly proud of the *Interahamwe* of the 1960s, while showing consternation for those of the 1990s – tend to render the name as 'those who aim to achieve the same objective' as suggested in the Abanyuramatwi song mentioned above. This, too, is correct from a grammatical and memory point of view.

Buckley-Zistel (206: 136) noted that although the racist rhetoric was significant, 'it only started after the Tutsi-dominated RPF invasion of 1990 had made the Hutu masses receptive to such propaganda'. It could be argued that the Hutu masses became receptive to the racist propaganda after discovering the coded memory messages behind the nickname *Inkotanyi*, another phrase-name that allows more than just one interpretation. The subject *I* – those who – is followed by a verb *kotona* – which I explain shortly, and the suffix *–yi* used in many nominalisation constructions. The verb *gukotana* itself contains another suffix *–na*, usually used to indicate that the action is being done together with someone else or is interactive. One has to begin with the verb *gukota*, which is generally used to describe the intermittent mouth movements a mouse or similar animals, and by extension people, make while eating raw, hard sweet potatoes or items that are similar. Two things are important in this explanation: the hardness and repeatedness of the action, and the sense of a need to complete that action.

Taken from the eating realm, this verb could be understood as meaning: engaging hard, constant actions to achieve something one considers of supreme importance. When the actions are conducted together with other people, or when resistance is opposed, then the verb takes the *–na* suffix. The first grammatical meaning of *Inkotanyi* would then be: those who conduct hard actions together for a supreme cause. The stress is on the hardness and the risk involved as well as the bravery needed to complete those actions and overcome resistance. In the case of Rwabugiri, those actions were wars to expand Rwanda and to impose Tutsi domination. In the RPF context, the Tutsi dominant narrative explains *Inkotanyi* as Brave/Redoubtable Fighters, which is grammatically correct. The Hutu repressed memories, on their part, go beyond grammar to link those fighters' ideology to Rwabugiri's, which is not incorrect from a memory point of view. The verb *gukotana* has now secured a new meaning in the Hutu memories. It means siding with the RFP to the detriment of Hutu interests. From this meaning, other terms were coined, such as *amakotanyi*, which refers to the money allegedly paid to Hutu political leaders to join, or support the cause of, the RPF-Inkotanyi.

## Summary

The aim of this part was to explore some of the channels through which memories relating to ethnic identities are mediated. Although often neglected or pushed aside as mere fiction, myths, tales, proverbs, and other oral memory texts have emerged from the above as interesting memory channels worth studying. The claim I made here is that those mythic, epic fictions were a way in which people in ancient Rwanda coded their experiences and feelings. The reasoning was: if they survived orally, it was because those who kept them alive believed that they represented a certain reality. From that perspective, then, they should serve not as unquestionable historical sources, but rather as clue providers. They should trigger questions like: if hundreds of age-old proverbs refer to Tutsi as untrustworthy, unpredictable, and wicked fellows, doesn't it suggest that the Hutu were behind these proverbs? If the Tutsi monarchs never fought against those Tutsi-demonising proverbs, doesn't it mean that they had some truth in them? If hundreds of other proverbs keep referring to the Hutu as nasty, unintelligent, good-for-nothing fellows, can't one conclude that the Tutsi were their originators since they seem to express their feelings towards the Hutu? If the Hutu never protested against these degrading descriptions, doesn't it suggest that in some way they agreed with them?

My concern in this part is not about agreeing or disagreeing with the message behind oral memory texts. It is rather about what they tell us about ancient Rwanda, however imperfectly. The reality is that the impasse of the late-1950s was largely rooted in those oral memory texts, which rendered it impossible to solve. More interestingly, tangible memory objects emerged in connection with the mythical past of Rwanda. The heavenly mythic origins of the Tutsi dynasty ended up with the latter viewing the royal Drum – the Kalinga – as a symbol of their might. At the same time, it was adorned with the genitals of slain Hutu kings. That drum turned out to be a Tutsi triumphant memory reminder, whilst at the same time it appeared to be a symbol of the Hutu's traumatic memory. More tangible ethnic reminders emerged in post-colonial Rwanda, this time in written texts, amongst other forms. I have chosen to discuss the two national anthems – the Parmehutu-inspired one and its RFP-inspired counterpart – in order to show how ethnic identities and related memories keep trapping Rwanda. Whilst the former proclaimed Hutu ownership of Rwanda, praising the Parmehutu for having restored that ownership, the latter implicitly refers to a similar ownership, insistently bringing back to the surface the blood-tainted Rwanda-making-process embodied by the Kalinga.

Another memory transmission channel I discussed is naming, both for individuals and for political organisations. The belief is that name is man and that the name tells the story of the bearer in a certain way. It summarises the bearer's memories in a few syllables, and in so doing, it captures the memories of the family and the community at that particular moment in time. Generally given by the father, the name reflects the bearer's gender. I have argued that naming in Rwanda is a memory act *par excellence*, as it meets most of the features of the memory processes: it is about the past, it is selective, presentist, futurist, and both personal and collective. The name involves much more than the story of the bearer, as the latter sees the light of the day in a community. Moreover, the memories coded into the name are meant both for the bearer but also for the community. The futuristic dimension of the name is a bit intriguing: it consists of a mission statement that tells the bearer what they are supposed to do in the future. It is also intriguing as it seems to have the power to seal and unseal the bearer's fate and guide, in some ways, their future actions. To complement the name, Rwandans use a self-introductory poem – *icyivugo* – in which [only] men assign themselves nicknames and tell about their real or exaggerated, or even fictitious past. The common feature in most of the poems is that they all praise violence as a virtue.

The above has also shown how the features of individual names applies both to the country as an entity and to political organisations. The name 'Rwanda' is like a memory book telling different stories to different ethnic groups. To the Tutsi, it reminds the heroic expansion of Rwanda that showed the bravery of their ancestors. To the Hutu, it reminds the assassinations of their own ancestors and the annexation of the Tutsi kingdom of Rwanda. The naming process becomes interactive when applied by political organisations. It has appeared that the name *Inkotanyi*, with its 19$^{th}$ century memories, called the names *Interahamwe* and MDR, which are equally loaded with the memories of the 1960s, amongst other names. While some seemed to be coding a memory message, others seemed to be deciphering it before responding in memory codes, turning the process into a memory dialogue. Both ethnic groups and the leaders claiming to represent them had the two tools they needed to code their messages: a memory reservoir and the Kinyarwanda language that allowed them to camouflage those messages and yet deny any memory connotation of those messages.

I started this book with post-genocide Rwanda and the dangers of remembering and forgetting. The main point was that there are at least two parallel memory lines stretching far back to times that are unmemorable. Surviving in post-genocide Rwanda appears to depend a great deal on which memory line one is following. In Part two, I attempted to understand how the memories relating to ethnic identities are transmitted through oral memory texts and names. Here, too, it appeared that Rwandans were trapped in their own memories and had not even began to tear the trap apart. In Part three, I explore some of the ways in which the memories relating to ethnic identities transpire through autobiographic accounts.

# Part Three

Memory at Work

*Chapter 9*

# Memories, the Self, and the Collectivity

Autobiographical accounts are a special form of memory in many respects: firstly, they are not spontaneous in the sense that the author has time to think and rethink what to write about, in what form and from which perspective, which is not the case for on-the-spot remembering. Secondly, they constitute a unified, coherent narrative as they are meant to be read as a whole and not as fragments. Thirdly, they are memories that are meant and designed for an unknown and unpredictable public, which considerably distinguishes them from those uttered to a familiar and predictable audience. Fourthly, they are generally submitted to a commercial system – the publishing industry – which turns them into a commercially viable and profit-making commodity;[109] amongst other reasons. However, they do present most features of other memory texts in that they, too, are selective, presentist, futuristic, and a version of the past amongst many other features.

The autobiographical accounts discussed in this and the next two chapters come from those who claim to be, or have been, victims of ethnic conflicts. I have selected two autobiographies, one by a Tutsi author: Scolastique Mukasonga's *Inyenzi ou cafard* (2006); and one by a Hutu author: Marie-Béatrice Umutesi's *Fuir ou mourir au Zaïre* (2000). I chose to consider these books because their authors present an almost-similar profile: they are both women, born in the late-1950s, who attended the same secondary school, to name a few similarities. Yet, the two authors produced two radically opposed accounts of the common past they witnessed. While these autobiographies only serve as the cornerstone, other autobiographical writings are referred to where more clarifications are deemed necessary. Before discussing these autobiographies in detail, I provide short summaries of both works followed by a brief theoretical discussion of the autobiographic genre as memory. I then analyse the Self-Society tandem,

---

109 The case of Julian Assange's *Julian Assange: The Unauthorised Autobiography* (2011) published by Canongate is a very interesting example of the interference of the profit-making side of published autobiographies. The contradiction in the title suggests that the author has refused to endorse his own account. The publisher gave the reason: the author, who was interviewed and recorded so that some one else would write the account, found it to be a form of 'prostitution'. In his view, he could not recognize himself in the account. My understanding of the publisher's note is that the publisher had managed to have [to turn the account into] a 'passionate, provocative and opinionated' [I am quoting the note] narrative which he proceeded to publish, since the author had already pocketed part of the money agreed upon and paid in advance for his legal bills.

looking into ways in which individuals pursue diverging routes simply because they identify with diverging memories. I explain this by showing the role low-age memory acquisition plays. The result of all this, is the two parallel memory lines I mentioned in chapter 1.

## 9.1 Autobiography as Memory

To begin with, I want to provide very short summaries of the two autobiographies right away, so to facilitate the understanding of comments and discussions made about them. These summaries are entirely the result of my reading and interpretation and, containing only a few lines, are far from doing justice to the hundreds of pages the authors produced. Mukasonga's *Inyenzi ou cafard* tells her family's story from the late-1950s, when her father was a secretary-accountant of the local sub-chief. She described the destruction of their property during the 1959 Hutu uprising, the deportation of the Tutsi close to the aristocracy to Nyamata, a malaria-infested place that was, until then, unoccupied because of its hostility. She managed to attend primary and secondary school despite discrimination against the Tutsi, but was later pushed to run away to Burundi following anti-Tutsi pogroms in the early-1970s. There she attended university, got a job, and married a French man, before moving to France. Her family were killed during the 1994 genocide.

Umutesi's *Fuir ou mourir au Zaïre*, like Mukasonga's account, begins in the late-1950s. The author tells of the prevailing oppression by the Tutsi, describing the case of her aunt who was whipped in public, for having taken sweet potatoes from her family's farm without the customary leaders' authorisation. The author discovered her identity during the 1960s, when Tutsi monarchist rebels were attacking, targeting her own region in the north. She later lived with the Hutu-Tutsi reality at school, including a few years at Lycée Notre Dame de Cîteau in Kigali – the same school Mukasonga attended in the same period –, at the National University of Rwanda in Butare, and even at the Université de Louvain in Belgium. In the early-1990s, her family fled to the camps for the internally displaced people, following the RFP attacks. Many of them died after being tortured. Umutesi fled to the Democratic Republic of Congo [called Zaïre at that time] after the RPF victory in 1994, worked in Bukavu, and was forced again to flee westward into the D.R. Congo's forests in 1996, when the Congolese Tutsi rebellion broke out with the support of Rwanda. She walked for months, witnessed deaths either 'natural' or by murder, and was miraculously rescued thanks to a former European colleague of hers who sent someone to fish her out of the bush.

These autobiographical accounts are part of what is referred to as *ego documents*, that is, documents by and about the author. Gusdorf, who dedicated most of his philosophical oeuvre to the Self and its relationship with memory, nicely called them *littérature du moi* (Gusdorf, 1991a: 168) or *écritures du moi* (*Ibid.*: 151–152). Written either in the first person or in the third singular (*Ibid.*: 147), these documents include autobiographies, diaries, aphorisms or short witty sentences, letters and correspondences, and….

all the texts authored by an individual acting on his own behalf to mention incidents, feelings and events that concern him personally. Such documents have the character of testimonies as they engage the author in facts that involve his private, and even public and social life... The length and the nature of the text do not matter... (*Ibid.*: 145).

Described like this, ego documents appear to have at least two common features: firstly, they are the articulation of the Self; and secondly, they are both private and collective. Of all the sorts of ego writings, I want to focus on autobiography and diary, since they seem to be very close to one another: the diary seems to be 'a day-to-day autobiography' (*Ibid.*: 151–152). Despite this closeness, diaries are a one-moment thought about a specific event or experience. Prior knowledge, post-event knowledge, memories, and assumptions play a role and influence the one-moment pictures as they interfere with perception and interpretation. For instance, from her hiding in Amsterdam during World War II, Jewish teenager Anne Frank (1997: 242) wrote one entry about how she and her family felt 'when *350 British planes dropped 550 tons of bombs* on Ijmuiden', [emphasis added] shaking houses 'like blades of grass'. Whilst the shaking of houses belongs to the one-moment picture, the weight of bombs and the number of planes as well as their origin certainly came from her prior knowledge – e.g., that morning's news – or from post-event knowledge – e.g., that afternoon's or evening's news. In his earlier work on *The Discovery of the Self*, Gusdorf (1948: 38–39) provided key features distinguishing diary from autobiography:

> The diary shows one along one's entire life, like memoires do, but without the same *retroactive* value and without any *illusion of coherence*, since it is not about the man of the entire life, but about the day-to-day man, the moment-to-moment man... This way, this new form of intimate writings preserves the spontaneity of the lived experience [Emphasis added].

The main point that emerges from this is that the diary is spontaneous, whilst the autobiography is retroactive and coherent. In other words, the compilation of all the diary entries do not make it an autobiography, as the retroactive element would be missing. Retroactivity is a form of presentism, as the author projects his or her current thoughts, concerns, and the prevailing atmosphere to their past experiences. With this retroactive or presentist dimension, autobiographical writings become 'a revised and corrected version' of the past, and autobiographers play a role of 'metteurs en scène' (Gusdorf, 1991b: 235; see also Assmann, [2006] 2008: 213). Whilst playing the role of *metteur en scène*, the author strives to produce a unified, coherent narrative. John Robinson and Leslie Taylor (1998: 127) called this effort of coherence 'continuity bias', which consists in smoothing a life history by omitting sidetracks, or of 'editing events to make them conform to a more predictable and culturally acceptable pattern'. It might be deduced that both the diary and the autobiography use the same raw material but result in different outputs. In autobiographies, 'life loses its initial nature, and is reoriented in the mental space of the writer... Writing creates the event by relating it; it creates history, a history, which follows the succession of events that it records under the writer's control' (Gusdorf, 1991b: 247). To borrow from philosopher of history George Collingwood ([1946] 1994: 293-294), the diary is about thinking, while autobiography is about re-thinking. From the new edited version of the past emerges a new portrait of the author, leading to observe with literary critic and theorist Paul de Man (1979: 920) that 'life *produces* the autobiography' [emphasis in original] but also 'the autobiographical project may itself produce and determine the life'.

Viewed from the perspective of memory theories discussed in this book's introduction, autobiographical writings result from, and are a manifestation of a memory process: the author remembers and forgets through the lenses of the present time and his or her writings are 'only the present thought of past experience' (Gusdorf, 1991b: 235). This makes autobiographical writings a special case of memory because 'what is remembered is an act of thinking' implying at least two tasks: on the one hand recollecting, i.e., searching memory for a vision of past experiences – a process that can be facilitated by other ego writings, among other things –; and on the other hand selecting relevant parts of one's past life (*Ibid.*: 295-296). The resulting narrative is, therefore, not like a 'police investigation' but rather one's testimony to oneself, proceeding not from the past to the present, but from the present to the past (Gusdorf, 1991b: 469). Being narratives, the two autobiographical accounts cannot escape selectivity because 'the idea of an exhaustive narrative is a performatively impossible idea' (Ricoeur, 2004: 448). The two accounts I have selected are, therefore, considered and studied as resulting from the authors' re-thinking of their past experiences. This is where ethnic identities and related memories inevitably sneak into the process. In the next two sections I track ways in which these memories result in diverging perceptions of the notion of happiness, thereby reducing Rwanda into a society of '*we*' and '*they*'.

## 9.2 Society and Pursuit of Happiness

Discussing memory, whether collective or private, is inevitably discussing society as the framework of memory. It is essential to first understand and map the concept of society before narrowing down to the Self. Dewey ([1899] 1927: 11) defined society as 'a number of people held together because they are working along common lines, in a common spirit, and with reference to common aims'. According to philosopher George Santayana ([1905] 1954: 152), these common aims revolve around happiness, which man can achieve only by relying on other men's acts. Three elements can be pointed out: firstly, the individual as the smallest unit; secondly, interdependence amongst individuals as a key element in any society; and thirdly, welfare as both an individual and collective aim. This view of the individual and society is not a recent invention. Ancient philosophers, too, viewed society not as 'any collection of human beings brought together in any sort of way', but as an association of large numbers of individuals based on an agreement and a partnership for the common good.[110] They acknowledged that

---

110  Cicero, *De Republica* ([54 & 51 B.C.] 1970), p. 65.

man is an animal distinguishable from other animals by its 'foresight and quick intelligence' and its possession of memory, which lead to 'fellowship and union with [his] fellow-men'.[111]

The recurring key words are togetherness, common lines or goals, striving for common happiness and interdependence. The above seems to take into account only peaceful societies and would make it difficult to call Rwandans a society: if any common lines exist, they are first and foremost, ethnic. The same goes for interdependence, and the struggle for happiness. To begin with, let me compare the two authors' dedications to study ways in which they relate to ethnic identities and corresponding memories. Announcing the tone quite from the start: Mukasonga (2006: 7) dedicated her book 'To all those who died during the genocide in Nyamata, to my father Cosma, to my mother Stefania, to my brother Antoine… '; while Umutesi (2000: 1) wrote her own account 'to the memory of Zuzu', who, like other children she had adopted, died whilst trying to escape war in Zaire [now DR. Congo]. I want to add two more dedications here to be able to draw some meaningful conclusion. Révérien Rurangwa (2006: 7), a Tutsi genocide survivor dedicated his heart-breaking narrative – *Génocidé* – to the 'forty-three members of my family, assassinated because they were Tutsi', and to 'All survivors who can neither mourn nor talk'. As for former Hutu army officer Lambertus Ntisoni (2007: 5), he dedicated his *J'ai traversé des fleuves de sang* to the 'Rwandan Nation', to the 'victims of war'.

These dedications tell which memory lines the authors followed. Rurangwa and Mukasonga are very explicit: they openly dedicated their autobiographies to fellow Tutsi victims of the genocide. Unlike them, Ntisoni and Umutesi made no clear reference to fellow Hutu, but left no doubt as to whom they dedicated their accounts: while Ntisoni adopted the all-inclusive pattern discussed in Section 2.4 – using phrases like 'the Rwandan Nation' and the 'victims of war' – Umutesi picked out one person – Zuzu – to represent hundreds of thousands of Hutu who died in the Congolese forests trying to escape RPF-supported rebels.

The same memory lines appear in the ways in which these autobiographies reflect the notion of the pursuit of happiness. The happiness of Sibomana, the direct Hutu neighbour and killer of Rurangwa's family – according to Rurangwa – resided in the zeal in which he and his children and relatives *macheted* the 43 people hiding in the Mugina church premises (Rurangwa, 2006: 47–55). Two decades before, a general movement by Hutu students had found it to be their duty to harass and, in some instances, kill Tutsi schoolmates (Mukasonga, 2006: 95–96; Umutesi, 2000: 12–14), as if both groups belonged to two different societies, with different goals and different ways of pursuing and perceiving happiness.

Similarly, around Christmas 1963, the Tutsi of Nyamata were excited to hear that the exiled King was triumphantly returning to re-establish the monarchy (Mukasonga, 2006: 40–43). Their happiness depended on the military victory of the monarchists, whilst the happiness of the Hutu depended on maintaining and reinforcing the new republican order. Either of these involved oppression

---

111 Cicero, *De Legibus* ([45–44 B.C.] 1970), pp. 321 & 329.

and killing of the members of the other group. Later on, the happiness and the goal of the Tutsi RPF fighters and supporters seemed to reside in the enthusiasm in which they killed Hutu populations after indescribable torture, including tying people to pillars with their own intestines and leaving them there for a slow death (Umutesi, 2000: 26–27). It also included testing portable missiles on the displaced people's camps, shooting Katyusha rockets in there and poisoning their water sources (Ruzibiza: 2005: 160–161). These methods 'were regularly applied on innocent civilians who fled war between the RPF and the government army' (*Ibid.*). Ruzibiza (2005: 170–171) – a witness and actor of those atrocities – maintained that this 'RPF's political error' of exterminating the Hutu in the north, put the Tutsi living inside Rwanda in danger, as a strong anti-Tutsi ideology was prevailing in the country. Umutesi contended that such ideology was not needed for the population of her home region, Byumba, where RPF guerrilla operations were the bloodiest. Starting from 1991, terrorised populations....

> started massively moving to non-affected areas. They told about the atrocities committed by the rebels. Women were disemboweled, men impaled. Other forms of torture, more barbarous as time went on, were perpetrated. These macabre stories created a feeling of terror among the populations of the communes bordering Uganda... Life changed; horror, anguish and fear became everyday companions (Umutesi, 2000: 26–27).

The accounts in these autobiographies lead to the conclusion that the Rwandan society, like Rwandans' memories, is fragmented in two major blocks, the Hutu and the Tutsi, with two ways of reconstructing the past, envisioning the future, and achieving happiness. It appears that whenever the Hutu are in control of power, the Tutsi are not happy at all, as they do not fully enjoy their rights, and vice versa. It is when each of the two blocks wants to reach that state of happiness that it pushes the other into unhappiness. Central to this process leading to hoped-for happiness is memory, which 'acts as a social, cultural, and political glue' amongst those who share it, and whose 'fundamental ironies' of being both 'collective' and 'not necessarily unified' (Zelizer, 1995: 230) are more obvious in Rwanda than anywhere else.

Sociologist Louis Wirth ([1936] 1966: xxv) maintained that society is imaginable only when 'individuals in it carry around in their head some sort of picture of that society'. It is worth asking if any picture of the Rwandan society exists. There is certainly the official promoted picture of a harmonious Rwanda, but there are more authentic though not publicly recognised ones that show a rather gloomy Rwanda, torn by ethnic hatred, and the two autobiographical accounts are there to demonstrate this. In any case, the picture put forward goes beyond the individual, as it necessarily takes into account the surrounding social environment. One way to explain why Rwandans present different pictures of their society and have different perceptions of happiness is the memory line they acquired quite early on from childhood. From that line, they quickly learn to distinguish 'we' from 'they'.

## 9.3 'We' and 'They'

Apart from serving as the framework for remembering, society serves as the framework for memory acquisition in the first place (Halbwachs, [1925] 1992: 38). Each individual has a family from which they come and in which 'parents lend children their experience and a vicarious memory' (Santayana, [1905] 1954: 104). Although his parents pretended that all was fine under the Hutu regime of President Habyarimana, Rurangwa (2006: 39) could detect their concerns and grave face expression just by observing their talks. This suggests that memory acquisition does not necessarily pass via storytelling, but also via perception and observation. Unlike him, Mukasonga (2006: 58) acquired her initial knowledge of the coming of the colonisers and their conflict-marked encounter with Rwandans from her mother's stories. She had acquired it herself from other sources – perhaps her own parents. Umutesi (2000: 8–10) and Ntisoni (2007: 32), too, acquired some knowledge of the past from the family framework. As discussed in chapter 5, one channel through which children become acquainted with the past is storytelling, a practice that is still observed in Rwanda. Mukasonga (2006: 58–60), for instance, got most of her knowledge of the past from her mother's stories:

> … on the way, at sunrise, my mother started telling me stories. She told me the story of Ruganzu Ndori, the great king, his stay in exile at his aunt's, the plots by his aunt's husband, the revelation of the kingdom's secrets, his return to Rwanda. The story was long, endless. I was half-asleep while walking and, sometimes, I had the impression of seeing afar Ruganzu holding his spear, Ruganzu Cyambarantama cy' I Rwanda [The-sheep-skin-clothed-man], who moved from one hill to another clothed with sheep skin… In the evening, when the time of tales came, my mother resumed where she had stopped with her endless story…

As this quote shows, it is through storytelling that Mukasonga came across one of the most crucial episodes of Rwanda's past. From the perspective of the Hutu identity and related memories, Ruganzu Ndori moved, indeed, from one hill to another not as a wanderer, but as a vengeance-driven killer who infiltrated Hutu King Nzira's court as a job-seeking poor man, clothed with sheepskin. He killed the naïve Hutu King, thereby pushing the Hutu to encode their conclusions in proverbs like 'When you lodge a Tutsi in your house, he chases you out of your bed' or 'What is in the heart of a Tutsi is known only to God and to himself' (Erny, 2005: 76). In his essay, *The Storyteller,* Benjamin ([1955] 1973: 86) came to the conclusion that all stories have at least one thing in common: 'any real story', he wrote, 'contains, openly or overtly, something useful', and this 'usefulness may, in one case, consist in a moral; in another, in some practical advice; in a third, in a proverb or maxim'. The story I have just discussed is a good illustration of Benjamin's remark.

Like Mukasonga, Ntisoni acquired his initial knowledge of the past through tales and stories. However, while Mukasonga appeared to be proud of the Great King Ruganzu and his triumphant move from one hill to the other, Ntisoni is disgusted, and is not at ease with his Hutu identity partly shaped by Ruganzu, his predecessors and his successors:

> My childhood was marked by the tales that I was told at sunset. Seated near the fireplace… listening to the narratives about my people's misfortunes made me sad. I grew up normally, but would not accept my Hutu identity with ease (Ntisoni, 2007: 32).

Mukasonga, a Tutsi, and Ntisoni, a Hutu, have both acquired the knowledge of the past during the traditional storytelling sessions, generally held in the evening after supper. Benjamin (1955] 1973: 91) rightly remarked that 'There is nothing that commends a story to memory more effectively' than the art of storytelling:

> … the more natural the process by which the storyteller forgoes psychological shading, the greater becomes the story's claim to a place in the memory of the listener, the more completely is it integrated into his own experience, the greater will be his inclination to repeat it to someone else someday, sooner or later (*Ibid.*).

The issues mentioned in the stories about the past were social and political in some way and were told in ways that reflect the teller's perspective, his or her ethnic identity. Once a version of the past has been acquired, it follows that the remembering subjects proceeds to position themselves vis-à-vis the actors of various events and experiences of the past, resulting in a 'we' versus 'they' situation. This identification leads to interesting phenomena observed in the autobiographies under consideration. Although not part of the focus of this analysis, Sebarenzi's autobiography is worth citing here. On hearing from a fellow Tutsi that the RPF was about to attack Rwanda back in 1990, Sebarenzi (2009: 47), who was not part of the attacking forces, wrote: '*I* was worried by the reality of a war *we* could not win…' [Emphasis added]. Eventually, the RPF won in 1994, prompting Sebarenzi to return home in 1995 from his Canadian exile. He described the situation he found in Kigali as follows:

> … *I* saw Tutsi men standing with guns. For the first time since I was a boy, since I had first learned what Hutu and Tutsi meant in the cooking house that night so long ago… *I* also realised the feeling for Hutu was just the opposite. Now it was *they* [emphasis in original] who felt fear (*Ibid.*: 82. Emphasis added).

Another example from Sebarenzi's autobiography is about the time he was receiving death threats in early-2000, after his controversial resignation as speaker of the National Assembly. After an intelligence officer had warned him that Paul Kagame, still Vice President at the time, wanted him dead, his wife could not believe the entire story. She said: 'But I cannot believe that he [Paul Kagame] would take your life, Papa Respect! Why would he do that? Kagame is a Tutsi like *us*. If you were Hutu, your life might be at risk' (Sebarenzi, 2009: 186. Emphasis added). The move from '*I*' to '*we*' and their opposition to '*they*' as well as how their distinction took place in the family setting, is a clear demonstration of the point

I am trying to make here: the acquisition of memories relating to ethnic identities through whatever channel most likely results into a 'we' versus 'they' pattern. Sebarenzi identified himself spontaneously with the attacking Tutsi forces, and once they had won, saw fear in those who were not part of '*we*'. Mukasonga also identified herself with the attacking Tutsi rebels in the 1960s, but refrained from giving a full context of the war. This could have revealed what the 'we' was doing when the 'they' behaved the way she described:

> Soldiers were patrolling everywhere, in houses, in bushes. *They* were no longer afraid. *They* were self-confident. *They* had helms on their heads. And in their eyes, that is at least what *we* thought, *we* could decipher an implacable hatred. *They* called *us* Inyenzi – cockroaches. The military arrested many people, especially teachers and the merchants who had opened their shops in the small centre of Nyamata (Mukasonga, 2006: 44. Emphasis added).

The clear use of 'they' and 'we' throughout this quote and the entire book is an indication that though the book is Mukasonga's story, it is first and foremost about a collective experience. The same is true for Rurangwa's *Génocidé*. Although in singular and thus referring to himself, Rurangwa's story involves in clearer terms, the distinction between 'they' and 'we'. The 'they' represents the Sibomanas – the neighbours who decimated his own family in a matter of minutes – but also 'each Hutu family' who were involved, closely or from afar, in the massacre and each Hutu who has dirty and blood-tainted hands (Rurangwa, 2006: 79–80). Rurangwa's 'we' referred to the Tutsi, *les bons* or the good guys, who should not be at the same table or in the same church as 'they', *les méchants* or the bad guys (*Ibid.*: 84–85). 'They' must have descended from Cain, the soil-worker and, like him, were cursed after killing 'we', their brothers the Tutsi – probably descending from Abel, the flock-keeper. Building on this Genesis (4, 1–15) story, Rurangwa found a satisfactory and prophetic explanation to the massive flight of the Hutu in 1994 and the killings by the RPF soldiers two years later in Zaire (*Ibid.*: 116).

It is this plight of the Hutu refugees in Zaire and their suffering, harassment, and massacre by the RPF and the rebels it supported that Umutesi narrated from her own perspective. On one hand, the story primarily turns around 'we', that is, herself, the few members of her family, and other children she had adopted, and the masses of Hutu refugees. On the other hand, 'they' refers to the rebels loyal to Laurent Désiré Kabila and their backers from the Tutsi-dominated Rwandan Army. Along more than 2,000 kilometers, each of 'we' had to struggle to survive, to bear the odor of decomposing corpses (Umutesi, 2000: 148). She was finally rescued *in extremis*, while hundreds of thousands of others died in that country of forests and giant rivers. Even before reaching the Zaire-part of the book, Umutesi's account presents many other instances of 'we' and 'they' as explicitly referring to the Hutu and Tutsi. One of them is her account of the 1963 Tutsi rebel attack:

> It was around 6:00 p.m. ... *We* heard whistles and my father came back home running. He told my mother: '*They* are coming!'... Those who were coming were the Tutsi rebels... *we* were far from the combat zones... The rebels had arrived at about twenty kilometers from Kigali. Popular rumors announced that *they* killed the Hutu... (Umutesi, 2000: 7 & 10–11. Emphasis added).

Ntisoni, too, found himself in the Congo, crossing rivers with waters that were red like blood. His autobiography metaphorically suggests that instead of water, those rivers channeled blood. Having lost no single milliliter of his own blood, Ntisoni implied that that blood belonged to other Hutu refugees, 'we', who crossed the same rivers, to escape from 'they', mentioned above. He wrote, for instance, that '*Our* fate was engraved in a stone: of the 1,500,000 Hutu refugees, one-third had to be repatriated by force, one-third had to be killed and the remaining one-third had to go "missing"' (Ntisoni, 2007: 78. Emphasis added), before adding that 'The vanity of the Tutsi is unequalled. *They* consider themselves as the reference for everything. All those who do not look like *them* are barbarous...' (*Ibid.*: 79. Emphasis added). The explicit or implicit use of 'we' and 'they' and all their derivative forms in these autobiographical accounts suggests that individual authors perceived their memories as being collective. In the next section, I discuss that collectiveness as being both horizontal and vertical.

## 9.4 Horizontality and Verticality

In his 1948 book, *Qu'est-ce que la littérature?* or *What Is Literature?*, Jean-Paul Sartre devoted a few pages especially to American novelist Richard Wright and his autobiography *Black Boy* (1945). He suggested that this work is better understood if one begins first by considering its target audience, namely 'educated Blacks in the North' of the United States, and 'good-intentioned Whites'. However, as each human work goes beyond its target audience, it would also land in the hands of the general public, amongst whom non-educated blacks who had had 'the same childhood, same hardships, same complexities [as Wright]' and who would understand his account with their heart: 'by attempting to clarify his own situation, he clarifies their own' (Sartre, 1948: 101–102). Sartre was rightly stipulating that an autobiographical account tells the story of many through one, which is the case for the two autobiographies on which I am focusing here.

With the title *Inyenzi ou cafard* – Inyenzi or cockroaches – Mukasonga told the story not only of her aristocratic family from Magi, where her father served as a secretary-accountant of the local sub-chief in the late-1950s (Mukasonga, 2006: 11–12), but also the one of all those who, after the 1959 Revolution, were deported to the Bugesera region to start a new life in that empty, inhospitable place. The collectiveness of the autobiographical accounts I am concerned with can be construed in two ways: firstly, like Wright's *Black Boy*, they are horizontally collective because, parallel to them, thousands, if not millions of other related but not necessarily similar memories were piling up. In this respect, Mukasonga and Umutesi, who have almost all in common (more in Section 10.1.), share somehow the memories of the attacks of the Tutsi exiles and subsequent pogroms against the Tutsi in the early-1960s, and those of the prevailing atmosphere at Lycée Notre Dame de Cîteaux in Kigali. Sharing in this sense is limited to the idea that the same event or experience had been witnessed by both authors. The rest depends on the author's background and ethnic identity, which largely interfere with the re-thinking process that takes place whilst writing the autobiographical account. In this process, posterior events like the defeat of the monarchist rebels in the 1960s, RPF attack, the genocide, control of power by the Tutsi, the D.R. Congo 'hunt-down', etc., push the writers to re-visit their first-hand eyewitness memories. In a way, each element has to fit in with the bigger picture that the writer wants to portray.

Secondly, the autobiographical accounts that I am concerned with are vertically collective, as they all dive into the past to provide a background that presents the succession of events that are presented as justifying the authors' current situation. That succession includes a chain of other people, especially parents, grandparents, and great-grandparents, who kept the memory alive until the author acquired it. Kajeguhakwa's autobiography reflects the best the verticality of his memory's collectiveness. He went as far as the late-10th century, discussed the connections between his ancestry and the dynasty, especially King Mibambwe III Mutabazi II Sentabyo and Yuhi IV Gahindiro in the late-18th century, and the turmoil of late-1959, amongst others (Kajeguhakwa, 2001: 9–13). It could therefore be suggested that Kajeguhakwa shares his memories with his earliest known ancestor, Mututsi, who lived 10 centuries ago, with the two above-mentioned kings, and so on.

Beside the verticality and horizontality of the collectiveness of autobiographical memories, two major trends have emerged from the theories about the collectiveness of memory in general. The first trend is best reflected in Halbwachs' ([1925] 1992: 39) view that....

> what we call the collective framework of memory would then be only the result, a sum, or combination of individual recollections of many members of the same society. This framework might then serve to better classify them after the fact, to situate the recollections of some in relation with others.

The collective nature of memory resides not in the fact that many people share the same recollections in some sense and to a certain extent, but in the fact that each individual recollection is part of a larger memory pool that includes other individual memories. To say otherwise, individual memories are part of collective ones because the latter are the sum of the former, and no procedures are needed to make it happen. 19th century thinker Ernest Renan (1869: 4–5) had a similar argument to explain why each person automatically acquires the membership of different communities at birth, whether they like it or not. Renan's observation could even be an explanation for Halbwach's standpoint: being an automatic member of a community automatically makes one's memory collective.

The second trend comprises theories from scholars who view memory as a social and collective phenomenon first, before having some specific meaning for individual members of society. Wells (1938: vi) considered individuals not as beings 'simply born or thrown together into association like a swarm of herrings', but rather as beings 'with a sense of collective activities and common ends'. This implies that nature has shaped man in such a way that his fellow men are constantly in his mind when he accomplishes each and every activity, including remembering.[112] Van Dijck (2007: 25) was even more categorical about the relationship between the individual and collectivity: 'in order to remember ourselves, we have to constantly align and gauge the individual with the collective, but the sum of individual memories never equals collectivity.' The latter argument supposes that both personal and collective memories exist, but implies that the former are but the ramifications of the latter, since 'personal memory can only exist in relation to collective memory,' and not the other way round (*Ibid.*).

The question that arises here is the following: how does it happen that the same memory lines discussed above are constantly observed both in the horizontal and vertical collectiveness of autobiographical accounts? Studying 'The Impact of the Concept of Culture on the Concept of Man', which, in a sense, could also be understood as the impact of the collectivity – since culture is collective – on Man or individual, cultural anthropologist Clifford Geertz (1973: 45) conceptualised culture as being a 'control mechanism'. That mechanism is based on the assumption that 'human thought is basically both social and public', and that each particular individual finds the symbols composing it already current in the community when they are born. While he lives, Geertz (1973: 52) suggested, he uses those symbols or some of them, either deliberately or spontaneously, 'but always with the same end in view: to put a construction upon the events through which he lives'.

There seems to be an inescapable cultural link connecting the individual to his community, and, logically, his personal memory inescapably has connections with, and is a ramification of, the community's thought or memory. The interpretation of Geertz's view would thus be that autobiographical memory operates 'under the guidance of cultural patterns'. Community's or society's thought supposes that the community or society thinks and, thus, has a sort of mind. As individuals, the authors of the two autobiographies I am considering seem to be wrapped up by their respective ethnic identities and related memories, which operate as a powerful control mechanism guiding not only their recollection process, but also their pens or keystrokes. This chapter discussed the theories about autobiographical memories, ways in which individual authors position themselves in society and vis-à-vis other members of society. The next chapter goes a step further, zooming in on ways in which ethnic identities and related memories serve as a background to the Self.

---

112  In his book *The Life of Reason or the Phases of Human Progress*, philosopher George Santayana ([1905] 1954: 38) suggested that 'nature has made man man's constant study. His thought, from infancy to the drawing up of his last will and testament, is busy about his neighbours.'

Chapter 10

# Backgrounding the Self

The concept of 'Self' and its relationship with ethnic identities and related memories are at the heart of this chapter. Whilst the concept of memory has been largely discussed, the Self still needs to be conceptualised. Ancient philosophy scholar Richard Sorabji (2006: 17) once wondered if there was 'such a thing as the Self', and if yes, what is it? (*Ibid.*: 20). The Self does exist, and is even indispensable for both humans and animals, who 'could not cope with the world at all unless they saw things in terms of *I*' (*Ibid.*: 20). That *I* 'has psychological states and *does* things… [and] is not just a stream of experiences and actions, but the owner of experiences and actions' (*Ibid.*: 21–22). Psychologist Mark Howe (2004: 55–56) held that the Self emerges as a viable entity at about the age of 2, and from then on serves as 'a new organiser of information and experiences… and facilitates the grouping and personalisation of memories for events into what becomes autobiographical memory'.

From this perspective, the Self means and implies 'being aware of oneself as a person with a certain standing, past history, culture, and aspirations… this identity is often considered part of the self' (Sorabji, 2006: 21–22). Other authors who explored this subject have almost come to a similar conceptualisation. For example, psychologist Mark Freeman (1992: 16) defined the Self as the 'integrated, consistent, and enduring identity', whilst philosopher Charles Taylor (1989: 36) explained it as one's identity, involving one's stand on moral and spiritual matters, and some reference to a defining community. Taylor (1989: 47) further suggested that there is no way one can make sense of life and the world without a Self:

> … in order to make minimal sense of our lives, in order to have an identity, we need an orientation to the good, which means some sense of qualitative discrimination, of the incomparably higher. Now we see that this sense of the good has to be woven into my understanding of my life as an unfolding story. But this is to state another basic condition of making sense of ourselves, that we grasp our lives in a *narrative*.

From these few theoretical definitions of the Self, the link between individuals, their past and their perception of the present world becomes obvious. The past – memory – has created a framework in which actions and experiences are interpreted. In the light of the discussion in previous chapters, this would mean that the Hutu and the Tutsi in Rwanda are likely to have different memory-inspired sets of criteria against which they weigh their experiences and other people's actions. This chapter sets out to explore how this worked in the two autobiographies. I first pose the question to understand why Umutesi and Mukasonga ended up viewing things very differently whilst they seemed to have all in common. I then try to find an answer, arguing that their Selves pushed them to accord different degrees of relevance to past experience. The result of this was that one event received two opposite interpretations.

## 10.1 All In Common Except...

Mukasonga and Umutesi are two interesting cases to study. The two women have almost all in common: they belong to the same generation – born in 1957 and 1959 respectively –; they both witnessed the Tutsi refugee attacks of the 1960s; they attended the Lycée Notre Dame de Cîteaux in Kigali (Mukasonga, 2006: 77; Umutesi, 2000: 15); they worked for rural development projects aimed to particularly help women in Burundi for Mukasonga (2006: 105–106), and in Rwanda for Umutesi (2000: 19). Moreover, both authored their autobiographies from Western Europe – Belgium for Umutesi and France for Mukasonga. Similarities stop there. Their sole apparent dissimilarity – ethnicity – seems to be an impassable river between the two ladies. Let me illustrate this with the choices they made to place their accounts in a certain historical context.

Both authors began with the inescapable period of the late-1950s but quickly diverged in the way they approached the dramatic events of 1959. Mukasonga (2006: 14) stressed 'the first pogroms against the Tutsi' that 'broke out on All Saints Day in 1959':

> I was three years old when the first images of terror landed on my memory. I remember... I was home with my mother. All of a sudden, we saw smoke rising from everywhere, on the sides of the Makwaza Mountain, in the Rususa valley... Then we heard noises, shouting voices... an overwhelming roar... at that time a gang appeared shouting, holding machetes, spears, bows, clubs, torches. We went quickly to hide in the banana plantation. The men, still roaring, rushed to our house: they burned the straw-roofed house, the barns with calves therein; they destroyed the granaries full of sorghum and beans; they ruthlessly destroyed the brick-walled house... Their intention was not to loot, they wanted to destroy, to remove all traces, to annihilate us (*Ibid.*: 13–14).

Umutesi, too, began with an account of the same events, not as someone who witnessed them, but as someone who heard from direct witnesses. Unlike Mukasonga, she preferred to mention the 1959 events only after highlighting the developments that, according to her, caused them:

> The revolution broke out in July [sic!] 1959, when I was only two months old. The Hutu protested against the Tutsi feudal power, based on servitude, exclusion, and disdain. ... The revolt had been brewing since the early-1950s... Hutu peasants revolted against the system imposed upon them... One of my aunts was involved in those revolts. Aged 16, and in the framework of the compulsory not-paid-for services, she accompanied one young Tutsi lady who was visiting her family. She spent three days there

without eating because she had to eat alone and only after all the family members had finished eating. She should not look into the mouth of the 'masters' when they are eating... On the way back, she refused to help the family [the mistress]... My aunt knew what the risk was but she preferred whipping to humiliation. Another time, she went to collect sweet potatoes from her farm without the authorisation of the customary authorities... her family was hungry, my grandfather was in jail. ... She received eight whips. In public... Other attitudes made her furious... She had to carry her master's tobacco leaves with two wooden sticks because Hutu hands would sully it... These individual revolts resulted in a larger movement only in the late-1950s, when they were organised by Hutu intellectuals, educated in seminaries. In 1959, the movement resulted in the toppling of the Tutsi feudal regime by the Hutu... In my region, houses belonging to the Tutsi were burnt. Their owners fled to the churches. A few people died (Umutesi, 2000: 8–10).

Two main things are important to underline in these two long quotes: firstly, the two authors considered the events of the late-1950s as the starting point, the one that is central to the understanding of the later stages of their memories. Secondly, the diverging approaches the two authors adopted reveal which aspect of the 1959 events each author considered the most relevant. These approaches correspond to, and reflect, the diverging visions of the world on the part of the two authors. Their Selves judged the 1959 riots based on totally different criteria. Referring to the analysis of a painting, Foucault (1969: 253) observed that each reflects the implicit philosophy that shapes the painter's vision of the world, his intentions. This implicit philosophy consists of what Freud ([1900] 1925: 27–29) called 'latent ideas', and is strongly marked by ethnic identities and related memories in Rwanda. Gusdorf (1991b: 247) nicely explained the process of autobiographical writing not as a loyal rendition of past experiences, but as new constructions, or even new creations.

From this perspective, the accounts of the late-1950s events by the two authors are their reinvention, and this reinvention took place under their control, that is, following their own Self-dictated plans. Mukasonga, whose family once belonged to the upper-class aristocracy, suddenly found herself in a camp for the displaced, where she and her family survived thanks to charity (Mukasonga, 2006: 21–22). This degrading experience certainly shaped her 'Self' to a greater extent. For Umutesi, that very change that resulted in Mukasonga's stay in the camp meant the end of non-paid labour and of public humiliation like the one in which her aunt had been victim. Both situations fed her Self and played an important part in her later account of the 1959 events. In the last analysis, the late-1950s events contain the material that has gone into the formation of the two ladies' character (Schachtel, 1959: 286). The next section suggests that once the character, the identity, and the Self have completely matured, individuals accord different degrees of relevance to past events and experiences.

## 10.2 The Relevant Past

Authoring an autobiography is an intellectual exercise that goes far beyond the mere processes of retrieving memories and ordering them in a certain way. It is 'a closed book... a project of totality' for which the author determines the point of departure and the point of arrival (Gusdorf, 1991a: 317–318). Within that closed book, only one person determines the path linking the two points, and the path is generally traced from the point of arrival toward the point of departure. In this sense, the authors are the *Omega* and *alpha* of their own autobiography as they create their own world, and position themselves at the centre (Gusdorf, 1991b: 225–228; 237 & 427), taking into account current needs, wishes, aspirations, and intents (Howe, 2004: 45). Autobiographical authors neither allow contradictory points of view in their accounts, nor do they accord any pages to self-questioning reflections. They generally filter out all they deem irrelevant and trace a straight, obstacle-free path from the point of arrival to the point of departure. This was the case for both Mukasonga and Umutesi, who just focused on those parts of the past that they deemed interesting for their stories.

For Mukasonga, a Tutsi whose life was in jeopardy during the 1959 riots, the most relevant part was the roars and the fury of the Hutu who invaded her home and set it on fire, not the reason why they were furious. For Umutesi, a Hutu whose parents suffered the Tutsi feudal regime, the reasons for that fury, namely the servitude system and the humiliation it created are the most relevant parts, not the burnt houses or the 'few people' who died. Two reasonings could stem from the two long quotes in the previous section: on one hand, the fury of the Hutu peasants could be explained by the fact that they could not harvest from their farms before their masters had filled their granaries with crops taken from those very farms. Luc de Heusch's documentary, *Ruanda: Tableaux d'une féodalité pastorale* (1955) – Rwanda: portrayals of a cattle-based feudality – commented by Maquet and based on the latter's research, shows a scene of Hutu peasants lining up with baskets full of crops and waiting for their turn to offer them to their Tutsi lord's wife.

In a different study, Maquet explained that prior to the coming of the colonisers, the Hutu were subjected to special forms of taxes, which were essentially agricultural – *uguhunika* – or putting into the granary, 'which consisted of a certain number of baskets of beans, peas, and sorghum to be delivered at harvest time' (Maquet, 1961: 102; also see Kagame, 1952: 125–126). On their side, the less powerful Tutsi had to contribute milk – *umusogongero*. The collected milk was meant for the Queen or her provincial representative (Kagame, 1952: 127–128). In another scene from Heusch's documentary, one Hutu serf, after consuming so much alcohol to forget about his dead cow – entrusted to him by his Tutsi master – lamented, insulted the master, and 'all the Tutsi of the Kingdom': 'Are *they* not humans like *we*? Why do *they* exploit *us*?' he wondered.[113] From this perspective, destroying the houses and granaries without first emptying them of their valuable contents, could mean that the furious Hutu no longer wanted to see those houses

---

113 Note the use of 'they', 'we', and 'us' already in the 1950s (see Section 10.3.).

and granaries they had built and filled with sorghum and beans for free, and which served as a sign of humiliation. This explains Mukasonga's (2006: 14) remark that 'Their intention was not to loot, they wanted to destroy, *to remove all traces*, to annihilate us' [Emphasis added]. This interpretation is implicitly favoured as relevant for Umutesi's approach to the 1959 riots.

The second reasoning could be around the following questions: if the Hutu were really furious about those granaries they had filled for centuries, those cows they had kept working for, and those houses they had built for free, would this justify that 'a few Tutsi' should pay for it with their lives? Would that mean that they should, from then on, be homeless as their houses were burnt? Should they, from then on, starve as all their granaries were reduced to ashes? While Mukasonga put these questions at the centre of her account, Umutesi handled them almost *en passant*, as they appeared irrelevant to her narrative.

Having two or more diverging approaches to the same event, which necessarily and unmistakably leads to different understandings of the events in question, is a common phenomenon in memory. Irwin-Zarecka (1994: 191) suggested that 'if "texts" generate multiple readings, and they do, focusing on how some of those readings are privileged over others is of considerable help'. The approaches of Mukasonga and Umutesi offer considerable help in shedding the light on the gap separating the visions of the past of the two ladies of the same generation and with no obvious political militantism. The part of that past that hurts one does not necessarily draw the attention of the other. Can anyone be blamed for the version of the past they have acquired? The easy, standard answer is 'No', even if in practice Umutesi's version in post-genocide Rwanda would be a typical example of genocide denial and, thus, punishable by law. The one that should be blamed is rather the one who identifies those with a different vision of the past as an enemy. Born from an aristocratic family who had little contact with the masses of Hutu peasants, Mukasonga was understandably far from imagining the extent of the peasants' suffering. It would hardly be her major preoccupation. This explains why the attack of the furious Hutu peasants fell like a bomb on her. Similarly, Umutesi, whose parents could not harvest because the aristocrats had first to fill their granaries, understandably ignored the feelings that were prevailing among the threatened Tutsi. The same remark is true for the next crucial episode of Rwanda's past – the monarchists' attacks of the 1960s – which the two authors witnessed, but related to in very different ways.

## 10.3 One Event, Two Perspectives

The two authors used the events of 1959 as a relevant background to the story of their respective 'Selves'. The accounts were authored by people who were in their 40s, yet they described an event that took place when they were approximately one [Umutesi] and three years [Mukasonga] old. One can assume that much of what they described was put together based on testimonies of those who had witnessed the event as adults on one hand, and through imagination on the other hand. Imagination from the perspective of memory should not be mistaken for pure invention or fiction. Gusdorf's (1991b: 487) claim that ego writings are situated in the intermediary zone between the imaginary and the real and, as such, could be misunderstood as meaning that autobiographical accounts are half-fiction, half-reality. From the Aristotelian perspective, imagination and memory belong to the same part of the soul, 'and those things that are essentially the objects of memory are also such of which there is imagination'.[114] Imagination is the process that gives meaning, or, as Nora (1984b: XXXIV–XXXV) suggested, a symbolic aura to memory events and objects. It is even inescapable when one is trying to make sense of past events, as one cannot bridge the gaps without imagining: 'it is not otherwise that we find ourselves obliged to imagine Caesar as having traveled from Rome to Gaul when we are told that he was in these different places at these successive times' (Collingwood, [1946] 1994: 241). In the last analysis, then, imagination and memory have the same concern: making the absent present (Ricoeur, 2004 : 44). In this section, I explore ways in which Mukasonga and Umutesi bridged the gaps in the 1960s, the decade marked by recurrent attacks by Tutsi monarchists against the Hutu-dominated Republic.

Once the monarchy was deposed, Mukasonga, her family, and thousands of other Tutsi were 'deported' to Nyamata in what the author described as a punishment. They had to begin a new life, as they had lost everything. Desperate, she, like other deportees, waited for a saviour who would put her back in the privileged position. That saviour was the deposed King Kigeri V Ndahindurwa, who, together with his men, was shortly to return from exile:

> In late-1963 a rumour circulated among the Nyamata refugees: King Kigeri was about to return and take the displaced home. In Gitwe, the rumour had come from our neighbour Sebeza. His oldest son Kazubwenge, had gone to Burundi and the parents had received news that he was about to return. And he would not return alone. He was to come with the King who was returning to rescue the unfortunate deportees of Nyamata and take them home. Everybody started getting ready to welcome the King who would then take us back home. Men made big bows in honour of the awaited monarch. They were not war weapons and nobody had the intention to use them. It was simply a sign to show the King that his fighters had remained loyal to him. My father had the biggest bow of the entire village… Women made hair bands from sorghum barks… They had chosen large barks which, when dried, took a beautiful golden color and on which they wrote with a hot piece of iron: 'Long live Kigeri!'… Each wore their best cloths… Nobody went to the farm. Men stood in the middle of the road… we, the children, were dancing without knowing why… It was the long-awaited day, the day of our rescue… (Mukasonga: 2006: 40–43).

I want to break this quote here for a few analytical comments. Mukasonga gave a number of details about the reasons why the refugees were excited, yet she claimed that 'we, the children, were dancing without knowing why'. The question would then be to know how and when she finally knew about what she described

---

114 Aristotle, *De Memoria et Reminiscentia*, p. 29.

in such a thorough way. This is where imagination and memory seem to meet: the remembering subject was too young to know exactly why things were happening the way they were. However, based on post-event information received from adults, the remembering subject was able to *imagine* the scene and to *imagine* her place in it. The description goes on:

> Nothing was coming… Later, in a distance, a roar was growing louder and louder… That was not the expected joyful clamours. All of a sudden black objects appeared in the sky, flying straight towards us. Helicopters… All of us ran away… Helicopters flew above our houses again and again… They [the Hutu military] were shooting indiscriminately, propelling grenades… In the evening, they drove away in trucks… At dawn, we saw Kazubwenge, the neighbour's son, coming back home, wild and exhausted, with cloths in pieces. He was with other youngsters, three or four, whom I did not know, armed with bows. They patrolled around houses and vanished again early in the morning (*Ibid.*).

This story from the deportees' perspective leaves a number of questions unanswered: why was the return so awaited? Was it a peaceful return? What role did the neighbour's son play? Why were helicopters deployed? The answers, which Mukasonga found irrelevant for her account, can be found in Umutesi's account of the same late-1963 events, which looked at this event from the opposite perspective:

> The first time I heard of the Tutsi refugee issue was in 1963. I was four years old. It was around 6:00 p.m. … We heard whistles and my father came back home running. He told my mother: 'They are coming!'… Those who were coming were the Tutsi rebels… For weeks, our lives were marked by fear for an attack. Although we were far from the combat zones, people were traumatised by the rebels… Hide-outs in the swamps or in the forests were ready… Initially located in the regions bordering Uganda and Burundi, the guerrilla war took huge proportions in 1963. The rebels had arrived at about twenty kilometers from Kigali. Popular rumours announced that they killed the Hutu on their way, and that the [internal] Tutsi were joining their troops. This attack was followed by reprisals against the Tutsi in many regions of the country (Umutesi, 2000: 7 & 10–11).

In this account, too, one sees a mixture of 'eye-witness' stories – the father running and telling the mother about the attack – and post-event information either from adult eyewitnesses or from other sources. The cartography of the attacks, their extent, and popular rumours thereabout are not something a four-year-old child can fully grasp. The readiness of hide-outs in the swamps and forests is most probably something Umutesi *imagined* based on post-event stories from adults.[115]

---

115 Psychologists suggest that infants, toddlers, and early-age children retain events but these become increasingly fragmentary with the passage of time (Howe, 2004: 54). Piecing these fragments together can be considered to be a form of imagination.

The concepts of 'imagination' and 'creation', which I mentioned in this and some of the previous chapters, and which emerge as inherent to autobiography, bring to mind the related concept of 'fiction'. De Man (1979: 920) maintained that autobiography 'seems to fade off into neighbouring or even incompatible genres', including fiction, tragedy, and novel, amongst other genres. However, borrowing from fiction does not equate the two genres, as

> Autobiography seems to depend on actual and potentially verifiable events in a less ambivalent way than fiction does… It [autobiography] may contain lots of *phantasms* and *dreams*, but these deviations from reality remain rooted in a single subject whose identity is defined by the uncontested readability of his [author's] proper name [Emphasis added].

The *imagined* scenes of preparations for the return of the King and of the readiness of the swamps, do not turn the two accounts into fiction or fantasy, even though forms of fiction and fantasy often appear in the process of remembering (Ricoeur, 2004: 48-49). Rather, they contribute to the authors' efforts toward 'self-portraiture' (*Ibid.*). They allow one to see how memories interfere with imagination, which both contribute to the autobiographic project. They indicate from which perspective the authors have chosen to look back at their own past. The chosen perspective driven by ethnic identities and related memories can further be detected by looking at ways in which the authors present various events. For instance, while Mukasonga presented the return of King Kigeri and his people as a peaceful one, Umutesi emphasised that the return was rather a war between the Tutsi monarchists and the former Hutu emancipationists who were then in control of the country. Umutesi stressed that it was a guerrilla war, which, as all guerrilla wars do, terrorised and traumatised the Hutu population.

Marcel Bertou's 1963 documentary titled *Une arcadie africaine: le Ruanda*, shows scenes of burning houses and terrorised Hutu peasants running away for safety, and those of real-life military operations. Commenting that scene, Bertou corroborated Umutesi's description of that period, saying that 'Tutsi commandos attack hills, churches, cut people's throats, burn houses, and swipe women and cattle'.[116] Mukasonga also signaled the presence of the neighbour's son – Kazubwenge – among the awaited rescuers, and his presence on the D-day, together with 'other youngsters, three or four, whom I did not know, armed with bows', who then vanished the next day. This leads to imagine that Kazubwenge and his companions were at war, just like the helicopters. However, Mukasonga refrained from calling it a war, which Umutesi did, without fully dealing with the other side of the medal. Umutesi also mentioned how popular rumours claimed that the Tutsi who had stayed in Rwanda were joining the rebels. Mukasonga's account seems to give credit to these rumours, as she wrote that the Tutsi of Nyamata had remained loyal fighters of the King, and were proud of it, thus joining the battle, like the neighbour's son, Kazubwenge.

---

116 Marcel Bertou, *Une arcadie africaine: le Ruanda* (1963) [documentary]

How can one explain that one event has received two opposite interpretations? Why are the details relevant in one story omitted in the other? The question can be answered either in a simple way or in a complex one. The simplest answer would be: 'because that is how memory traps remembering subjects'. The abuses and killings committed by the Tutsi rebels are not relevant to Mukasonga, whose focus is on the harsh reaction to those attacks by Hutu soldiers. Reversely, the indiscriminate bombing of the Nyamata refugees, though responding to a guerrilla war allegedly supported by Tutsi inside Rwanda, did not deserve more than the 'reprisals against the Tutsi' description in Umutesi's account. The complex answer is that the memories relating to ethnic identity exert a considerable influence on remembering subjects and, before they even realise it, 'dictate' to them the events and experiences to compile in their straight path linking their point of arrival and their point of departure.

This effort to trace the path from the point of arrival to the point of departure is what Ricoeur (2004: 26–27) called 'search' or 'recall', whilst memories relating to ethnic identity and similar influence fall under what he termed 'evocation'. Emanating from a discussion on Aristotle's categorisation of memory into *mneme* – 'the simple presence of memory' – and *anamnesis* – 'the act [or effort] of recollection' (*Ibid.*: 19), Ricoeur's analysis helps understand the interference of memories relating to ethnic identity with autobiographical accounts: 'There is… "affection" in "searching". In this way, the intellectual and the affective dimensions of the effort to recall intersect with one another…' (*Ibid.*: 30). From this perspective, the two authors' search for their past experiences can be said to have been guided by the affections stemming from ethnic identities and related memories, in the sense that the Self's suffering leaves no room to the Other's suffering, which it relegates either to the status of minor, insignificant happenings, or simply the one of non-happening.

## Summary

In this part I was concerned with ways in which the memories relating to ethnic identities sneak into autobiographical accounts in Rwanda. Autobiography, as a genre, is itself a memory process as it is primarily about retrieving, ordering, and giving sense to one's past experience. Like other memory processes, autobiographies look into the past from the present. However, unlike most other ego memory documents, they offer a unified, coherent and linear narrative, cleared of any dissonance. I selected two autobiographical accounts, one by a Tutsi author and another by a Hutu author to try and explore the manifestations of ethnic identities and related memories therein. At first sight, the two authors present an almost similar profile: same gender, same age, similar schooling amongst other similarities. The sole difference – ethnicity – seems to have been decisive in the way they looked back at the past. In their accounts, it appeared that the happiness of the Hutu seemed to be the reverse for the Tutsi and vice-versa. It was also observed that society, especially its subcomponents served as the framework in which ethnic identities and related memories are acquired. In that framework, individuals learn to distinguish between 'we' and 'they'. These, and their various derivative forms populate the accounts and unambiguously make reference to ethnic groups in Rwanda. I have suggested that based on the 'we-versus-they pattern', ethnicity-tainted memory lines stretch both horizontally and vertically: regardless of who is behind 'we' or 'they', individuals share the memories of the events they witnessed, hence the horizontality of memory. However, sharing those memories does not mean assigning them the same meaning, significance and relevance. The relevance of each event or experience depends on the inherited memories, since current events are part of a continuous chain that started long before today's remembering subjects were born.

I have also discussed the ways in which the two authors connected their Selves to a certain background coloured by ethnic identities and related memories. The Self, i.e., the awareness of oneself, one's history, one's moral values, and one's belonging and identity gets much of its material from memory. If memory is ethnically coloured, it follows that the Self, too, will be ethnically coloured, which seems to be the case in the two autobiographies on which I focused. Otherwise, there would be no other way to explain how the two authors – despite being born in the same period, having attended the same secondary school, had an almost similar professional trajectory, experienced harsh exile conditions before settling in the West – would produce mutually-contradicting accounts of the same past. The sole major difference among the two is their ethnicity, and that was enough for them to trace different paths from their present position to their point of departure. The authors, each on her side, presented just one perspective to the story, or slightly mentioned the other perspective *en passant*. The blame of dramatic events seemed to be put on the Other, one described as 'they'. The most illustrative example of this was the accounts of the late-1959 Hutu uprising, which served as a point of departure for the two authors. Whilst one author witnessed and described the events from the position of an innocent target, the other presented them as justified, as offering relief and better perspectives to 'we'. Given the very low age at the time of the events, there is no doubt that post-event stories contributed to this double interpretation, which I keep calling memories relating to ethnic identities throughout this book.

Chapter 11

# Concluding Remarks

I started this book with an oral memory text about 19th-century Rwanda (chapter 0); I closed it with written memory texts about the late-20th and early-21st-century Rwanda. The journey between my point of departure and my point of arrival took me to many areas and regions of memory that had remained unexplored. It was at the same time an exploratory and analytical journey meant to go beyond the surface of myths, tales, memory-driven judicial measures, names, memory objects, autobiographical texts and other sorts of memory texts. My main aim was to map the complexities of remembering and forgetting in Rwanda, and in doing so, pointing out the dangers that such complexities entail. My journey was not linear. In some moments it took me to other places far from Rwanda. These detours were meant to show that while some complexities are typically Rwandan, many others appear in those other places that I visited. Now that I am preparing to land the plane, I have a feeling that I have created a sentiment of fear and pessimism by suggesting that behind the memory texts – oral, written, or otherwise – that I discussed, there is a potentially hidden, hatred-loaded message. I can therefore anticipate that the reader legitimately expects me to offer some paths to explore if Rwanda and Rwandans are to [start] tear[ing] apart the memory traps in which they have been stuck for long. That is what I am setting out to do in this concluding chapter. I first reflect on the concept of remembering, then on forgetting, before discussing [re]conciliation. At the end, I suggest a way that could help break the trap.

## 11.1 Remembering

The concept of remembering was one of the key concepts at the centre of this book, and it is not without a reason that it appears in this volume's title. RTLM journalist Gahigi was asking listeners to *remember* the arrogance of the Tutsi and inviting them to *remember* King Rwabugiri's defeat in the 19th century as illustration of his point. The Tutsi-dominated RPF regime keeps reminding the Hutu to *remember* that the RPF did nothing else but praiseworthy acts. The judicial systems kept reminding the Hutu genocide suspects that they should *remember* the [new] definition of innocence, which implied denunciation and self-flagellation. The royal drum Kalinga was designed to help people constantly *remember* the Rwanda-in-making process, whilst myths, tales and other oral memory texts help people *remember* those long-gone times in a coded way. Names, either those of individuals or political organisations, are meant to send people back to a past they are supposed to *remember*. Autobiographies, finally, show what authors preferred to *remember*. What, then, should Rwandans do to make sure that *remembering* is not taking a risk or imposing one's terror, but rather a right to position oneself in time and space?

One urgent way to solve this is to *demystify* memory. Rwandans need to be memory literate before anything else. It is good and fine to have all those stories from and about the past, but at the same time it is crucial to understand ways in which they should handle them, to keep control over them [rather than the other way round], to question them critically, to weigh them against one another [if they are conflictual], and, above all, to stop thinking of them as irremovable monuments representing unquestionable, to-be-followed truths. This is true for both memories of ancient Rwanda and those of modern Rwanda. With memory literacy, Rwandans would learn to be above their memories rather than their prisoners. With the memory literacy approach, children could learn about the story of the Kalinga, its adornments, its significance, but *should* at the same time explore the other side of the medal, i.e., the slain kings and their descendents, and the annexation of their kingdoms. The most important element here is the way that the stories are told: is it in a truncated and triumphalistic way as has so far been the case? Then, the trap gets tightened. Is it a balanced way that shows *all* the sides of the story and the traps that subsequent ideological interpretations have set? Then there is chance that those children will grow with a new perception of society, one in which no one needs to hide his face to express one's memory-related feelings.

In this way, memories themselves would cease to set traps and become a source of scientific and linguistic curiosity. For example, linguists and philologists could valuably track language evolution through old, but still-in-use proverbs and adages. [Oral] Historians could study oral memory texts to 'ascertain what in a testimony belongs to a tradition, whether the tradition really goes back to its supposed point of origin in time and space, and what distortions may have occurred between the first testimony and the last' (Vansina, 1971: 445). Narratologists and memory scholars could detect in more detail how memory narratives worked through historical tales for instance.[117] Scientists, like the Italian archaeologists who found the Lupercale

---

117 One example to illustrate my point is the historical tale titled 'The [hi]story of Ruganzu' – *Igitekerezo cya Ruganzu* (Coupez & Kamanzi, 1962: 222 –253. See more about King Ruganzu Ndoli in Section 6.2, p.101). The tale opens with a war poem allegedly authored by Ruganzu, and which goes like this:
*Ruganzu Cyitatire cya Mutabazi*
*Nyir'intorezo y' inganzamarungo [sic!]*
*Yayikubise Nyagakecuru mu Bisi bya Huye...*
Author's translation:
Ruganzu, the one who spies for himself, son of the Conqueror
Owner of the giant-tree-cutting axe
The one that hit Nyagakecuru at Bisi bya Huye...
What is very interesting for narratologists is the anachronism in the three verses of this war poem. Nyagakecuru is reported [by other tales] to have been a contemporary of King Yuhi II Gahima [*circa 1520*] (see Section 7.3, p.114), the grandfather of King Ruganzu II Ndori [*circa* 1580]. Ruganzu's killer-axe also appears in the zither tune by singer Sabatunzi (see Section 5.1, p. 91) who, by the way, attributed a different war poem to Ruganzu. One interesting research subject – from a narratology perspective – would be exploring the possible confusion in the storyteller's mind between the death of King Nzira – killed with Ruganzu's axe – and the death of Nyagakecuru, killed almost a century before.

sanctuary (Section 4.1.), could inspire themselves with the oral memory texts and find both the various *Rwanda rwa...* locations and the various ancient Hutu kingdoms. For that to be possible, of course, there must be no political motivation behind the move. The archaeological excavations should not be meant to prove the bravery of the Tutsi ancestors. The mapping of Hutu kingdoms should not aim to present the Hutu as the victims of their 'age-long enemies,' the Tutsi.

The process would be more helpful if applied to the most recent memories of war and genocide, whereby remembering implies asking for justice. But this all depends on where the process starts. The memories from the 1990s become sensible because they are viewed as a culmination/continuation of a process. As Mamdani (2001) suggested, it has been a succession of victims and killers changing roles. The process should start with the lesser fresh memories so that the concept of memory literacy itself can be given a chance to make its way. At a later stage, when it has proven its efficiency – i.e., when the memories previously dubbed Hutu and Tutsi, can cohabitate, contradict or complement each other in the classroom or in public media, without exposing anyone to danger – then the most recent memories [from the 1950s onwards] could be tackled. Parallel to that would be a process of fair justice that would leave no one frustrated. Perhaps it appears utopian now, but it will have to happen, at least if Rwandans want to free themselves from the grasp of their ethnic identities and related memories.

## 11.2 Forgetting

Forgetting is the other key concept discussed in this book. The Hutu have to *forget* their loved ones killed by the RPF, the way the Tutsi were forced to *forget* the victims of the pogroms in the late-1950s through to the 1970s. Any ethnic group that happens to control power makes sure that the previously dominant narrative is *forgotten*. Names highlight selected aspects and events, and *forget* others. Autobiographical authors *forget* to take into account the other side of the story, preferring to focus on the relevant parts that contribute to their narrative. In many cases, forgetting has emerged as a way to survive and to live a peaceful life. Forgetting in this sense is linked to victory: the winner dictates what should be forgotten, namely his own abuses and killings. Any solution, therefore, should start by exploring this relationship between forgetting and victory.

The success – if one can talk of success – of the South African Truth and Reconciliation Commission was first and foremost based on the idea that no one had won. In Rwanda, notions of victory and defeat have marked ethnic relationships for ages, and power has always been associated with victory – not electoral but military victory. Victory gives privileges to the winner – including remembering and forgetting at will – and means the beginning of oppression for the loser. The 1959 events and the 1961 proclamation of the Republic, and later the 1994 seizure of power by the Tutsi-dominated RPF were all instances of ethnic victories that meant nothing but privileges for some and oppression for others. To cite Benjamin ([1955] 1973: 258; see also Debord, 1967: 119–120), 'Whoever has emerged victorious participates to this day in the triumphal procession in which the present rulers step over those who are lying prostrate'. The solution-seeking process, then, should start with forgetting that any one has won or lost. This would be the most important step towards the creation of a state where friendship and goodwill would prevail. Chanting and celebrating ethnic victories – either through calendrical commemorations, coat of arms, or national anthems, among other ways – do nothing but revive old memories of enmity and violence.

The case of Norway is interesting to explore. In 2006, there was debate on the total removal of all wars and related developments from history textbooks. The ministry of education wanted no World Wars, no Communism, no Russian Revolution, no Nazism, no Cold War, no United Nations, no European Union, no Berlin Wall, etc., in short, no victory or defeat, no winners or losers, in the curriculum. All these subjects can hardly be handled without alluding to the most devastating wars humanity has ever witnessed. After protests and fierce criticism, the ministry made a few concessions and slightly changed its initial plan: the pupils learnt about 20$^{th}$-century international conflicts, but to a lesser extent, and in a less general way (Kester, 2006: 7). In the Netherlands, the process of ridding textbooks of some forms of victory-stressing World War II representations was gradual: in the 1950s and 1960s, the emphasis was on the liberation of 'an innocent nation' as essentially a military operation – a military victory. The decade thereafter witnessed a change in the approach that left aside military triumphalism to present the War as pitting values like freedom, equality, mutual respect and democracy on one hand, against their opposites on the other – a moral victory. From the 1990s onwards, the liberation has been conceptualised in relation to general concepts such as freedom under its various forms, in various places and times (Van Boxtel, 1995: 20–21) – victory was removed.

Both the Norwegian move and the Dutch approach to teaching about war-related episodes could be interpreted as avoiding any conflict-generating attitude, or any spirit of triumphalism. Removing the notion of victory and defeat from their history textbooks is a way of forgetting victory in times when celebrating victory would do more [economic, diplomatic, social, political, etc.] harm than good. Rwandans can learn from these experiences and ponder Wells' (1938, 76) wise reflection in the late-1930s: 'I think we underrate the formative effect of this perpetual reiteration of how we won, how our Empire [ethnic group] grew and how relatively splendid we have been in every department of life…'. As discussed in Section 5.3 both the pre-genocide Hutu leaders and their post-genocide Tutsi counterparts have not managed to go beyond their ethnic identities and relating memories by keeping the symbols of ethnic supremacy and triumphalism in the symbols of the Nation. For instance in the old anthem, the Hutu celebrated Rwanda as being 'theirs', which the Tutsi repeated in the new anthem. The old anthem praised the Hutu emancipationists who had toppled the Tutsi monarchy; the new one celebrates '*Our* brave ancestors [who] Gave themselves bodies and souls | As far as making you a big nation…' [Emphasis added]. The pervasive presence of victory is obvious in both anthems, and through it, Rwandans are/were told which part of the story to forget.

If forgetting is part of the medicine I am proposing, then the name 'Rwanda' should be the first to be forgotten. As Section 7.3 has shown, it implies military victory of the Tutsi over the Hutu. It should be the first one to join the scientific and curiosity areas of Rwandans' memories discussed in the previous section. Section 7.3 showed how, by expanding the initial tiny territory of Rwanda, the Tutsi kings killed Hutu kings and their male progeny, and mutilated their bodies to adorn the royal drum Kalinga. To go on with Wells, current efforts should aim to get 'the criminal history of the royalty, the murder of the Princes in the Tower... the scandals and revenges' out of history and people's minds (Wells, 1938: 76). This cannot happen when the Nation itself and its inhabitants bear the name that reminds them how violent they have been [can be] against one another for the conquering of power.

There is even a psychoanalytic argument to further back up my point. As Ricoeur (2004: 79–80) observed, many nations and historical communities were born out of a situation comparable to war, which is celebrated as the founding event. The above has stressed that Rwanda is no exception. Discussing the transposition of pathological categories to the historical, collective plane, Ricoeur contended that celebrating that founding event is legitimating the violence, glory, and humiliation they implied, which, from a psychoanalytic point of view, does not facilitate the process of mourning but rather perpetuates 'wounded memory'. The name 'Rwanda' being a permanent celebration of the violent process that led to the country's current state and shape, its removal would trigger a new perception of the past, where victory, glory, and triumphalism, on one hand, and humiliation on the other hand, would have a different significance.

Conducted in all fairness, the *forget Rwanda* move would set some unprecedented processes in motion: all ethnic ideologies, emancipationist or supremacist as conveyed by myths, proverbs, dynastic poems, political organisations' names, etc., would immediately become irrelevant and, in the long run, be harmless. They would refer to a non-existent entity and would become epics. The new name should be neutral and immune of memories relating to ethnic identities. It could describe the country's geo-morphology on the model of the Netherlands or Low Countries – and here the legendary thousands hills, the beautiful great lakes, or the volcanoes could serve as a source of inspiration. It could reflect the regional location on the model of the *Central* African Republic or *South* Africa; the constitutional system, on the model of the *United States* of America; or simply refer to *Imana*, the God that spends the day abroad but always comes back to spend the night in Rwanda, as a popular saying suggests.

This move could set in motion another process, one of unsealing the country's fate (see Section 7.1), but here much prudence and vigilance would be needed to avoid hidden, coded, agendas, which Rwandans have so far proven to be keen on, both at the individual and political levels. I am basing this part of my reflection on the popular belief amongst Rwandans that 'name is man', which can be extended to mean 'name is country'. The name Rwanda seems to have deemed the country to be in perpetual cycles of violence either to *expand* itself in size or to *increase* control of power by those already occupying it. The hope is that by changing that name, the war-and violence-implying fate would be unsealed, which the name has proven capable to achieve in some ways.

## 11.3 Conciliation

If one sentence could summarise this book, that sentence would be: Rwanda is and has been trapped by its own ethnic identities and related memories. Some old memories relating to ethnic identities get repressed, amnesia is imposed, and the result is nothing else but resentment of those prevented from enjoying their right to remember. That resentment leads to violence aimed at reversing the order. That way the loop keeps on and on. Those who attempted to understand the relationships between the Hutu and the Tutsi after the genocide came to the conclusion that the situation looked like 'a time-bomb' (Buckley-Zistel, 2006: 147) or like 'a simmering volcano' (Mamdani, 2001: 282). These two descriptions imply that the situation seems under control, but all the needed ingredients – frustration, resentment, partial memory-driven justice, etc.– are there for yet another shock. From the observation by Buckley-Zistel and Mamdani, the sole unknown element is when. This takes me to the other key concept at the centre of this book, namely the dangers of ethnic identities and related memories in Rwanda. It has appeared in this book that remembering and forgetting can cost lives and that to live in peace one has to know which past to remember and which one to forget. To try and reverse this unacceptable situation that turns Rwanda into a time-bomb or a volcano, I am suggesting that Rwandans explore the 'conciliation' path.

I am using the term 'conciliation' on purpose because the more popular 'reconciliation' seems not to be applicable in Rwandans' case. As far as I understand, that word turns the reconciling subjects to their past, to the golden age they would like to return to. In this book I have contended that there has never been a golden age common to the Hutu and Tutsi. The Tutsi claim has been that the colonisers destroyed harmony amongst Rwandans, one fostered by the *Ubuhake* system. Indeed, as Maquet (1961: 139) explained, that cattle-based feudality ensured social harmony as 'two castes whose interests were so often divergent or opposed could constitute a stable unitary structure'. The Hutu 'had at their disposal some cattle', while the Tutsi 'consumed agricultural produce and had their fields cultivated by their clients and servants'. The system allowed the participation of both groups in the country's economic growth and, to some extent, to political power, as 'almost any Hutu was linked to a Tutsi, and partook in the social power of the upper caste' (*Ibid.*: 150). This apparent harmony was not marked by any overt conflict and, indeed, could lead to the misleading conclusion that in the system 'Tutsi cattle herders and Hutu farmers complemented each other' (Caplan, 2007: 21), and that hatred among the two groups would need careful nurturing. The Hutu serfs even voluntarily sought protection of someone in the pyramid with the King on the top (Kagame, 1954: 284).

This, undoubtedly, turned the entire population in one unitary block, sticking together behind the King, because 'everyone [was] in their place, their class, taken up with the duty allocated to them' (Rancière, 2009: 42). In chapter 5, I fought this oversimplified view that presents pre-colonial Rwanda as a paradise lost. The situation perceived as social harmony was a deceiving one, marked by acceptance of injustice in order to live a peaceful life. Breaking the *Ubuhake* contract very often meant returning all the received cows and troubles coming from the frustrated master, and even fatal torture (Kagame, 1954: 284–285; also see Vansina, 1962: 58). That was an artificial harmony or even no harmony at all, because it was based on inequality and injustice.

On their side, the Hutu mostly think that the two decades of the Habyarimana regime, that is the 1970s and 1980s, could be a common golden age both for the Hutu and the Tutsi. But again, this is another deceiving oversimplification as perceptible harmony among the Hutu and the Tutsi covered interiorised acceptance of injustice on the part of the Tutsi. Sebarenzi (2009: 44) nicely qualified this type of harmony as 'cosmetic peace' or 'negative peace' (*Ibid.*: 43), one whereby the Tutsi were safe but treated as second-class citizens. Cross-marriage is an often-cited example of that harmony between the Hutu and the Tutsi under Habyarimana. The two autobiographic authors I focused on in part two agreed that interethnic marriages intensified in that period, but cite different reasons. For Umutesi (2000: 14), a Hutu, it was a sign that tensions were easing up, as even army officers could get married with Tutsi women. For Mukasonga (2006: 72) 'marrying a Tutsi woman was part of the victor's rights', and senior leaders had to set examples by taking those women against their will and that of their parents. They would repeat: 'The Tutsi and their girls are no longer entitled to pride'. This, obviously, is far from being a paradise lost for all Rwandans. One popular tune of the Hutu emancipationists pointed to the pre-Ubuhake period as the absolute Hutu golden age, where even democracy, harmony, and social understanding prevailed among the subjects of the small and peaceful Hutu kingdoms.[118]

Simply defined, reconciliation means the **re**turn to **conciliation**.[119] To conciliate, according to most reference dictionary definitions, means 'to gain (as goodwill) by pleasing acts',[120] 'To end a disagreement or someone's anger by acting

---

118 The Abanyuramatwi's song is titled *Turate twogeze Demokarasi*, meaning 'Let us praise and promote democracy'. The refrain of this song goes:
*Turate twogeze demokarazi*
*Imaze gushinga imizi mu Rwanda*
*Mbe mbere Yarihe?*
*Ntiyarizwi*
*Gihake yari yarayimize.*
Translation:
Let us praise and promote democracy
It is now deeply rooted in Rwanda
Where was it before [the coming to power of Parmehutu?]
It was unknown
The Ubuhake system had swallowed it.
119 *Encyclopedia Britannica Ultimate Reference Suite* [Computer-based – version: 2010.00.00.000000000]
120 *Ibid.*

in a friendly way or slightly changing your opinions, or to satisfy someone who disagrees with you by acting in this way'.[121] Conciliation, thus, is the 'state of being brought to friendship or goodwill'.[122] The question would then be: has there been any genuine conciliation amongst the Hutu and Tutsi to which the current or future generation should strive to return to? I am afraid that there has been none. The history of Rwanda presents no single instance of such a state of *true* friendship and goodwill amongst the Hutu and the Tutsi. The Tutsi believe it was before colonisation; the Hutu believe it was before Tutsi invasions and occupations of their kingdoms. President Kagame is of the opinion that *true* friendship and goodwill amongst the Hutu and Tutsi never existed after 1959, that is, when the Hutu took control of the country:

> There was no single day in the history of post-1959 Rwanda, on which the above-mentioned groups [the State, the Church, and the Belgians] worked to achieve national unity. Never! No single statement can be found showing that the State, the Church or the Belgians have strived to achieve the unity of the Rwandan people. If you know any, let me know! Instead of that, from 1959 until 1994, when Habyarimana died, there was hatred and manipulation, either on the part of the clergy, or of certain Belgians who were here at that time: priests or governors (Misser, 1995: 89–90).

Paul Kagame's point is debatable as to the role of the institutions he blamed, but has the merit of being clear and categorical: there has never been any form of conciliation between the Hutu and the Tutsi as far as the 1959 – 1994 period is concerned. The preceding period too, as far as the Hutu memories are concerned, were far from being one of harmony and unity amongst the Hutu and the Tutsi. Basing his contention on popular culture, especially the proverbial part of it, Higiro (1996: 177) held that 'there was no harmony between the Hutu, Tutsi, and Twa social groups' before the coming of the colonisers. Hence, efforts should be directed not to the return to a non-existing anterior conciliation, but to the creation of friendship and goodwill, the latter more than the former, amongst the current generations of the Hutu and the Tutsi.

The duty of current generations should be one of creating a golden age, achieving conciliation that would serve as a reference for future generations whenever they seek re-conciliation. What is worrying is that efforts to create goodwill and friendship seem not to be on the political agenda of the current regime of President Kagame. He is implementing a strategy he once defined in an interview with *La Libre Belgique* back in June 1991, when he was still a rebel commander. He was considering the eventuality that 'Tutsi and Hutu could live in Rwanda without necessarily being friends. What holds them together is their

---

121 *Cambridge Advanced Learner's Dictionary. 3rd Edition* (Cambridge: Cambridge University Press, [1995] 2008), p. 288.
122 A.S. Hornby *et al.*, *The Advanced Learner's Dictionary of Current English* (London: Oxford University Press, 1957).

common interest, which is their country'.[123] About 17 years later, he claimed that he had brought back the conciliation that the colonisers, the Church, and post-independence leaders had destroyed: 'We are nine millions of Rwandans living in peace and harmony'.[124] The RPF regime has achieved that [seeming] reconciliation but, as Caplan (2007: 31) wrote, 'on its own terms', that is, based on its own reference and standards.

The most cited reconciliation initiative remains the South African TRC [Truth and Reconciliation Commission]. The TRC strove not to return to any previous state of conciliation among the non-White and the White communities, but focused its efforts on 'offering a road map to those who wish to travel into our past' by providing 'a perspective on the truth about a past that is more extensive and complex than any one commission could, in two and a half years, have hoped to capture'. The Commission's chairperson, Archbishop Desmond Tutu defined the body's ultimate goal as 'helping our nation to come to terms with its past, and in so doing, reach out to the future.' This goal-framing made the past-future bridging function the essence and the justification of the Commission's existence. It also stressed that its [legal] work provided just 'a perspective on the truth', an interpretation of the past based on 'material that passed through our hands', and which 'others will inevitably critique'.[125] Here, too, the term reconciliation refers to a sort of dive into the past not in search for a golden age to return to, but in search for *a* past on which to base a better future, that is a past on the basis of which present-day conciliation can be built. That process implied the acceptance to sacrifice justice [in the legal sense] for long-term racial conciliation. The TRC was not expected to render justice to the long-oppressed non-Whites. First post-apartheid President Nelson Mandela accepted to put in brackets abuses and crimes of which he and his fellow Blacks had been victims, and the ones they had themselves committed against the Whites, preferring to focus on the hard-won social justice. This is certainly an interesting path to explore in Rwanda.

## 11.4 The Way Forward

So far, I have suggested three paths to explore in an attempt to tear the memory ethnic traps that keep Rwanda in a constant loop of ethnic conflict. The first is that memory should be demystified so that remembering can cease to be 'a criminal act' to become a right. The second is forgetting victory and all its reminders that keep legitimising ethnic triumphalism. The third is building a favourable atmosphere for a state of genuine friendship and goodwill between the Hutu and the Tutsi, which imperatively requires that Rwandans stop cheating on themselves. Efforts in these directions would lead to a *re-membering* and *re-invention* of the Nation based

---

123 Marie-France Cros, '*Le chef des rebelles rwandais s'explique. Une interview exclusive du mystérieux Paul Kagame: "nous ne combattons pas pour la suprématie"*', *La Libre Belgique*, 13 June 1991, reproduced in Misser (1995: 145-148), p. 146.
124 President Paul Kagame's interview with François Soudan, in *Jeune Afrique, 2466*, (13–19 April 2008: 24–32), p. 29.
125 Truth and Reconciliation Commission, *Truth and Reconciliation Commission of South Africa Report, Volume One* (1998), pp. 1–2 http://www.doj.gov.za/trc/report/ (Accessed 24 November 2008).

on a more sound and long-term-oriented base. For the purpose of my reflection, I want to borrow two aspects from Derrida's theory about the concept of invention, mainly the invention of the Other. Firstly, invention supposes some 'illegality, the rupture of an implicit contract... introduces a disorder in the peaceful order of things... disturbs prevailing hierarchies' (Derrida, 1987: 11). Secondly, placing the term 'invention' side by side with other terms belonging to the same etymological family, Derrida (1987: 16) established the relationships within that web of words, and went beyond the lexical game that revolves around the Latin verb *venire: invention* involves an event [*événement*] consisting in breaking some *convention*, the coming [*avènement*] of a certain future [*avenir*], the entire process having the features of an adventure [*aventure*].

In this respect, Rwanda has achieved drastic cultural inventions. On independence, Rwanda was among the rare African nations that legally forbade polygamy, whilst it was part of Rwandans' culture and tradition. More recently, the straw traditionally used to share locally brewed beverages from the calabash was banned. Until the last decade, one straw was used to pass from one mouth to the other, and that was a sign of friendship and brotherliness. Wiping or cleaning the straw before introducing it to one's mouth was the most unacceptable insult. Due to the threat such a practice posed to public health, the entire cultural, and friendship-building philosophy behind the straw was sacrificed for the good of the people, who have to *invent* new cultural ways of exteriorising friendship. Besides, each baby boy has now to be circumcised at birth in an effort to slow down HIV/AIDS. According to the ministry of public health, a massive education program on circumcision was expected to kick off in early-2010, to call a maximum of male adults to volunteer.[126] Until recently, circumcision was almost exclusively practiced by the Moslem community, hence its Kinyarwanda name – *gusiramura* –, with the *Rwandicised* radical of Islam [–*siram*–] in that word. In the mind of Rwandans, the 'islamisation' or male circumcision is being forced into their mind and culture by law, once again for the common good.[127]

Heavier sacrifices are needed at the memory level and for the common good. Like the straw was spotted out as a potential spreader of tuberculosis and other contagious infections, I have depicted the memories relating to ethnic identities as the spreader of ethnic hatred and violence. Banning the straw was easy because the process took place more outside than inside the psyche, even though it affected it to some extent. Changing ways Rwandans look at the past, the credit and belief they accord mythic and myth-inspired memories could be done through laws, education, and other political measures. I have pointed out the obstacles such symbols as the coats of arms, the national anthem, the name of the country, might pose to the process. Changing the attitudes vis-à-vis ethnic identities and related memories implies stripping them of their magic power, a task that requires compromise. That compromise, as Mboninama rightly noted, requires that the

---

126 Irene Nambi, 'Massive circumcision drive on the books', *The New Times,* 28 August 2009. http://www.newtimes.co.rw/index.php?issue=14001&article=19286 (Accessed 29 August 2009).
127 BBC News, 'Rwanda in mass circumcision drive' (22 January 2008) http://news.bbc.co.uk/2/hi/africa/7202487.stm (Accessed 9 July 2009)

Hutu and the Tutsi sit on a round table and agree on a certain past.[128] Since it is a matter of life or death for the Nation, the round table needs political support and a huge amount of confidence and, of course, of freedom of speech and thought.

One important step is the redefinition of terms like 'extremism', 'moderation', 'negationism',[129] 'revisionism', 'divisionism', 'genocidaire', 'liberation' currently used in Rwandan political discourse. It was frequently observed that one could be moderate today and extremist tomorrow, depending on their loyalty towards those in control of power. This was the case for former president Pasteur Bizimungu, former prime ministers Faustin Twagiramungu and Pierre Célestin Rwigema, and former National Assembly speaker Alfred Mukezamfura. All were initially labeled moderate Hutu and were presented as embodying the successful Hutu-Tutsi reconciliation. As soon as they started raising obvious ethnicity-related issues, they were suddenly removed from the list of moderates and were added to the one of 'dangerous' Hutu extremists. This process often ends with legal prosecution and jail, which was the case for Bizimungu and Mukezamfura.[130]

In a rather eulogistic article, *The Economist* reported that 'In practice, the government can label any criticism against it as "divisionism", which entitles it to lock up the offenders'.[131] This description empties the term of its meaning, as divisionism seems to equal criticism. 'Liberation' is another controversial term. The Hutu claim that they liberated themselves from Tutsi feudal monarchy in the early-1960s. But that liberation forced many Tutsi into exile. On their side, the Tutsi claim that they liberated themselves in July 1994, but that liberation left at least a million Tutsi and hundreds of thousands of 'non-remembered' Hutu dead, and forced many others into exile. Those terms are other ways of fostering ethnic identities and related memories and ethnic triumphalism, as they only apply to 'we', different from, and in conflict with, 'they'. As Foucault (1969: 32) suggested, 'We have to re-question these before-hand made syntheses, these groups of concepts that one has to admit before any further inquiry, these links whose validity is recognised from the start'. Instead, 'we have to chase them from the shadow from where they operate... We also have to worry while faced with these categorisations or groups of concepts which have become so familiar to us'. At a theoretical level, Foucault (1969: 37) suggested not to completely and definitively reject those concepts, 'but to shake the ease with which they are accepted; show

---

128 Gamaliel Mbonimana speaking in *Hopes on the Horizon* (2001), a documentary by Onyekachi Wambu
129 The label 'negationist' is also used as a don't-look-into-my-past weapon targeting international scholars and institutions. Brandstetter (2010: 15) observed that 'Human right organisations, the International Criminal Tribunal for Rwanda (ICTR), international scholars, and other individuals and organisations who question this official story [that most of those killed by RPF soldiers were killed in combat, and were not civilian casualties] risk being reproached as genocide deniers or genocide ideologists'.
130 Edwin Musoni, 'Former Speaker gets life sentence', *The New Times*, 4 September 2009.
http://www.newtimes.co.rw/index.php?issue=14008&article=19554 (Accessed 4 September 2009).
131 The Economist, 'Middle East & Africa: Progress and repression in Rwanda Divisionists beware', *The Economist*, 4 March 2010.
http://www.economist.com/world/middle-east/displaystory.cfm?story_id=15622375
(Accessed 4 March 2010).

that they are not self-evident, that they are always the result of a construction the rules of which are to be identified, and its justifications controlled'.

Two things seem certain and obvious, and should be taken into account whenever such a compromise-seeking round table takes place: firstly, the Hutu and the Tutsi versions of the past are not mergeable, and any attempt to merge them would simply be vowed to fail and to lead to more cultural hypocrisy. The best would not be throwing away one of the conflicting and unmergeable memories and keeping the other, but 'bringing the two to a productive crisis' (Spivak, 1990: 111). Secondly, all the conflicts and turmoil, including those that marked the making process of Rwanda centuries ago, the 1959 events, the rebellions and reprisals of the 1960s as well as the 1990 to 1994 war, massacres, and genocide, are all rooted in ethnic identities and related memories. What is more, each of them is recorded and transmitted to the future generations along ethnic lines, which tightens the trap.

Like the physician who proceeds to finding the cure after identifying the pathological agent causing the disease, the Hutu and the Tutsi should ask themselves the question to know which cure can prevent future wars, massacres, and genocides. Was the *Gacaca* going in that direction? Will there be other *Gacaca* courts to judge the Tutsi if ever the Hutu come back to power? Have the potential causes of the genocide been removed?[132] Is the replacement of ethnically biased machete and hoe in the old coat of arms by the equally ethnically oriented and war-evoking shields a move to the right direction? Is the 'beatification' of King Rudahigwa, who defended the Kalinga – and thus the memories behind it – or of the slain RPF commander Fred Rwigema – whom the Hutu blame for starting a disastrous war that killed hundreds of thousands – a step towards a new Nation? Reversely, would it be wise to canonise Kayibanda while the Tutsi consider him as the initiator of their plight, as the one who predicted 'a total and precocious end of the Tutsi race' if ever they kept attacking Rwanda? Would it be a good idea to accord President Habyarimana the status of hero when the Tutsi felt discriminated under his regime?

Another set of questions could be asked as well: Would it not be a wiser idea to not canonise anyone? To commemorate no date at all? No 1959? No 28th January and 25th September 1961? No 5th July 1973? No 1st October 1990? No 6th or 7th April 1994? No 4th July 1994? Those dates, amongst many others, are references of ethnic victory and triumphalism and constitute a huge obstacle – a handbrake – to the invention of a new society, and its new members. In his time Cicero ([54 and 51 B.C.] 1970: 15) wisely refrained from speaking 'of the men, numerous in number, who have been each the salvation of this republic' because mentioning their names – I should add the dates of their celebrated accomplishments – would prompt some to complain of the omission of themselves or of some member of their family – or ethnic group, to bring it back to the Rwandan context.

---

132 This question was asked by Paul Rusesabagina during the 25 April 2009 Africa Day event in The Hague http://www.olny.nl/RWANDA/Videos/rusesabagina_rwanda_back_to_feudality.html (Accessed 2 July 2009).

The questions posed above have to be honestly discussed if Rwanda has to abandon the status of 'land of blood' (Kajeguhakwa, 2001: 347). Addressing them and taking responsible, fair decisions about them, implies heavy sacrifices and new beliefs. The to-be-defined members of the to-be-invented society will have to realise that [self-] imposed amnesia observed in one ethnic group whilst the other promotes the memories relating to its own identity should be replaced by a self-imposed compromise, costs what it costs. Contrary to what is frequently suggested, Rwanda's future does not primarily lie in the democratisation of the country's political system, but mainly in the democratisation of its memory system, as the latter would pave the way to the former.

# *References*

Aghion, Anne (2002) *Gacaca: Living Together Again in Rwanda?* [Documentary]

Aghion, Anne (2005) *In Rwanda We Say...The Family That Does not Speak Dies* [Documentary]

Aghion, Anne (2009) *My Neighbor My Killer* [Documentary]

Althusser, Louis ([1985] 1992) *L'avenir dure longtemps* (Paris: Stock/IMEC)

Amnesty International (2010) *Rwanda: Safer to stay silent: The chilling effect of Rwanda's laws on 'genocide ideology' and 'sectarianism'* (London, August) < http://www.amnesty.org/en/library/asset/AFR47/005/2010/en/ea05dff5-40ea-4ed5-8e55-9f8463878c5c/afr470052010en.pdf >

Aristotle (2007) *De Memoria et Reminiscentia* [384 B.C. – 322 B.C.] in Bloch, David, *Aristotle on Memory and Recollection* (Leiden: Brill)

Assange, Julian (2011) *Julian Assange: The Unauthorised Autobiography* (London: Canongate)

Assmann, Aleida (2006) *Four Formats of Memory: From Individual to Collective Forms of Constructing the Past* (May)

Assmann, Aleida ([2006] 2008) 'Memory, Individual and Collective', in Goodin, Robert & Tilly, Charles (Eds.) *The Oxford Handbook of Contextual Political Analysis* (Oxford: Oxford University Press), pp. 210–224

Assmann, Jan & Czaplicka, John (1995) 'Collective memory and cultural identity', in *New German Critique*, 65, pp. 125–133

Bamusananire, Emmanuel, Byiringiro, Joseph, Munyakazi, Augustine & Ntagaramba, Johnson (2006) *Primary Social Studies. Pupil's Book 4* (Kigali: MacMillan Rwanda)

Bank, Jan & Rooy, Piet de (2004) 'Wat iedereen moet weten van de vaderlandse geschiedenis: Een canon van het Nederlands verleden', in *NRC Handelsblad* (30 October), p. 3

Barthes, Roland (1970) 'Science versus Literature', in Lane, Michael (Ed.) *Structuralism: A Reader* (London: Jonathan Cape), pp. 410–416

BBC Great Lakes, 19 December 2007 [Radio news]

BBC Great Lakes, 30 June 2009 [Radio news]

BBC Great Lakes, 10 March 2010 [Radio news]

BBC Great Lakes (2010) *Imvo n' Imvano* (29 May) < http://www.bbc.co.uk/greatlakes/meta/tx/nb/greatlakes_0530_au_nb.ram >

BBC News (2005) 'Madrid removes last Franco statue' (17 March) < http://news.bbc.co.uk/2/hi/europe/4357373.stm >

BBC News (2008) 'Rwanda in mass circumcision drive' (22 January) < http://news.bbc.co.uk/2/hi/africa/7202487.stm >

BBC World News, 9 October 2008 [TV news]

BBC World – Hard Talk (2006) *'Stephen Sackur talks to Rwanda's president, Paul Kagame'* (7 December)

BBC World Service (2009) Interview Paul Kagame [by Owen Bennett-Jones] (6 November) <http://downloads.bbc.co.uk/podcasts/worldservice/interview/interview_20091106-2332a.mp3 >

Becker, Carl ([1931] 1960) *Everyman His Own Historian* (El Paso: Texas Western College Press)

Becker, Carl (1955) 'What are Historical Facts?', in *The Western Political Quarterly*, Vol. 8, No.3 (September), pp. 327–340

Becky Anderson (2010) 'Connector of the Day: Paul Kagame', *CNN* (16 Septembre) <http://videos.wittysparks.com/id/36028863582739599 >

Bellefroid, Bernard (2005) *Les collines parlent* [Documentary]

Benjamin, Walter ([1955] 1973) *Illuminations* (London: Collins/Fontana Books)

Bertou, Marcel (1963) *Une arcadie africaine: le Ruanda* [Documentary]

Bigirumwami, Aloys (1971) *Ibitekerezo: Indirimbo – imbyino – ibihozo – inanga – ibyivugo –ibigwi – imyato – amahamba n'amazina y' inka* (Nyundo)

Bloch, David (2007) *Aristotle on Memory and Recollection* (Leiden: Brill)

Bloch, Marc (1949) *Apologie pour l'histoire ou métier d'historien* (Paris: Librairie Armand Colin)

Bonaparte, Napoléon ([1806] 1939) *Vues politiques* (Paris: Librairie Arthème Fayard)

Bourdieu, Pierre & Passeron, Jean-Claude (1977) *Reproduction in Education, Society and Culture* (London: SAGE)

Boxtel, Carla van (1995) 'Vijftig jaar bevrijding in de schoolboeken', in *Kleio* 3, pp. 20–21

Brandstetter, Anna-Maria (2010) *Contested Pasts: The Politics of Remembrance in Post-Genocide Rwanda* (Wassenaar: NIAS)

Brockmeier, Jens (2002) 'Remembering and Forgetting: Narrative as Cultural Memory', in *Culture & Psychology*, Vol. 8 –1, pp. 15–43

Buckley-Zistel, Susanne (2006) 'Remembering to forget: Chosen amnesia as a strategy for local coexistence in post-genocide Rwanda', in *Africa: The Journal of the International African Institute,* 76 - 2, pp. 131–150

Caplan, Gerald (2007) 'Rwanda: Walking the Road to Genocide', in Thompson, Allan (Ed.) *The Media and the Rwanda Genocide* (Ann Arbor: Pluto Press), pp. 20–37

Carey, James ([1989] 2009) *Communication as Culture: Essays on Media and Society* (New York: Routledge). Revised Edition

Castelot, André (1978) *DE L'HISTOIRE et des histoires…* (Paris: Librairie Académique Perrin)

Certeau, Michel de (1974) 'L' operation historique', in Goff, Jacques le & Nora, Pierre (Eds.) *Faire de l'histoire: Nouveaux problèmes* (Paris, Gallimard), pp. 3–41.

Chrétien, Jean-Pierre, Dupaquier, Jean-François, Kabanda, Marcel, & Ngarambe, Joseph (1995) *Rwanda: Les médias du génocide* (Paris: Karthala)

Chrétien, Jean-Pierre (2007) *RTLM Propaganda: The Democratic Alibi* (AnnArbor : Pluto Press), pp. 55–61

Citron, Suzanne (1987) *Le mythe national: L'histoire de France en question* (Paris: Editions ouvrières)

Cicero, Marcus Tullius ([45–44 B.C.] 1970) *De Legibus* (Cambridge: Harvard University Press. Translated by Clinton Walker Keyes)

Cicero, Marcus Tullius ([54 -51 B.C.] 1970) *De Republica* (Cambridge: Harvard University Press. Translated by Clinton Walker Keyes)

Collingwood, Robin George ([1946] 1994) *The Idea of History* (Oxford: Oxford University Press. Edited with an Introduction by Jan van der Dussen). Revised Edition with Lectures 1926–1928

Confino, Alon (1997) 'Collective Memory and Cultural History: Problems of Method', *The American Historical Review*, Vol. 102, No.5, pp. 1386–1403

Connerton, Paul (2004) *How Societies Remember* (Cambridge: Cambridge University Press)

Coser, A. Lewis (1992) 'Introduction: Maurice Halbwachs 1877–1945', in Coser, A. Lewis (Ed.) *Halbwachs, Maurice On Collective Memory: The Heritage of Sociology* (Chicago: The University of Chicago Press. Edited & translated by Lewis A. Coser), pp. 1–34

Coupez, Andé & Kamanzi, Thomas (1962) *Récits historiques Rwanda* (Tervuren: Musée Royal de l'Afrique Centrale)

Creswell, John (2007) *Qualitative Inquiry and Research Design: Choosing Among Five Approaches* (London: SAGE). Second edition

Davies, Aull Charlotte ([1998] 2008) *Reflexive Ethnography: A Guide to researching selves and others* (New York: Routledge). Second edition

Debord, Guy (1967) *La société du spectacle* (Paris: Buchet/Chastel)

Derrida, Jacques (1987) *Psyché: Inventions de l' autre* (Paris: Editions Galilée)

Derrida, Jacques ([1994] 1996) *Archive Fever: A Freudian Impression* (Chicago: The University of Chicago Press)

Derrida, Jacques ([1993] 2002) 'Artifactualities', in Derrida, Jacques & Stiegler, Bernard *Echographies of Television. Filmed Interviews* (Cambridge: Polity), pp. 1–27

Dewey, John ([1909] 1933) *How We Think: A Restatement of the Relation of Reflective Thinking to the Educative Process* (New York: D.C. Heath and Company)

Dijck, José van (2006) 'Record and Hold: Popular Music between Personal and Collective Memory', in *Critical Studies in Media Communication*, 23: 5, pp. 357–374

Dijck, José van (2007) *Mediated Memories in the Digital Age* (Stanford: Stanford University Press)

Dunk, Hermann von der (2005) 'Geschiedenis als bijsluiter: Historisch besef in de schaduw van de actualiteit', in *Spiegel Historiael* 4/5 – 40 (April/May), pp. 214–218

Durkheim, Emile ([1922] 1966) *Education et Sociologie* (Paris: PUF)

Edy, Jill (2006) *Troubled Pasts: News and the Collective Memory of Social Unrest* (Philadelphia: Temple University Press)

Emerson, Ralph Waldo ([1872] 2010) 'Poetry and Imagination', in Emerson, Ralph Waldo, *The Collected Works of Ralph Waldo Emerson. Volume VIII. Letters and Social Aims* (Cambridge: Harvard University Press) pp. 1–42

Erny, Pierre (2003) *L'enseignment au Rwanda après l'indépendance* (Paris: L'Harmattan)

Erny, Pierre (2005) *L'éducation au Rwanda au temps des rois* (Paris: L'Harmattan)

Fèbvre, Lucien (1948) 'Avant-Propos', in Morazé, Charles, *Trois essais sur histoire et culture* (Paris: Librairie Armand Colin). Collections Cahiers des Annales

Fontaine, P.F.M. (1991) 'Het onopgeloste cryptogram', in *Kleio* 10, pp. 10–14

Forges, Alison des & Longman, Timothy (2004) 'Legal responses to genocide in Rwanda', in Stover, Eric & Weinstein, Harvey (Eds.) *My Neighbor, My Enemy: Justice and Community in the Aftermath of Mass Atrocity* (Cambridge: Cambridge University Press), pp. 49–68

Forster, Peter, Hitchcock, Michael & Lyimo, F. Francis (2000) *Race and Ethnicity in East Africa* (London: MacMillan Press Ltd.)

Foucault, Michel (1969) *L' archéologie du savoir* (Paris: Editions Gallimard)

Frank, Anne ([1942–1944] 1997) *The Diary of a Young Girl* (London: Penguin Book Ltd. Edited by Otto H. Frank and Mirjam Pressler & translated by Susan Massotty). The Definitive Edition

Freedman, Sarah Warshauer, Kambanda, Déo, Samuelson, Beth Lewis, Mugisha, Innocent, Mukashema, Immaculée, Mukama, Evode, Mutabaruka, Jean, Weinstein, Harvey & Longman, Timothy (2004) 'Confronting the past in Rwandan schools', in Stover, Eric & Weinstein, Harvey (Eds.) *My Neighbor, My Enemy: Justice and Community in the Aftermath of Mass Atrocity* (Cambridge: Cambridge University Press), pp. 248–265

Freeman, Mark (1992) 'Self as Narrative: The Place of Life History in Studying the Life Span', in Brinthaupt, Thomas & Lipka, Richard (Eds.) *The Self: Definitional and methodological Issues* (New York: State University of New York Press), pp. 15–43

Freud, Segmund ([1900] 1925) *Le rêve et son interprétation* (Paris: Gallimard. Translated from German by Hélène Legros)

Gakusi, Albert-Enéas & Mouzer, Frédérique (2003) *De la révolution à la contre-révolution: Contraintes structurelles et gouvernance 1950–2003* (Paris: L' Harmattan)

Gasana, James (2002) *Rwanda: du parti-Etat à l'Etat-Garnison* (Paris: L'Harmattan)

Goff, Jacques le (1988) *Histoire et mémoire* (Paris: Editions Gallimard)

Gourevitch, Philip (1999) *"We Wish to Inform You That Tomorrow we Will be Killed with our Families"* (New York: Picador)

Gusdorf, Georges (1991a) *Les écritures du moi. Lignes de vie 1* (Paris: Editions Odile Jacob)

Gusdorf, Georges (1991b) *Auto-bio-graphie. Lignes de vie 2* (Paris: Editions Odile Jacob)

Halbwachs, Maurice ([1925] 1992) 'The Social Framworks of Memory', in Coser, A. Lewis (Ed.) *Halbwachs, Maurice On Collective Memory: The Heritage of Sociology* (Chicago: The University of Chicago Press. Translated by Lewis A. Coser) pp. 35–189

Haley, Alex (1977) *Roots* (London: Hutchingson & Co)

Hall, T. Edward ([1959] 1981) *The Silent Language* (New York: Anchr Books)

Heiden, Konrad ([1935] 1971) *A History of National Nationalism* (New York: Octagon Books)

Heusch, Luc de (1955) *Ruanda: Tableaux d'une féodalité pastorale* [Documentary]

Higiro, Jean-Marie Vianney (1996) 'Distortions et omissions dans l'ouvrage "Rwanda. Les medias du Génocide', in *Dialogue*, 190 (April–May), pp. 160–178

Higiro, Jean-Marie Vianney (2007) 'Rwandan Private Print Media on the Eve of the Genocide', in Thompson, Allan (Ed.) *The Media and the Rwanda Genocide* (Ann Arbor: Pluto Press), pp. 73–89

Himmelfarb, Gertrude (1999) 'Postmodernist History', in Fox-Genovese, Elizabeth and Elisabeth Lasch-Quinn (Eds.) *Reconstructing History: The Emergence of a New Historical Society* (New York: Routledge), pp. 71–93

Hobsbawm, Eric ([1983] 2012) 'Introduction: Inventing Traditions', in Hobsbawm, Eric & Ranger, Terence (Eds.) *The Invention of Tradition* (Cambridge: Cambridge University Press), pp. 1–14

Hooper, John (2007)'Rome uncovers its founding moment', in *The Guardian* (21 November) <http://www.guardian.co.uk/world/2007/nov/21/italy.archaeology>

Hope, Valerie (2003) 'Remembering Rome: Memory, funerary monuments and the Roman Soldier', in Williams, Howard (Ed.) *Archaeologies of Remembrance: Death and Memory in Past Societies* (New York: Kluwer Academic), pp. 113–140

Howe, Mark (2004) 'Early Memory, Early Self, and the Emergence of Autobiographical Memory', in Beike, Denise, Limpinen, James & Behrend, Douglas (Eds.) *The Self and Memory* (New York: Psychology Press), pp. 45–72

Huizinga, Johan (1936) *In the Shadow of Tomorrow* (New York: W.W. Norton & Company, Inc. Translated from Dutch by J.H. Huizinga)

Huizinga, Johan ([1940] 1988) *Hoe bepaalt de geschiedenis het heden?* (Amsterdam)

Huyssen, Andreas (2000) 'Present Pasts: Media, Politics, Amnesia', in *Public Culture* 12, 1, pp. 21–38

Huyssen, Andreas (2003) *Present Pasts: Urban Palimpsests and the Politics of Memory* (Stanford: Stanford University Press)

Iggers, Georg (1999) 'The Role of Professional Historical Scholarship in the Creation and Distortion of Memory', in Ollila, Anne (Ed.) *Historical Perspectives on Memory* (Helsinki: SHS), pp. 49–67

Ingimundarson, Valur (2007) 'The Politics of Memory and the Reconstruction of Albanian National Identity in Postwar Kosovo', in *History & Memory*, 19, 1, pp. 95–123

Inkiko Gacaca (2012) *Gacaca Report Summary* (Kigali) < http://inkiko-gacaca.gov.rw/English/wp-content/uploads/2012/06/Gacaca-Report-Summary.pdf >

Irwin-Zarecka, Iwona (1994) *Frames of Remembrance: The Dynamics of Collective Memory* (New Brunswick: Transaction Publishers)

Kagame, Alexis (1947) 'La Voix de l'Afrique. Un Poème du Rwanda Avec Traduction par l'Abbé Alexis Kagame', in *Africa: Journal of the International African Institute*, Vol. 17, No. 1 (January), pp. 41–46

Kagame, Alexis (1951) *La poésie dynastique au Rwanda* (Bruxelles: IRSAC)

Kagame, Alexis (1952) *Le code des institutions politiques du Rwanda précolonial* (Bruxelles: Institut Royal Colonial Belge)

Kagame, Alexis (1954) *Les organisations socio-familiales de l' ancien Rwanda* (Bruxelles: Institut Royal Colonial Belge)

Kagame, Alexis (1956) *La philosophie bantu-rwandaise de l' Etre* (Bruxelles : Académie royale des Sciences coloniales)

Kagame, Alexis (1959) *La notion de génération appliquée à la généalogie dynastique et à l'histoire du Rwanda des Xe –XIe siècles à nos jours* (Brussels : I.R.S.A.C.)

Kagame, Alexis (1969) *Introduction aux grands genres lyriques de l' ancien Rwanda* (Butare: Editions Universitaires du Rwanda)

Kagame, Paul (2007) Speech commemorating the 13th anniversary of the genocide (7 April) [Recording from *Radio Rwanda*]

Kagame, Paul (2010) Speech commemorating the 16th anniversary of the genocide (7 April) [Recording from *Radio Rwanda*]

Kajeguhakwa, Valens (2001) *Rwanda: De la terre de paix à la terre de sang. Et après?* (Paris: Editions Rémi Perrin)

Karekezi, Urusaro Alice, Nshimiyimana, Alphonse & Mutamba, Beth (2004) 'Localizing justice: gacaca courts', in Stover, Eric & Weinstein, Harvey (Eds.) *My Neighbor, My Enemy: Justice and Community in the Aftermath of Mass Atrocity* (Cambridge: Cambridge University Press), pp. 69–84

Kaschuba, Wolfgang (2000) 'The Emergence and Transformation of Foundation Myths', in Strath, Bo (Ed.) *Myth and Memory in the Construction of Community. Historical Patterns in Europe and Beyond* (Brussels: Presses Interuniversitaires Européennes), pp. 217–226

Kayumba, Charles (2005) *La poésie héroïque rwandaise 'ibyîivugo'* (Butare : IRST)

Kester, Windy (2006) 'Geen wereldoorlogen meer voor Noorse scholieren', in *Historisch nieuwsblad* (March), p. 7

Ketelaar, Eric (2005) 'Sharing: Collected Memories in Communities of Records', in *Archives and Manuscripts,* 33, pp. 44–61

Ki-Zerbo, Joseph (2008) *Regards sur la société africaine* (Dakar : Panafrika)

Kinzer, Stephen (2010) 'The limits of free speech in Rwanda', in *The Guardian* (2 March) <http://www.guardian.co.uk/commentisfree/libertycentral/2010/mar/02/rwanda-free-speech-genocide>

Kors, Alan Charles (1999) 'The Future of History in an Increasingly Unified World' in Fox-Genovese, Elizabeth & Lasch-Quinn, Elisabeth (Eds.) *Reconstructing History: The Emergence of a New Historical Society* (New York: Routledge), pp. 12–17

Kovach, Bill & Rosenstiel, Tom ([2001] 2007) *The Elements of Journalism: What Newspeople Should Know and the Public Should Expect* (New York: Three Rivers Press). Completely updated and Revised.

Lemarchand, René (2004 ) 'Mythologie et violence politique', in *Bulletin des séances* 50-3, pp. 309 –317

Lévy, Pierre (1998) *Becoming Virtual: Reality in the Digital Age* (New York: Plenum Press)

Lévy, Pierre (2010) 'Building a Universal Digital Memory', in Parry, Ross (Ed.) *Museums in a Digital Age* (London: Routledge), pp. 107–115

Lewis, Bernard (1975) *History Remembered, Recovered, Invented* (Princeton: Princeton University Press)

Li, Darryl (2007) 'Echoes of Violence: Considerations on Radio and Genocide in Rwanda', in Thompson, Allan (Ed.) *The Media and the Rwanda Genocide* (Ann Arbor: Pluto Press), pp. 90–109

Lippmann, Walter ([1922] 1997) *Public Opinion* (New York: Simon & Schuster)

Longman, Timothy & Rutagengwa, Théoneste (2004) 'Memory, identity, and community in Rwanda', in Stover, Eric & Weinstein, Harvey (Eds.) *My Neighbor, My Enemy: Justice and Community in the Aftermath of Mass Atrocity* (Cambridge: Cambridge University Press), pp. 162–182

Lowenthal, David (1985) *The Past is a Foreign Country* (Cambridge: Cambridge University Press)

Mamdani, Mahmood (2001) *When Victims Become Killers. Colonialism, Nativism, and the Genocide in Rwanda* (Princeton: Princeton University Press)

Man, Paul de (1979) 'Autobiography as De-facement', in *MNL*, Vol. 94, No. 5, *Comparative Literature* (December), pp. 919–930

Mannheim, Karl ([1936] 1966) *Ideology and Utopia: An Introduction to the Sociology of Knowledge* (London: Routledge & Kegan Paul Ltd)

Maquet, Jacques (1955) commenting in Heusch, Luc de, *Ruanda: Tableaux d'une féodalité pastorale* [Documentary]

Maquet, Jacques (1961) *The Premise of Inequality in Ruanda: A Study of Political Relations in a Central African Kingdom* (London: Oxford University Press)

McKenzie, Donald Francis (1999) *Bibliography and the Sociology of Texts* (Cambridge: Cambridge University Press)

Michaux, Léon (1974) *La mémoire* (Paris: Librairie Hachette)

Mill, John Stuart ([1831] 1963), 'The Spirit of the Age', in Mill, John Stuart, *Essays on Politics and Culture* (Peterborough: Anchor Books. Edited and with an introduction by Gertrude Himmelfarb)

Misser, François (1995) *Vers un nouveau Rwanda? Entretiens avec Paul Kagame* (Paris: Editions Karthala)

Misztal, Barbara (2003) *Theories of Social Remembering* (Philadelphia: Open University Press)

Morris, Henry Francis (1964) *The Heroic Recitations of the Bahima of Ankole* (Oxford: The Clarendon Press)

Muhongerwa, Florence (2010) 'Inyangamugayo 40.000 za gacaca ziraregwa kugira uruhare muri Jenoside', in *Izuba Rirashe* (13 July) <http://www.izuba.org.rw/i-419-a-15592.izuba >

Mukasonga, Scholastique (2006) *Inyenzi ou les Cafards* (Paris: Gallimard)

Mulihano, Benedigito (1980] 2005) *Ibirari by' insigamigani*, Vol. 1 (Butare: Ingoro y' Umurage w'u Rwanda [Rwanda National Museum]). Third Edition

Nahimana, Ferdinand (1993) *Le Rwanda: Emergence d'un Etat* (Paris: L'Harmattan)

Nahimana, Ferdinand (2007) *Rwanda: Les virages ratés* (Lille: Editions Sources du Nil)

Narotzky, Susana & Smith, Gavin (2002) '"Being político" in Spain: An Ethnographic Account of Memories, Silences and Public Politics', in *History & Memory*, 14.1/2, pp. 189–228

Newbury, Catherine (2002) 'Ethnicity and the Politics of History in Rwanda', in Lorey, David & Beezley, William (Eds.) *Genocide, Collective Violence, and Popular Memory: The Politics of Rememberance in the Twentieth Century* (Wilmington: Scholarly Resources Inc.), pp. 67–83

Ngangura, Mweze Dieudonné (1994) *Le roi, la vache et le bananier: chronique d'un retour au Royaume de Ngweshe* [Documentary]

Ngarambe, Karirima, 'Twabaye Inkotanyi tutaramenya ko ziriho-Sebasoni', in *Igihe* (7 December 2012) <http://www.igihe.com/politiki/amakuru-124/twabaye-inkotanyi-tutaramenya-ko-ziriho-aho-tuzimenyeye-ni-cyo-cyatumye-tuzikunda-cyane-sebasoni.html >

Nietzsche, Friedrich ([1874] 1980) *On the Advantage and Disadvantage of History for Life* (Cambridge: Hackett Publishing Company, Inc. Translated with an introduction by Peter Preuss)

Nkundabagenzi, Fidèle (1961) *Rwanda politique 1958–1960* (Brussels: Centre de Recherche et d'Information Socio-Politiques)

Nkurunziza, Charles (2004) *Ubwami mu Rwanda* <http://www.olny.nl/RWANDA/Histoire_History/C_Nkurunziza_Ubwami_mu_Rwanda.html >

Nkurunziza, Charles (2005) *Le Bugara et les Bagara* <http://www.olny.nl/RWANDA/Histoire_History/C_Nkurunziza_Le_Bugara.html>

Nkurunziza, Charles (2006) *Le conflit rwandais* <http://www.olny.nl/RWANDA/Histoire_History/C_Nkurunziza_Conflit_Rwandais.pdf >

Nora, Pierre (1984a) 'Présentation', in Nora, Pierre (Ed.) *Les lieux de mémoire I- La République* (Paris: Editions Gallimard), pp. VII–XIII

Nora, Pierre (1984b) 'Entre Mémoire et Histoire : La problématique des lieux', in Nora, Pierre (Ed.) *Les lieux de mémoire I- La République* (Paris: Editions Gallimard), pp. XV–XLII

Nora, Pierre (1986a) 'L'Histoire de France de Lavisse', in Nora, Pierre (Ed.) *Les lieux de mémoire II- La Nation* (Paris: Editions Gallimard), pp. 317–375

Nora, Pierre (1986b) 'Introduction' in Nora, Pierre (Ed.) *Les lieux de mémoire II- La Nation* (Paris: Editions Gallimard), pp. X–XXX

Ntampaka, Charles (1997) 'Le role des règles issues de la culture rwandaise dans la promotion de la justice et de la démocratie', in *Dialogue*, 197 (March–April), pp. 7–18

Ntisoni, Lambertus (2007) *J' ai traversé des fleuves de sang: Le calvaire d' un officier des ex-Forces Armées Rwandaises* (Paris: L' Harmattan)

Nyirubugara, Olivier (2008) 'Interview with Faustin Twagiramungu' (16 March) <http://www.olny.nl/RWANDA/Videos/Nahimana_book_conference_15_march_2008.html#faustin >

Nyirubugara, Olivier (2008) 'Interview with Paul Rusesabagina' (26 April) <http://www.olny.nl/RWANDA/Videos/Hague_Peace_Conference_26_April_2008.html#rusesabagina >

Nyirubugara, Olivier (2009) 'Rusesabagina: Rwanda back to ethnic servitude system' (29 April) <http://www.olny.nl/RWANDA/Videos/rusesabagina_rwanda_back_to_feudality.html >

Paternostre de la Mairieu, Baudoin (1994) *'Pour vous mes frères!' Vie de Grégoire Kayibanda, premier Président du Rwanda* (Paris : Pierre Téqui)

Péan, Pierre (2005) *Noires fureurs, blancs menteurs: Rwanda 1990–1994* (Paris: Mille et une nuits)

Plato ([ca 385 BC] 1999) *Symposium* (London: Penguin Books. Translated by Christopher Gill and Desmond Lee)

Rancière, Jacques (2009) *The Emancipated Spectator* (London: Verso)

Renan, Ernest (1869) *La part de la famille et de l'État dans l'éducation* (Paris: Maurice Loignon et Cie)

Reyntjens, Filip (1985) *Pouvoir et Droit au Rwanda. Droit public et evolution politique, 1916–1973* (Tervuren: Koninklijk Museum voor Midden Afrika)

Ribuffo, P. Leo (1999) 'Confessions of an Accidental (or Perhaps Overdetermined) Historian', in Fox-Genovese, Elizabeth & Lasch-Quinn, Elisabeth (Eds.) *Reconstructing History: The Emergence of a New Historical Society* (New York: Routledge), pp. 143–163

Richters, Annemiek (2010) 'Suffering and Healing in the Aftermath of War and Genocide in Rwanda: Mediations Through Community-Based Sociotherapy', in Kaptein, Lidwien & Richters, Annemiek (Eds.) *Mediations of Violence in Africa: Fashionning New Futures from Contested Pasts* (Leiden: Brill), pp. 173–210

Ricoeur, Paul (2004) *Memory, History, Forgetting* (Chicago: The University of Chicago Press. Translated by Kathleen Blamey & David Pellauer)

Ricoeur, Paul (2006) *On Translation* (London: Routledge)

Robinson, John & Taylor, Leslie (1998) 'Autobiographical Memory and Self-Narratives: A Tale of Two Stories', in Thompson, Charles, Hermann, Douglas, Bruce, Darryl, Read, Don, Payne, David & Toglia, Michael (Eds.) *Autobiographical Memory: Theoretical and Applied Perspectives* (Mahwah: Lawrence Erlbaum Associates), pp. 125–143

Roncayolo, Marcel (1986) 'Paysage du savant', in Nora, Pierre (Ed.) *Les lieux de mémoire II- La Nation* (Paris: Editions Gallimard, pp. 487–528

Roth, Kenneth (2009) 'The power of horror in Rwanda', in *Los Angeles Times* (11 April) <http://www.latimes.com/news/opinion/la-oe-roth11-2009apr11,0,5732620.story>

Rousseau, Jean-Jacques ([1768] 1966) *Émile ou de l'éducation* (Paris: Garnier-Flammarion)

RTL4 , 19h30' News edition (20 November 2007) <http://www.rtl.nl/(vm=/actueel/rtlnieuws/)/system/video/html/components/actueel/rtlnieuws/miMedia/2007/week47/di_1930_romulus.avi_plain.xml>

Rugamba, Cyprien (1981) *Contes Ruandais* (Paris: Edicef)

Rurangwa, Révérien (2006) *Génocidé* (Paris: Presses de la Renaissance)

Ruzibiza, Abdul (2005) *Rwanda: Histoire secrète* (Paris: Editions du Panama)

Ryback, Timothy (2009) *Hitler's Private Library: The Books that Shaped his Life* (London: Vintage)

Santayana, George ([1905] 1954) *The Life of Reason or the Phases of Human Progress* (New York: Charles Scribner'Sons)

Sartre, Jean-Paul (1948) *Qu'est-ce que la littérature?* (Paris: Gallimard)

Saussure, Ferdinand de ([1916] 1967) *Cours de linguistique générale* (Göttingen: Otto Harrassowitz, Wiesbaden). Edition critique par Rudolf Engler

Schachtel, Ernest (1959) *Metamorphosis: On the Development of Affect, Perception, Attention, and Memory* (New York: Basic Books, Inc.)

Scherrer, Christian (2002) *Genocide and Crisis in Central Africa: Conflict Roots, Mass Violence, and Regional War* (Westport: Praeger)

Schudson, Michael (1995) *The Power of News* (Cambridge: Harvard University Press)

Sebarenzi, Joseph (2009) *God Sleeps in Rwanda: A Journey of Transformation* (New York: Atria Books. With Laura Ann Mullane).

Shuman, Daniel & McCall, Smith Alexander (2000) *Justice and the Prosecution of Old Crimes: Balancing Legal, Psychological, and Moral Concerns* (Washington, D.C.: American Psychological Association)

Shyaka, Anastase (year ?) *Le conflit rwandais: origines, développement et stratégies de sortie*

Smith, Pierre (1975) *Le récit populaire au Rwanda* (Paris: Armand Colin)

Sorabji, Richard (2006) *Self: Ancient and Modern Insights about Individuality, Life, and Death* (Chicago: University of Chicago Press)

Soudan, François (2005) 'Paul Kagame: "Pourquoi la France nous hait"', in *Jeune Afrique l' Intelligent, 2302* (20–26 February), pp. 40–46

Soudan, François (2008) 'Paul Kagame: pour en finir avec le génocide', in *Jeune Afrique, 2466* (13–19 April), pp. 24–32

Spielmann, Peter James (2009) 'War: Is it getting more hellish, or less?' [Associated Press] (12 July) <http://www.cbsnews.com/stories/2009/07/12/ap/national/main5153528.shtml>

Spivak, Gayatri Chakravorty (1990) *The Post-Colonial Critic: Interviews, Strategies, Dialogues* (London: Routledge. Edited by Sarah Harasym)

Spradley, James (1980) *Participant Observation* (London: Thomson Learning)

Strath, Bo (2000) 'Introduction: Myth, Memory and History in the Construction of Community', in Strath, Bo (Ed.) *Myth and Memory in the Construction of Community. Historical Patterns in Europe and Beyond* (Brussels: Presses Interuniversitaires Européennes), pp. 19–46

Taylor, Charles (1989) *Sources of the Self: The Making of the Modern Identity* (Cambridge: Harvard University Press)

Thoreau, Henri David ([1854] 1983) *Walden* (New York: Pinguin Books Ltd.)

Trachtenberg, Marc (1999) 'The Past Under Siege', in Fox-Genovese, Elizabeth & Lasch-Quinn, Elisabeth (Eds.) *Reconstructing History: The Emergence of a New Historical Society* (New York: Routledge), pp. 9–11

Truth and Reconciliation Commission (1998) *Truth and Reconciliation Commission of South Africa Report, Volume One* <http://www.doj.gov.za/trc/report/ >

Twagilimana, Aimable (2003) *The Debris of Ham: Ethnicity, Regionalism, and the 1994 Rwandan Genocide* (Lanham: University Press of America)

Umutesi, Marie-Béatrice (2000) *Fuir ou Mourir au Zaïre: Le vécu d'une réfugiée Rwandaise* (Paris: L'Harmattan)

Ungor, Ugur (2004) 'Justifier l'injustifiable: Ideologie en genocide in Rwanda', in *Vrede en Veiligheid*, 33, 3, pp. 342–358

Valéry, Paul (1931) *Regards sur le monde actuel* (Paris: Librairie Stock)

Vansina, Jan (1962) *L'évolution du royaune rwanda des origines à 1900* (Brussels: Editions J. Duculot)

Vansina, Jan (1971) 'Once upon a Time: Oral Traditions as History in Africa', in *Daedalus*, Vol.100, No. 2, pp. 442–468

Vansina, Jan (1985) *Oral Tradition as History* (London: James Currey)

Vansina, Jan (2000) 'Historical Tales (Ibiteekerezo) and the History of Rwanda', in *History in Africa*, Vol. 27, pp. 375–414

Vivanti, Corrado (1986) 'Les Recherches de la France d'Etienne Pasquier', in Nora, Pierre (Ed.) *Les lieux de mémoire II- La Nation* (Paris: Editions Gallimard), pp. 215–245

Wambu, Onyekachi (2001) *Hopes on the Horizon* [documentary]

Waugh, Colin (2004) *Paul Kagame and Rwanda: Power, Genocide and the Rwandan Patriotic Front* (London: McFarland & Company, Inc.)

Wells, George (1938) *World Brain* (London: Methuen & Co. Ltd)

Wendt-Kellar, Elizabeth (2005) 'Family's hopes of staying in U.S. dwindling', in *Naples News* (25 July) <http://www.naplesnews.com/news/2005/jul/25/ndn_family_s_hopes_of_staying_in_u_s__dwindling/>

White, Hayden (2000) 'Catastrophe, Communal Memory and Mythic Discourse: The uses of Myth in the Reconstruction of Society', in Strath, Bo (Ed.) *Myth and Memory in the Construction of Community. Historical Patterns in Europe and Beyond* (Brussels: Presses Interuniversitaires Européennes), pp. 49–74

Wilkinson, James (1996) 'A Choice of Fictions: Historians, Memory, and Evidence' in *PMLA*, Vol. 111, No. 1: pp. 80–92

Williams, Howard (2003) 'Introduction: The archaeology of Death, Memory and Material Culture', in Williams, Howard (Ed.) *Archaeologies of Remembrance: Death and Memory in Past Societies* (New York: Kluwer Academic), pp. 1–24

Willis, Paul (2000) *The Ethnographic Imagination* (Cambridge: Polity Press)

Wineburg, Sam (2001) *Historical Thinking and Other Unnatural Acts: Charting the Future of Teaching the Past* (Philadephia: Temple University Press)

Woolley, Leonard ([1930] 1954) *Digging up the Past* (Harmondsworth: Pinguin Nooks Ltd.)

WRR [De Wetenschappelijke Raad voor het Regeringsbeleid] (2007) *Identificatie met Nederland* (Amsterdam: Amsterdam University Press)

Zelizer, Barbie (1995) 'Reading the Past Against the Grain: The Shape of Memory Studies', in *Critical Studies in Mass Communication*, 12, pp. 214–239

Zerubavel, Eviatar (2003) *Time Maps: Collective Memory and the Social Shape of the Past* (Chicago: The University of Chicago Press)